IMPERATIVE

Studies from the Book of James

ISMAEL BERLANGA

CYPRESS

The views presented in this book are those of the author and do not represent the views of the Department of Defense, it's components, or the United States Government.

Manufactured in the United States

Cataloging-in-Publication Data

Berlanga, Ismael.

Imperative: studies from the book of James/ by Ismael Berlanga

p. cm.

Includes Scripture index.

ISBN: 978-1-956811-33-9 (pbk.); 978-1-956811-34-6 (ebook)

1. Bible. James—Commentaries. I. Author. II. Title.

227.9107—ddc20

Library of Congress Control Number: 2022912934

Cover design by Brad McKinnon and Brittany Vander Maas.

For information:

Cypress Publications
3625 Helton Drive
PO Box HCU
Florence, AL 35630

www.hcu.edu/publications

DEDICATION

To Brigette, the wife of my youth.
Thank you for everything. I wish I had the words, but you already know. Your precious light has helped many find their way out of the seas of chaos. I am thankful for your strength and humbled by your gracious spirit.

To my children, Judah and Hadassah.
May this book be a reminder to you that with God, all things are possible. Keep Him first and foremost in your life and live humbly under the shadow of His wing. Do not forget our story, how our God led us through the wilderness to a good land. He said, "Never will I leave you nor forsake you." You heard how the Lord was true to His promises and now you have seen this first-hand. Hold our family story close to your hearts. He blessed us beyond measure, but the best is yet to come!

ACKNOWLEDGMENTS

To Heritage Christian University.

Enrolling was uncharted territory for me, having been the first in my family. You welcomed and accepted me where I stood, but challenged me to grow. Thank you for being a blessing to me and so many others!

To my Copy Editor, Marlena Gibson.

I am so thankful for your professionalism, talents, and patience. I look forward to working with you on future projects to come.

CONTENTS

BIBLE ABBREVIATIONS

Old Testament

Gen	Genesis
Exod	Exodus
Lev	Leviticus
Num	Numbers
Deut	Deuteronomy
Josh	Joshua
Judg	Judges
Ruth	Ruth
1–2 Sam	1–2 Samuel
1–2 Kgs	1–2 Kings
1–2 Chr	1–2 Chronicles
Ezra	Ezra
Neh	Nehemiah
Esth	Esther
Job	Job
Ps	Psalms
Prov	Proverbs
Eccl	Ecclesiastes

Song	Song of Solomon
Isa	Isaiah
Jer	Jeremiah
Lam	Lamentations
Ezek	Ezekiel
Dan	Daniel
Hos	Hosea
Joel	Joel
Amos	Amos
Obad	Obadiah
Jonah	Jonah
Mic	Micah
Nah	Nahum
Hab	Habakkuk
Zeph	Zephaniah
Hag	Haggai
Zech	Zechariah
Mal	Malachi

New Testament

Matt	Matthew
Mark	Mark
Luke	Luke
John	John
Acts	Acts
Rom	Romans
1–2 Cor	1–2 Corinthians
Gal	Galatians
Eph	Ephesians
Phil	Philippians
Col	Colossians
1–2 Thess	1–2 Thessalonians
1–2 Tim	1–2 Timothy
Titus	Titus
Phlm	Philemon
Heb	Hebrews
Jas	James
1–2 Pet	1–2 Peter
1–2–3 John	1–2–3 John
Jude	Jude
Rev	Revelation

INTRODUCTION

One of the amazing aspects about the original language of the New Testament is that verbs could be intensified from simple action words to commands or imperatives by their inspired authors. Because of this, you may be surprised to learn that of the 108 verses that make up the book of James, over half of them contain imperatives! No wonder James has long been known as the book of Proverbs of the New Testament, since, like its Old Testament counterpart, it contains clear guidance for those seeking to find meaning, purpose, and connection to God.

In *Imperative: Studies from the Book of James*, we are going to allow James's imperatives to drive our study. I will offer a reading of the book of James that incorporates the entire redemption story of the Bible, and I will connect that powerful message to each section of the book of James and its imperatives. Christians everywhere have a deep yearning to be connected to God and to have an enriched relationship with Him. We desire spiritual connection to God, but at times lack direction as we navigate through life's difficult choices. It is my hope and prayer that this unique reading of James will surface his voice and be a strong source of support and direction for you on your daily Christian walk!

CHAPTER 1

JAMES: THE RISE FROM EARTHLY BROTHER TO SERVANT

JAMES 1:1

INTRODUCTION

Let's begin this amazing journey with James, the earthly brother of Jesus, and the rise that James experienced from estranged brother to servant of the Lord Jesus Christ. As we will see, James himself is a model of what the Lord can do for the lost, even for those that turn their backs on the Lord. His story is truly one of hope and growth. May the Lord bless this journey that we are about to embark upon!

I. *"A PROPHET IS NOT WITHOUT HONOR, EXCEPT AMONG HIS OWN FAMILY"* (MARK 6:44)

James 1:1, begins, *"James, **a servant of God and of the Lord Jesus Christ ...***" While there are several men in the Bible named James, there is only one that is ever mentioned without suffix, and that is James, the Lord's earthly brother. Such a close relative of Jesus would have needed no introduction to His followers. Notice the similarity between James's introduction and that of his other brother Jude in his own book: *"Jude, a servant of Jesus Christ and brother of James."* Their status as earthly siblings of Jesus was well known, but rather than use their physical kinship to Jesus as a badge of honor and authority, they both simply refer to themselves as *"servants of Jesus Christ."* This is a sign of true spiritual maturity, but as we're about to see, James, the servant of God and of the Lord Jesus Christ, wasn't always a giant in the faith.

The name "James" as we know it comes from the changes that occur with translating a Hebrew name into Greek and Latin, and then into English. But James's original name is *Yakobos*, which should be translated, "Jacob." Matthew 1:6 tells us that there was a Jacob in the family genealogy: Joseph's father. This gives us some insight into how excited Mary and Joseph must have been to have had a son after Jesus — a son with a name of their own choosing. After all, the name Jesus was given to Mary and Joseph by God (Matt 1:21), but with James, they were now free to decide for themselves what to call their baby and they took the opportunity to honor Joseph's father.

Not much is known about the childhood of Jesus and even less is known about James's, but it's not hard to imagine how tough it would have been to have the Son of God as your older brother. That's a pretty long shadow. The first time we really receive insight into Mary and Joseph's family dynamics is at Jesus's first recorded miracle at a wedding in Cana. Mary, who was probably part of the wedding party, saw that they had run out of wine and asked Jesus for help. Famously, He told her, *"What does this have to do with me; my time has not yet come,"* (a phrase that will return later in this study) (John 2:4). We know that eventually, albeit reluctantly, Jesus agreed to honor His mother's request and performed His first miracle of turning water into wine. What we can gather from this conversation is that His family was well aware of Jesus's abilities. Jesus's response when He said, *"My hour has not yet come,"* also tells us that the family knew, too, that He had a mission and a time frame for that mission. Yet what happens next in Mark chapter 3 tells us that neither James nor the rest of the family fully understood what Jesus was seeking to do with His earthly ministry.

In Mark 3, Jesus's fame had begun to spread, and He eventually caught the attention of those in power in Jerusalem. The Pharisees, a powerful religious sect, formed an unlikely alliance with the Herodians, a party loyal to Herod, to put Jesus to death (verse 6). The Pharisee-Herodian alliance dispatched scribes from Jerusalem, presumably to record the events that they observed regarding the man who was said to have power over unclean spirits and who was gaining a large following (verse 22). Imagine how worried the family must have been at this time, knowing that Jesus was receiving this kind of attention from powerful political and religious leaders. With Jesus's absence from the home, this must have put James, as the younger brother, in a family leadership role before his time. With pressures building, Jesus's family became so worried for His safety that they took matters into their own hands and attempted to seize Him forcefully, even going so far as to say that He was out of His mind (verse 21). James, Mary, and the rest of the family were not denying Jesus or His ability, or even His timeline. I believe they were acting out of fear for what would happen to Him if these powerful leaders continued to mark Him an enemy. Their emotion and love for Jesus prevented them from seeing that Jesus's plan was ultimately to die on the cross, and that the prophecy about the rejected stone later becoming God's Cornerstone was referring to their older brother (Ps 118:22; Acts 4:11). Acting from a place of panic prevented them from seeing that God was working something much bigger than they believed possible! Unfortunately, the sadness and heartache the family was experiencing was only just the beginning.

Mark 3 closes with the family frantically seeking to speak to Jesus outside of a house filled to the brim with His new followers, even sending a disciple in to tell Jesus that they wanted to talk to Him. In a move meant to clear the issue once and for all for His family, Jesus responded by saying: *"Who are my mother and my brothers? ... Here are my mother and brothers, the ones who do the will of God,"* (Mark 3:33–34). He was indicating that His followers were his family. The hope of bringing Jesus home and having their routine revert to normal was gone. Imagine hearing your brother say, "Who are my brothers?" as if He did not know He had an entire family waiting on His return! For James, visions of everything they had been through growing up together must have flashed before him and in their place was the reality that things were never going to be the same again. It was a painful realization that the two brothers must now go their separate ways. James was counting on Jesus, as the eldest brother, to take His place at the head of the family, but instead, James just heard Jesus say, "My ministry is more important."

The brothers' relationship reached a breaking point in John 7. At this time, over a year had passed since Jesus first left home for good, and He now had powerful groups who were actively seeking to kill Him. Imagine how the year of absence would have taken its toll on the family. They would have been constantly on edge, not knowing if a message would arrive telling them that Jesus had been captured or killed. Wondering each day if that day was going to be your beloved brother's last. The constant fear and anxiety that Jesus's absence brought would have taken a toll on everyone. John 7 records the last encounter the family had before Jesus's death. The strained relationships are about to collapse.

Having just arrived home, you would think this moment would be overflowing with happiness, given that the family was together again. They are about to make the annual traditional family trip to Jerusalem for the festival of Booths. This was Jesus's chance to bring back the normalcy that they so desperately wanted. For over a year, Jesus had been missing from the regular family routine. Daily worry and dread had hung over their home like a cloud, and now, all of a sudden, Jesus finally comes home. As they're about to leave, Jesus gives the family the news that He can't go with them because there are people waiting to kill Him. Their hopes are dashed one last time, and this proves too much for the brothers to handle. What happens next speaks volumes regarding where James and his brothers were mentally and emotionally at this point. They're the ones who had to step up in Jesus's absence. They were the ones who comforted and cared for their mother as she cried for Jesus. His brothers had enough. John 7:1, 3–6 reads:

> *After this, Jesus went about in Galilee. He would not go about in Judea,* **because the Jews were seeking to kill him** *... So his brothers said to him,* **"Leave here** *and* **go** *to Judea, that your disciples also may see the works you are doing. For no one works in secret if he seeks to be known openly. If you do these things, show yourself to the world.'"* **For not even his brothers believed in him. Jesus said to them, "My time has not yet come, but your time is always here."**

"*Leave here and go,*" is an imperative command statement, meaning that this exchange was forceful and emotionally driven. His brothers, James included, essentially told Jesus, "Get out of here; just go already! If you're the Messiah, the Christ and Savior of Israel, then what are You doing performing miracles for Galileans? Jerusalem is the capital and that's on the other side in Judea. You say You are the Messiah and that when the time is right, You're going to save us, so then Judea is where You need to be, not here. You've put us through enough already."

Their pain is understandable, but rather than chide them for their short-sightedness, Jesus simply repeats what He told the family in John 2, "My time has not yet come." The Scriptures indicate that this is the last time Jesus would speak to His brothers before His death. Psalm 69 gives us a glimpse into the heaviness of Jesus's heart when this fallout happened. Verses 7–9 say, "*I endure insults for your sake; humiliation covers my face.* **I have become estranged** *from my brothers and* **a foreigner to the sons of my mother.**" Jesus hid this sadness in His heart and pressed on because His love for you and me was greater.

Later, on the cross, before He took His last breath, John 19:25–27 tells us,

> *Standing by the cross of Jesus was his mother ... When Jesus saw his mother and the disciple whom he loved standing nearby, he said to his mother, "Woman, behold, your son!" Then he said to the disciple, "Behold, your mother!" And from that hour the disciple took her to his own home.*

This was Jesus's way of saying, "John, a mother is about to watch her child take his last breath; a mother is about to bury her firstborn child and son. Watch over her like she was your own mother."

Tragically, Jesus felt like it was John, His true follower — and NOT Mary's other sons — who could provide her with the spiritual care and compassion that she would need to get through the shock of the next few days before His resurrection. Jesus chose John over James because James was not ready. James, at this point, was still the estranged brother and had not yet risen to become the servant of the Lord Jesus Christ. Thankfully, though, James's story does not end here. This is only the beginning!

II. THE RISE FROM BROTHER TO SERVANT

It is the Apostle Paul, in his appeal to the Corinthian brethren for support for the Jerusalem church (the church where James was later a prominent figure), who gives us a little window into the moment that changed the course of James's life.

For I delivered to you as of first importance what I also
received: that Christ died for our sins in accordance with the
Scriptures, that he was buried, that he was raised on the third
day in accordance with the Scriptures, and that he appeared
to Cephas, then to the twelve. Then he appeared to more than
five hundred brothers at one time, most of whom are still alive,
though some have fallen asleep. **Then he appeared to James,**
then to all the apostles (1 Cor 15:3-7).

I love how the fact that Jesus appeared to James is
mentioned just in passing, but the implication is so much
weightier! Something happened here that profoundly
altered James's life. Something transformed James from
being the estranged brother of Jesus to a Servant of God and
of the Lord, Jesus the Christ. This was a reunion that wasn't
just meaningful for the brothers themselves, but also had
far-reaching consequences for the entire world! First, James
finally realized that Jesus was who He had said He was the
whole time, and that he had misunderstood the nature of
his brother's mission. In one quick moment, James would
have realized that when he and his family pushed away
Jesus and told Him to go, they hadn't just alienated their
brother, they had pushed away and doubted God Himself.
It's easy to think how mortified James must have been at the
thought that those critical years had been wasted in conflict
and non-support. Instead of standing in Jesus's way, he
could have used the time he had to help Him. It can be guar-
anteed that Jesus accepted this penitence with love and
forgiveness; even at the time of his brother's rejection, He
had continued His mission, knowing that James would one
day understand. Jesus was patient with James, despite his
unbelief, and no doubt rejoiced to see His brother come to

the truth at last. Life is hard, but God's grace redeems our lost years.

This resurrection meeting was the moment when James realized that Jesus was the Son of God and the Messiah, not only of the people of Israel, but of the whole world. James's transformation didn't just stop there, however. The next time we hear of James, he is back with his mother Mary, and with his other brothers and they are in an upper room (Acts 1:14). He's right by His mother's side, with the rest of Jesus's closest followers, in a sacred place, surrounded by people whose lives were fundamentally changed by Jesus, the Son of the Living God! James's presence signified that he too was ready to be changed, ready to redeem lost time.

As we've read in John 7, Judea and Jerusalem were the locations that the brothers felt Jesus should be if any true change was going to occur. Jerusalem was a very important place for the Jewish people, and remained such for the early church. It would have been the place containing the most believers since arguably it was the spot where it all began. It's no surprise then that James stayed in Jerusalem and began to be a force for good there. The work that James was doing was of tremendous importance, so it is understandable how significant it was for Paul, as a new apostle and still struggling with his past, to visit here and meet Peter and James (Gal 1:18–19). By this time, I calculate that James was in his thirties and still strengthening the church in Jerusalem while the gospel continues to spread. He has become a powerful leader in early Christianity.

But the transformation of James wasn't done just yet. When James was around his late forties, a new contention arose that would push him to once again rise up and continue his growth in Jesus on a higher level. Paul, in his letter to the Galatian churches, writes:

> But when Cephas came to Antioch, I opposed him to his face, because he stood condemned. For before **certain men came from James,** he was eating with the Gentiles; **but when they came he drew back** and separated himself, fearing **the circumcision party** (Gal 2:11–12).

Under the old law, it had been the custom of the Jews not to eat with Gentiles, so there were some in Jerusalem who continued this custom. Notice where they came from: "from James." This does not mean that they were sent by him, but it certainly means that they were known as members of his flock and that this practice was prevalent in Jerusalem and was not being addressed. By not eating with the Gentiles, these early Christians were still outlining a distinction between themselves and those who were not previously of the nation of Israel. The conflict escalated when it reached Jerusalem, as seen in Acts 11:1–2:

> Now the apostles and the brothers who were throughout Judea heard that the Gentiles also had received the word of God. So when Peter went up **to Jerusalem, the circumcision party** criticized him, saying, "You went to uncircumcised men and ate with them."

This tension came to a head at the Jerusalem Council, where the early church leaders assembled to address the issue of whether Gentiles needed to obey the Law of Moses, and if so, which laws did they have to keep to be right with God. This was a tough transition time for the church, and it was a moment that required strong and respected leadership. During that meeting, Paul and Barnabas spoke, and even Pharisees had a say (Acts 15:5), but the one who finally settled the issue was James in Acts 15:19, when he said, *"My judgment is that we should not trouble those of the Gentiles who turn to God."* James provided solid leadership during this moment of tension, and his counsel was honored by all, including Paul. It was now clear that the message of salvation was for Jews and Gentiles alike, with no preferential distinction. After the Jerusalem Council concluded, Paul recounted that it was James, among other voices, that bid them godspeed on his mission to preach to the Gentiles, putting a public seal of approval on Paul's work. In a nod to James's own humble upbringing, and in an affirmation of Jesus's mission (Luke 4:18), James told Paul to continue his good work, but never forget about the poor (Gal 2:10).

For the duration of his ministry, James continued to bring good news to the poor in Jerusalem, even dedicating a quarter of the book of James to the discussion of their fair treatment.

James appears again for the last time in Acts 21. By now, he must have been in his late fifties. Although he had been a follower of Jesus for a significant amount of time, this final passage showed that he still had more growth to do. He, along with the other elders in the church at Jerusalem, greeted Paul, who had just arrived for another visit. They are excited to hear about all the good work that he has been doing among the Gentiles since their last encounter, but they're concerned that Paul has developed a reputation for abandoning the Law of Moses. Although previously they had agreed that the Law of Moses was no longer in effect, they no doubt worried that Paul might agitate those devout

Jews in their city with this controversial message. In a move that showed a lack of trust in the Lord, James and the elders came up with a plan to "fix" Paul's reputation and appease any who were worried that he'd abandoned the Law of Moses altogether. They planned for Paul to pay for the sacrifices needed in the purification ceremony for four men who were going through a Nazarite vow. By doing this, Acts 21:6 says that Paul would be "purifying himself with them ... declaring the fulfillment of the days of purification, until the offering was made for every one of them."

The idea was that if Paul did this, he wouldn't be seen as an enemy of Judaism any more. Paul agreed and followed through, but the plan failed and he was arrested in the Temple. Some have wondered about the wisdom of James's plan, while some still attempt to rationalize his actions. But no matter how we view it, James should have been firmly planted in Jesus and trusted in God's providence. Perhaps the city would have been agitated, but this too would have been an opportunity to glorify God. As so often happens in life, a fear of conflict can be allowed to hamper God's truth unless Christians have the spiritual maturity to stand strong in their convictions.

About four years later, according to tradition, James was led to the pinnacle of the temple, perhaps to the very place where his oldest brother stood at His temptation (Luke 4:9). With his final words, he proclaimed that Jesus was the only true and living way. According to tradition, he was pushed from this ledge and survived the fall, only to be beaten to death shortly after. He who had previously wavered because he wanted to avoid difficulty was now willing to die for speaking the truth of salvation without compromise. It's clear from this part of James's life that even mighty Christian heroes are human. They, like today's Christians, faced tough decisions and pressures from society to conform. James was a giant in the faith, not because he never made mistakes, but because he never lost sight of the Lord. James's path wasn't straightforward, and he didn't always make the right decisions, but the book that he wrote before his death was born out of his incredible story and lessons that he learned along the way, lessons that ensured he ended his race well (2 Tim 4:7).

James's life is an incredible story of transformation. Just like every single one of us, his story wasn't always easy, but the growth he experienced made everything worthwhile. James's life and work continue to shine through the pages of his book.

Sound and healthy Christian living are, at its very heart, about having a strong and healthy relationship with God on both an individual and collective level. We accomplish this through knowledge of His Word and His will, and through the constant molding process that comes with His Word. We also develop a sound relationship with God through love, gratitude, and reverence for Him as our Creator. This involves a humble submission to Him and His guidance. Where are you on your walk before God? Are you estranged from the Lord? Have you risen to a servant of God yet? Like James, the process of becoming more and more Christ-like is a lifelong process. What did your Story of Transformation look like? How have you changed over the course of your spiritual walk with God? What changes do you still need to make?

SPIRITUAL FORMATION SECTION

Read Psalm 69:7–9, *"I endure insults for your sake; humiliation covers my face. I have become estranged from my brothers and a foreigner to the sons of my mother."* Close your eyes and envision Jesus watching His family leave for Jerusalem. Feel the sadness in Jesus's heart as they leave without Him. Then, let humility and gratitude fill your heart, knowing that Jesus experienced estrangement and division in His own earthly family so that you could spiritually become a part of His.

CHAPTER 2

THINK THROUGH YOUR TRIALS

JAMES 1:2-3

Imperative 1: Consider

INTRODUCTION

It is now time to begin our journey deep into the book of James. We will work through the book of James in a way that is different from the standard commentary. Starting right now, we are going to reveal which verbs have been enhanced into an imperative form and allow those imperatives to lead the way forward. Reading the book of James this way will allow us to hear his voice more clearly and see his teachings as lessons that he first learned himself: hard-fought lessons that he is placing into our hands. Commands are often seen in a negative light, but at the completion of this book, you will have a whole new perspective on the benefits that come from these clear spiritual directives. Additionally, James's character and words give us greater insight into who he was as a person and how passionate he was for God! As we begin, may his passion become our passion, and may we humbly sit at the feet of an individual who knew Jesus both spiritually as Lord and personally as a brother.

Imperative 1: Consider

Our very first imperative is found in James 1:2–3 with the command to "Consider."

Consider it pure joy, my brothers and sisters, whenever you face trials of many kinds, because you know that the testing of your faith produces perseverance.

Immediately we see James call us "his brethren." This is amazing because if you remember in Mark 3, this was precisely the lesson that Jesus was trying to teach His own family when they begged Him to leave His followers and return home to Nazareth. Through his own spiritual transformation, James finally came to learn the true meaning behind Jesus's words that day, when He said, *"Here are my mother and my brothers! Whoever does the will of God."* Incorporating verses 1 and 2, we can hear James saying: "First and foremost, I am a servant of the Lord, Jesus the Christ, and the rest of us who hold faith in Jesus and are doing the will of God, we are brothers and sisters." Acknowledging this not only pulls each Christian into a close relationship with Jesus, but it also invites us into God's story of redemption!

Our first imperative to "Consider," should be understood as the act of thinking through an event. Look at this not as a single, one-time response, but as a process. Consideration involves giving thought to or weighing out a situation. Then, once the situation has been carefully evaluated, we arrive at a decision on how we ought to proceed. "Consider it joy," is James's way of saying that for the family of

God, there is no guesswork involved in how we should react to life's trials. Our response has already been given to us: Joy. The imperative to consider is the deliberate process of arriving at that blessed state of joy.

For James, this first imperative to "consider," was deeply personal and something he learned firsthand. If he and his siblings had paused long enough to weigh the spiritual significance of Jesus's ministry rather than allow themselves to act from a place of fear, anger, and anxiety, perhaps they could have done more for Jesus in those final three years. But the lesson was learned, and now he implores us to go through the process so that we arrive at joy and not sadness and heartache. What does that process look like? First, we are faced with a hardship of some kind, a trial of life. Second, we are to stop and think it through carefully in order to be spiritually deliberate and intentional with our reaction, taking into account multiple spiritual perspectives. Finally, we arrive at the conclusion of the matter: a joy-filled response to our trial.

Responding to our trials from a place of intention and deliberation is challenging because we are living beings comprised of two natures. We are an outer being, which the Bible calls the flesh, possessing its own earthly desires, fueled by emotion and guided by earthly instincts. But we also have an inner being that is spiritual in nature. The two are always at odds against one another (Rom 7:14–25), because they're motivated from contradictory sources. These two natures cannot peacefully co-manage normally, let alone in the midst of trials. One must dominate the other with each decision that we make. What James is really asking us to do is ensure that our actions flow from the right source. We choose whether we will respond to our trials from the rational and intentional inner being (spirit), or the irrational, short-sighted, and selfish flesh.

This is why joy, the Christian response to trials, is listed as one of the attributes of the Fruit of the Spirit (Gal 5:22) because Christian joy is the result of a decision made by the inner spiritual being. Christian joy is not based on the fleeting circumstances of life or the unstable and constantly changing emotions of the body. Instead, true spiritual joy is a thoughtful and intentional product of the inner being's decision to honor God and be filled with His blessings.

Unfortunately, our outer nature (the body), is always going to feel and react first before our inner spiritual self can fully consider the situation. This is because it takes less time for our fight or flight response to respond than it does to think through a situation and decide on a God-honoring path forward. James is calling Christians everywhere to take the time to move past the feelings of the flesh and be purposeful and thoughtful in the Spirit towards our trials. If we follow the process, we will be firmly planted in the Lord, regardless of the trials of life.

This ability to move past the flesh and be guided by the Spirit is a special spiritual power that is unique to God's people. It is only possible because of a spiritual connection to God that strengthens our will and resolve. Where the world just acts according to whatever feels good, Christians are commanded to be more purposeful and thoughtful about how we live and how we respond to trials, knowing that we represent a God who loves us deeply and has equipped us to do better. Our power comes from the fact that both our relationship to God and our Christian conduct toward others are not based on how well things are going in our lives, nor is it based on how we feel at any given moment. Our Christian conduct is informed and shaped by a connection to a righteous and eternal God who transcends this earth and the hope we have in Him. God is infinite and eternal, so in like manner, our decisions should also be eternity-informed.

THE REASON FOR JOY

When people think of joy they often equate joy with happiness, but the two are not the same. Happiness fluctuates because it is a reaction to temporary circumstances which change from day to day. That's why happiness often becomes a rollercoaster ride. Joy, on the other hand, is the peaceful and content state of being that comes when we've broadened our perspective to such a degree that we've surrendered to God's care and grace. It comes from having God as our Father, the Holy Spirit as our Comforter, and Jesus as our Advocate and Savior. Joy results when a person partakes in *all* the blessings of God, in the manner that He intended. A Christian whose heart is filled to the brim with thankfulness, appreciation, and love to God for all His blessings can see that they are always surrounded by blessings. From that heart-filled place, Christians can find peace regardless of life's circumstances. Fear, panic, anxiety, mishaps, and misfortunes can compound and give us tunnel vision, causing us to see only the bad in life and feeling as though there is no escape. Going through the consideration process and intentionally recognizing the blessings that surround us breaks that downward spiral. Through it, we are reminded that God's presence always surrounds us and that the ways in which we have been blessed signify that we are loved beyond measure and in good hands.

There's something else at work here in this first imperative verse that can be easy to miss, but I want to make sure that it is covered. James says, *"Consider it all joy, my brethren, when you fall into various trials."* The trials of life are numerous and they come in all shapes and sizes. "All" and "various" are connected in the sense that different trials will yield some form of joy. Lean into that truth! No matter the circumstances of the trial, joy should be a constant companion within our hearts; a constant reminder that we belong to God and we are loved. Thus, Christian joy can and should be a constant source of strength in our lives, regardless of the trials of life, because it transcends the ups and downs of life. That doesn't mean that we won't go through heartache and sadness; that is inevitable as long as we exist in a fallen and sinful world. But Paul says that Christians can be *"sorrowful, yet always rejoicing"* (2 Cor 6:10). What this means is that through consideration of our trials, our heart's response to trials will be God-glorifying — ever thankful and always appreciative of the reminders that we have of God's presence. With that mindset, some form of joy and peace will always be found in any state of sadness or difficulty.

When we're in the midst of a trial and we're thinking through our blessings, it is imperative (no pun intended!) that we are also thinking of what we're going to gain when we get to the other side of it. James addresses that in verse 3, saying, *"... you know that the testing of your faith **produces steadfastness**."*

A trial or hardship is usually associated with loss. But here, James is guiding us as faithful followers of God to view each trial not as a loss, but as a gain. During the consideration process, we are not only thinking about God's faithfulness, looking for blessings, and choosing joy, but we are also reminding ourselves that no trial is ever in vain. (In fact, no action taken is ever in vain, when done with the glory of God in mind: *"So, whether you eat or drink, or whatever you do, do all to the glory of God"* (1 Cor 10:31)!)

What exactly are we gaining, then? At a minimum, we will have achieved steadfastness or endurance: two elements critical to spiritual longevity. That is only a starting point, however. There are infinite possibilities of how God can use a trial for the greater good and for our growth.

When we patiently endure the trials of life, never yielding in our joyful response, we also let others know that no situation, insult, circumstance, or trial is greater than the God we serve and that we, as His children, will not be robbed of our peace in Him. Our joy-filled responses are like seeds that we plant in those who take notice of our behavior. That seed produces the hope that they too can find peace in this difficult life. In a lost and ever-fluctuating world, Christians ought to be circles of peace and stability, showing the world that it is possible to maintain a deep state of joy, contentment, and gratitude no matter what. This will cause the lost to want to know more about how we are able to endure our trials in this way and (most importantly) it will cause God to be glorified!

In addition to James, another fantastic example of these spiritual truths is the Apostle Paul. The context of the following passage is a sad one. Paul is writing his letter to the Philippians from prison, where he has been condemned for preaching the cause of Christ. It is difficult to see how any blessing could come from imprisonment, but watch

how Paul perfectly demonstrates James's first imperative. He says,

> *I want you to know, brothers, that what has happened to me*
> *has really served to advance the gospel, so that it has become*
> *known throughout the whole imperial guard and to all the rest*
> *that my imprisonment is for Christ (Phil 1:12–13).*

In other words, "As I sit here locked up, suffering for the
cause of Christ, it has occurred to me that this terrible
circumstance has actually been to the glory of God because
it has advanced the gospel." We know from other passages
(Acts 18:2; Phil 4:22) that all the Jews had been commanded
to leave Rome. His chains eventually served as a way to
maintain a presence for Christ in Rome, ensuring that the
gospel went forward into the city, even into Caesar's own
home. The ability to think through a trial, search for the
blessings of God, and act in a joy-filled and spiritually
informed way, takes practice and it takes spiritual strength.
Paul, like James, had his own deep valleys but he serves as a
reminder to us that with God, all things are possible!

God's ultimate will for us is not that we would live
struggle-free lives here on earth. His will for us is to persevere until the end. In that regard, even though the trial may
bring us pain or hurt, our inner man can use it to draw us
closer to God and potentially reach others for Him. In the
end, that is why we can and are commanded to rejoice in
these circumstances.

Remember, though, this type of spiritual thinking is not
going to happen by accident. We must be prayerful,
thoughtful, and intentional about the way that we endure
every trial that we go through. Try this the next time you

go through a trial — or if you are currently experiencing one as we speak. Pause for a moment. Take a pen and paper out and begin to list the blessings that you are thankful for. This will help break the downward spiral of negativity and tunnel vision and turn your mind toward God and hope. Then, weigh those blessings against the trial. Begin to think through the trial and see what blessing can be found in the midst of this suffering. Is it teaching you a new lesson? Have you grown in virtues like patience, humility, and empathy? Have you felt God's presence even more while leaning into Him during this time? Are there any ways to use your experience as a testimony to help others? Remind yourself that your trial is not in vain and that you will come out on the other side with greater perseverance and steadfastness than before. Go through this considera-tion process as many times as you need until you arrive at that peaceful and contented state before the Lord that is called joy. And do not forget that one of the blessings that the Lord sends in orders to bring us joy is community. Do not suffer in silence. There is strength in that upper room, together with other believers. James invites you to join him there!

SPIRITUAL FORMATION SECTION

Write down *ALL* the stressors and weights that you are carrying on pieces of paper. Do not leave a single one out. If it is weight you are carrying, no matter how great or how small, put it on a page and then tear it out. Collect your many weights and spread them out on the floor so that you can see the full scope of the burden you are carrying. Pray over it and incorporate Matthew 11:28–29 into your prayer.

Recognize that you do not have to carry these burdens alone.

If you are a visual learner, or for maximum effect, take each note and safely burn it. Watch the smoke rise up as if to symbolize the burden being lifted to the presence and throne of God.

CHAPTER 3

TRIALS: THE SPIRITUAL GYM

JAMES 1:4

Imperative 2: Allow

INTRODUCTION

As we saw in the previous chapter, consideration is the process of thinking through our trials in order to give ourselves enough time to move past the immediate emotions felt in the body and respond to our trials in a spiritually-informed and well-reasoned manner. Christians are called to be a people of reasonableness and that reasonableness ought to be well-known (Phil 4:5), but we've all been in a situation where this isn't the case. Someone insults us, we receive an unexpected phone call, or an announcement is made and our hearts start racing and the blood gets pumping! The body's fight or flight response will always kick in first, and the temptation is to respond to the trial with those instincts. James's imperative to "consider" calls us to exercise self-control and draw strength from our spiritual/inner man to respond to our trials in a deliberate and intentional way, searching for the joyous blessings found even in the most challenging moments. When we respond to our trials with joy and when we arrive on the other side, we will be that much stronger. Each hurdle we overcome allows us to face the next challenge with greater confidence. This is the definition of steadfastness: the ability to overcome and persevere, no matter what valley we face in this life. Our second imperative from James is found in verse 4, and it builds on these powerful truths.

I. IMPERATIVE 2: ALLOW

James begins by saying, *"Allow steadfastness to have its full effect ..."* If we are using the inner being (our spiritual side) to consider our trials, thinking through how we're going to respond to those trials, and then deciding to be joyful during them, then we must also purpose in our hearts to allow the trial to run its course and glorify God in the process.

We are a society that rejects anything that is uncomfortable. We despise pain, and we live as though challenges will never come. We don't plan for the future, and we do not live within our means. Instead, we live day to day, being guided by what we think will make us happy. We prefer to communicate through carefully manicured text messages and social media posts because face-to-face conversation requires "real-time" communication exchanges that can be exhausting and challenging; so we avoid it. Even our parenting styles can reflect our stance on pain avoidance. We hover over our children and often remove their ability to choose and learn autonomy because we want to save them from consequences that we know they will not like. While this is healthy in some regards, what happens when our children's decision-making abilities are stunted? What happens when the difficulty of life catches them off guard as they enter into the world?

As a child in grade school, I remember hearing how chicks have to force their way out of their shell so that they can gain the strength to survive once they are out. Without this difficult task, the chick would be too weak to live. This example fits with the great irony of what James is teaching us about what to do with trials. Trials are necessary for us to gain the strength we need to increase in steadfastness and perseverance. We do ourselves no favors when we do not allow the trial to have its full effect. It is no wonder that James is commanding (not suggesting!) us to allow the process to work: it is that vital to our Christian development.

When a trying moment comes up in our life, there are three main ways in which we can respond. The first is in defeat: by choosing to give up, or by abandoning the situation altogether. Now, this is obviously the worst possible response for a Christian to have but unfortunately, it is a path many take. Second, we can choose to stumble through a trial. This is when Christians experience a trying event and engage in a sinful response that dishonors God. This can take on many different shapes and sizes. For example, it includes numbing or blunting the effects of the situation by abusing harmful substances like alcohol and drugs, to artificially endure the trial. Some give in to various other addictions and negative behaviors like pornography, infidelity, gambling, binge eating, and over-spending, which are all meant to accomplish the same thing: a temporary relief or reprieve from the suffering. Stumbling through a trial also includes any other negative reactions such as complaining, retaliating, taking vengeance, wrath, blame, resentment, and doubt. The third option we have is the response that James gives in verse 4: to *"allow the trial to have its full effect."* This is the choice that leans into both the trial and the Lord and it is the only one that produces a positive outcome.

To achieve this best-choice result, we have to do something that our outer being/body is not going to understand! We're going to have to intentionally choose to walk into the fire, rather than avoid it. Like I said, we don't like pain. We don't like to be uncomfortable, and we especially don't like to be in a position of weakness. But regardless of the discomfort, we must "bear up" under the trial and "patiently endure" through it—without giving up, and without dishonoring God. When we do that, we find that the struggle will produce something that we didn't have before it: greater patience, endurance, steadfastness, and perseverance.

There is an important point to clarify, however. In no way is it true that because these blessings are a result, the trial itself was sent by God. On the contrary, many of our trials are the result of the sins of others, our own missteps, or just the result of living in a broken world. Regardless of the source, trials for a Christian are opportunities for God to produce good out of any situation.

Endurance, patience, steadfastness, and perseverance are not simple traits for us to adopt; they are earned, and more importantly, developed through a trial-infused process. In order for patience, endurance, steadfastness, and perseverance to grow, they have to be flexed in the spiritual gym. Listen to Paul's words carefully:

Train yourself for godliness; for while bodily training is of some value, godliness is of value in every way, as it holds promise for the present life and also for the life to come (1 Tim 4:7–8).

The word "train" is **gym***nazo* — and we all know what happens in a gym. People sacrifice and exercise, breaking down their muscles and rebuilding them stronger and stronger. Food and special nutrients are also included in the process to support these efforts. Similarly, each trial will have a certain weight associated with it that acts upon on our spirituality. Some will be light, and others will be very difficult to carry and bear up under — but when carried in a godly way, every repetition will make us stronger than we were before. This is how spiritual giants are created.

On the other hand, stumbling through a trial or throwing in the white flag of defeat is equivalent to picking up a weight in the gym and then immediately dropping it to the ground and walking away. How can our spiritual muscles ever be trained and grow if that is how we bear that weight? Similarly, if you simply buy a membership to the gym and never attend, or if you watch television programs about fitness but never participate yourself, you will not achieve any results. The mind plays a large role in discipline, but muscle gain happens when the mind's decisions turn into actions.

Spiritual giants in the faith are at that level because they *chose* (actively decided) to walk, one foot in front of the other, into the deep valleys and up the mountains of life. They may have stumbled a time or two, but the one thing they all have in common is that they did not give up and they chose to honor and trust God. They not only are able to reap the benefits of having done this, they are uniquely qualified to assist others. This is the embodiment of Paul's message to the Colossian church to *"bear with each other."* (Col 3:13). The experienced Christian is strong enough to carry weaker brethren along, weathering offenses and insults that may come (Prov 19:11), not because it's enjoyable, but because at one point in time, they themselves were in that very same place of misery. They know what it's like to stumble, but out of their spiritual strength they are able to encourage others to choose forbearance because that is what creates opportunities for growth and learning. Spiritual giants in the faith are truly "clothed" with *"compassion, kindness, humility, gentleness, and patience"* (Col 3:12). They look like the Lord because they've traveled with Him through thick and thin!

A faithful Christian must be willing to courageously, patiently, and honorably endure the trials of life otherwise they will not grow. We do this by following James's command to allow the trial to work on us no matter how heavy the burden may be. And even though we know the results are worthwhile, allowing the trial to work is not easy because suffering is not easy. That is why we have to be constantly reminded of what James says next.

II. THE SPIRITUAL REFINING PROCESS

*Allow steadfastness have its full effect, so that **you may be perfect and complete**, lacking in nothing* (vs. 4b).

This describes the spiritual end-state that we all ought to aspire to — the motivation we need to keep at the forefront of our minds when we are discouraged or find ourselves weakening and considering an easier way out. We will get into this in greater detail at a later time, but for now, I will simply say that the word "perfect" does not mean sinless perfection, but is instead referring to a state of being that is fully equipped. That is why "complete, lacking in nothing" are paired with "perfect." The purpose of the spiritual gym is not just to build Christian "muscle," but to bring us to the next level of spiritual maturity that is needed to be prepared for whatever is to come in our lives, positive or negative.

It's not uncommon to find pictures of athletes or body-builders on the walls of a gym; these are individuals that people want to emulate. The pictures are there for motivation, to help the trainee power through the intense workout and stay focused on what they want to achieve. Similarly, Christians have a great cloud of witnesses to look to for inspiration and for encouragement. The great cloud of witnesses went on before us and lived through the same hardships of life and yet, they persevered (Heb 12:1–2).

Giants in the faith are forged in fire. Trials are not unique to Christians; all people go through difficult moments. But Christians are uniquely capable of walking through the trial of fire and coming out stronger and more equipped on the other side. Our connection to God and the great cloud of witnesses gives our suffering meaning and purpose. James is telling us that it is worthwhile to follow this path and that recalling these truths will help us in the moment of testing. When we have exercised enough self-control to be intentional about how we respond to our trial, and have determined in our hearts to find joy and to use all that we endured for our growth and learning, we will grow and we will honor God in the process. I love how Peter describes this spiritual development process in 1 Peter 1:6–7:

> ... *though now for a little while,* (*if it is essential*), *having been sorrowful in various tests, that the trial of your faith,* (*being more precious than gold, which is perishing*), *even now being* **proven through fire, may be found for praise and honor and to glory in the revelation of Jesus the Christ.**

Tests and trials put pressure on our faith in the Lord and pressure on our spiritual strength, but that pressure is like a refining process. Every trial can be met with joy if we intentionally approach it as an opportunity for refinement. Refinement equips us with the strength needed to run our life race with endurance and steadfastness and brings us to the finish line. As Peter said, when Jesus comes again, we will be inspected, and if we have endured through the refining process of life, we will "receive honor and glory and praise" from the Lord. He's referring to the moment when we will be told by Jesus, *"Well done good and faithful servant, well done! Enter into my rest!"* (Matt 25:23) Is that not a reward worth any trial we may face?

Also, notice the way that Peter describes the trials that take place in this refining process. He says that they were for a "little while" and he acknowledges that they made his readers "sorrowful." The sorrow mentioned is another reference to the immediate bodily response to suffering and trials. Before our inner man is allowed to thoroughly consider and come to a decision about our trials, our outer nature/body will be experiencing every kind of emotion and physical pain imaginable — and that is normal! Peter is describing the same dynamic as James did in his first imperative, but he's adding an additional piece that we can take courage from: "Yes, you went through some difficult trials and it grieved you and hurt you, but the trial (as we now know) was only temporary; it was only for a moment, but push through and do not give up! Do not forget that we are just passing through, on our way toward the presence of God!"

When we're in the middle of a trying situation, we must remind ourselves that it will not last forever, and that it will all be worth it! It can be difficult to maintain this perspective. When the refining fire is turned all the way up, minutes seem like hours. Time seems to slow down to a crawl. In the heat of the trial, it may feel as though it will never end and it may not turn out alright. Do not give up! We do not know what the future holds. We do not know what the Lord will do with this season of our lives, but take comfort knowing that it will not be in vain!

III. HOW TO "ALLOW"

I want to share a few thoughts on how to navigate tough moments in life. As I have mentioned, our trials are never in vain. Blessings can flow from even the deepest valleys. If this sounds cliché and too simplistic, let me assure you it is not: it requires quite a bit of intentionality on our end to drive these truths to heart. Here are a few ways to help with this feat.

FIRST: REMEMBER THE STORY YOU TELL

As spiritually-recreated people, born of water and the Spirit and made alive in Christ, our actions ("fruit") tell a story about the God we serve. This is a concept that you will see throughout this book, but it is one that we must always be aware of. Our mission as God's New Covenant people is to shine a light for all to see, not for our own glory, but to direct those who are lost in darkness toward God! Earlier, I referenced the spiritual "clothing" that giants in the faith wear: "clothing" made of compassion, kindness, humility, gentleness, and patience. God's intention for these qualities was for them to tell a story. Isaiah 61:9–10,

> *Their offspring shall be known among the nations, and their descendants in the midst of the peoples; all who see them shall acknowledge them, that they are an offspring the LORD has blessed. I will greatly rejoice in the LORD; my soul shall exult in my God, for he has clothed me with the garments of salvation; he has covered me with the robe of righteousness, as a bridegroom decks himself like a priest with a beautiful headdress, and as a bride adorns herself with her jewels.*

Christians are a reflection of God here on earth and our actions, like visible clothing, are often how people notice or recognize us, causing them to acknowledge the blessed nature of being His children. That is a very humbling thought and one that we ought to never forget. The way that we respond to our trials is one way to tell a story to the world around us about the God we serve. If we are people of fear and anxiety in the face of trials, the message we are sending to our community is that we are not confident in our Lord. We imply that He is not trustworthy enough for us to be at peace in the real world outside of Bible study and sermons. If we are a people of anger, contention and complaint, then the message that we are sending is two-fold: either the God we serve has taught us to be this way, or we are not satisfied with the Lord and are unhappy with the life that He given us. We should be very conscious of what we are telling others about our Lord through our own reactions to life's ups and downs; it often could mean the difference between salvation of a soul or the repelling of one.

But what a joy it is to be able to give a lost and dying world a glimpse of something bigger and better and more everlasting than what exists in the day-to-day pain and struggle! What a gift it is to have the ability to show them what it means to have a true relationship with the Lord! Trials are perfect opportunities to demonstrate our love, trust, and confidence in the Lord. People will be astonished when they see a Christian go through difficult moments and still praise God. They will recognize a source of strength that they themselves lack, opening up opportunities to reach them for Christ.

SECOND: FIND A GYM PARTNER

Paul himself is the one who said that godliness training is like "gym" training. As one who frequents the gym, I can tell you that it is always good to have a partner/spotter for encouragement, motivation, and safety. A gym partner inspires you with their own work and stamina and cheers you on as you press through with yours. A gym spotter is a person who stands behind the weightlifter, ready to step in and take the weight if the lifter is unable to finish the rep.

Even the most active and experienced weightlifter requires a spotter from time to time because muscles can fail unexpectedly. A spotter is the one who is standing tall, ready to help raise the weight and put it back on the rack. If we are going through a trial and the trial has become too much for us to bear alone, it is important to find a gym partner — someone who is strong enough to help us so that we are not crushed under the weight of our trial. Colossians 3:13 isn't the only place where Paul talks about this supporting of our brethren. In Romans 15:1–2, he says:

> We who are strong have an obligation **to bear with** the failings of the weak, and not to please ourselves. Let each of us please his neighbor for his good, to build him up.

The word "failing" above means "to lose strength." The imagery brings the words muscle fatigue to mind. Our muscles have a certain amount of strength in them before they weaken and can no longer perform at the same levels without rest and recuperation. But the point at which this happens differs for each person. In the same way, not all of us are at the same level of spiritual maturity; some of us are just starting our growth process, while others are spiritually established and strong.

If we are at the point of feeling as if we are spiritually mature and strong, Paul is saying that we have an obligation to "spot" a believer who may be weakening in their trial (Gal 6:1–2). If they begin to fatigue and thus to stumble, we are to reach out and help them. Notice that the phrase is "bear **with**" them, not "carry their burdens **for** them." We are to strengthen them with support and encouragement, drawing their eyes up to the finish line and helping them to develop their spiritual muscles. It is not our role to fight their battle for them or attempt to remove the trial from their lives, but to partner with them through it. A spiritually mature Christian recognizes when and how much assistance must be given. Too much help and the individual will only grow weaker, but without enough support and encouragement, and they may stumble. Much prayer should go into this entire process.

If we are the ones who are struggling and experiencing weariness, our obligation is to let someone know we need help. We cannot and should not suffer in silence. Remember, joy is the peaceful and contented state that comes when we are filled with all of God's blessings. Some of the blessings that God has given to us come only through community. Spiritual partnership is an aid He meant for us to utilize. Victory in trials and full joy cannot be experienced if we are disconnected from the body of believers and on our own. Don't let pain and suffering cause you to believe that you are all alone, or to place unwarranted shame on asking for help!

I'm reminded of Jesus's own disciples who about to have to branch out on their own, into new territory. Just before Jesus's arrest and crucifixion, Jesus famously told His disciples, *"A new commandment I give to you, that you love one another: just as I have loved you, you also are to love one another"* (John 13:34). The word new is *kainos*, which means something familiar that is used in an unprecedented way. Every trial we go through is new and unprecedented, just like the new territory that Jesus's disciples would find themselves in without Jesus by their side. What Jesus was telling them and what both He and James are telling us today, is that if we take the same love and support that we have for one another and we take it into new territory, no matter what happens, we will make it through together! You are never alone with Christ Jesus and His children!

THIRD: MAINTAIN A PROPER CHRISTIAN PERSPECTIVE

As we saw in this chapter, we allow our trials to work on us because we know that they will help us become stronger. That's part of what we're thinking about as we are going through the consideration process, but in addition to that, we should also be thinking about the life to come. Doing so will also help us to maintain perspective as we are faithfully enduring through our trials. 2 Corinthians 4:8–10 and 16–17, speak to this very point:

> *We are afflicted in every way, but not crushed; perplexed, but not driven to despair; persecuted, but not forsaken; struck down, but not destroyed; always carrying in the body the death of Jesus, so that the life of Jesus may also be manifested in our bodies ... . So we do not lose heart. Though our outer man is wasting away, our inner man is being renewed day by day. For this **light momentary affliction is preparing for us an eternal weight of glory beyond all comprehension.***

Clearly, it is not enough to just know the purpose behind our struggles; we must go a step further and apply it as a tool for endurance. Even though we may be crushed, driven to despair, persecuted, or struck down in this life, Christians are told to press on, always carrying the death of Jesus with us and proclaiming the good news of salvation so that the life of Jesus is demonstrated in us. Every hardship we go through ... every trial that we overcome ... every day that passes in which we do not give up ... brings us closer to a glory that is beyond all comparison! That is why, although the outer man may be wasting away, the inner man is renewed day by day in the knowledge that the refining fire lasts only for a moment compared to eternity with God. A Christian's suffering, when endured in a God-honoring way, is never in vain because it is bringing us closer to our Creator. Using this motivation as a way to keep perspective during trials enables us to "let steadfastness have its full effect, [so that we] may be perfect and complete, lacking in nothing."

SPIRITUAL FORMATION SECTION

There is a stronger, more equipped, and more spiritual end-state that the Lord is bringing you to through your trials! It does not mean that the Lord is the one who caused the trial, but it absolutely means that He can bring about much good from any and all situations!

Take a moment to reflect on your life. Grab a blank sheet of paper and draw a vertical line down the middle of it. On the left side, write *ALL* of the challenges that you have experienced in your life, starting at the first one that you can remember. Leave nothing out because each of these challenges and valleys is part of your story. On the opposite side, write about whatever lessons you learned and what skills you developed when you came out on the other side of the correlating challenge. If the challenge is still ongoing, simply write the word "patience" on the other side. See if you can discern the providential hand of God working in your life through this exercise.

Once you have completed the lists on both sides, say a prayer of thanksgiving to the Lord for all that He has done for you. Make sure to tell your story to someone else!

For an added layer of meaning, memorize Psalm 145:4–5:

One generation will commend Your works to the next, and they shall proclaim Your mighty acts, the glorious splendor of Your majesty. And I will meditate on Your wondrous works.

CHAPTER 4

FULLY COMMITTED

JAMES 1:5-8

Imperatives 3–5: Let Him ask (vs. 5 and vs. 6) Must Not Suppose (vs. 7)

INTRODUCTION

S piritual endurance and steadfastness require a fully committed mindset, leaving no room for backpedaling or keeping open the possibility of doing things our own way if the plan doesn't work out. Because of our human weakness, we often struggle with this. We fear what can happen when we give up control over decision-making. As human beings, we're also notorious for padding potential failure with caveats and conditions ("Plan Bs") before we ever even try something new because we fear shame and vulnerability. With God, there is no reason to prepare for failure or hesitate when it comes to yielding to Him. He has shown us over and over again that He can be trusted. He has also already won the victory (Col 2:15; 1 Cor 15:57) and all we have to do is follow in Jesus's footsteps! The Psalmist says,

"In you, Lord my God, I put my trust. I trust in you ... No one who hopes in you will ever be put to shame ..." (Ps 25:1–3).

This portion of James offers three bold imperative statements that speak to the unashamed and fully committed Christian mindset. Fear and doubt, especially during trials, will naturally be our greatest enemy but, as James is going to show, with the correct mentality we can overcome every deep valley that this difficult life can bring.

I. IMPERATIVES 3–5

"Let Him Ask" and "Must Not Suppose"

> *If any of you lacks wisdom, **let him ask God**, who gives generously to all without reproach, and it will be given him. But **let him ask** in faith, with no doubting, for the one who doubts is like a wave of the sea that is driven and tossed by the wind. For that **person must not suppose** that he will receive anything from the Lord; he is a double-minded man, unstable in all his ways (Jas 1:5–8).*

What is being described in this scene is a turbulent ocean with powerful waves overtaking each other. The doubter is in the midst of the waves, being thrown around from side to side. With each crashing wave, death draws near. James declares that the doubter *"must not suppose that he will receive anything from the Lord."* This is a very strong and seemingly harsh statement considering the fact that every person on earth has experienced doubts at one time or another! We all know what it feels like to be that person caught in the raging storm, being overtaken by waves from all sides. Verse 8 clarifies what James means when he speaks of the one he calls the doubter.

James explains that this storm of doubt isn't caused by a lack of belief in the existence of God, but rather, it is the product of attempting to navigate life with two sets of competing values and interpretive lenses. The real issue at hand is not just an instance of shaky trust, but a self-created ocean of chaos. A true doubter is not someone who experiences a qualm or two under stress; rather, he or she is what is dubbed "double-minded." This kind of person cannot suppose that he will arrive at victory or receive any answers from the Lord because he is seeking to interpret life through two very different lenses: a spiritual one and a physical one and it's that conflicting thinking that is preventing him from moving forward in faith. He has his foot on both the brake and the gas pedal at the same time, resulting in waves of confusion. How we interpret the world around us will have a significant impact on how we understand our trials. How we understand our trials will determine whether we move forward in a God-honoring way. This is crucial to walking in faith but be warned, the spiritual path takes work! Let's look at how Jesus addressed this very issue.

II. SEEING BUT NEVER PERCEIVING

There's a famous exchange that happened in the life of Jesus when He was asked by His disciples why He taught in parables instead of just speaking to them plainly. Jesus's teachings required another level of thinking and interpretive lens in order to properly discern His meaning. The disciples were frustrated with Jesus, clearly not used to this style of teaching. Jesus's response to their exasperation is powerful! He said,

> The mystery of the kingdom of God has been given to you, but to those on the outside everything is expressed in parables, so that, **they may be ever seeing but never perceiving**, and **ever hearing but never understanding**; otherwise they might turn and be forgiven (Mark 4:11–12).

The parable was a tool to teach a message to a group of people, but with different results. Although all would "see" and "hear" the same message, not all would "perceive" and "understand" the true meaning of the parable. Using parables was a way of sorting the true followers of Jesus from those who had ulterior motives. Those who truly hungered and thirsted for righteousness (Matt 5:6) would have the type of spiritual discernment needed to perceive Jesus's meaning and, consequently, understand what they must do. All others would walk away either confused, frustrated, or oblivious, despite having heard the same message. Jesus's intention was not to prevent people from being saved, but to teach only those who desired to learn: people whose hearts were primed and ready to receive His pearls of spiritual truths. Salvation does not hinge on the presentation of information alone. If that were the case, then we would now be living in an age of unprecedented church growth since information is more readily available now than it has been at any point in our history. Unfortunately, as we see here, relaying information or teaching truth will not determine whether a person will comprehend and turn from their sin; the heart must be ready to receive and make that kind of commitment.

Thus, Jesus was addressing the lack of spiritual discernment and insight here, which is exactly what James is referring to as well when he talks about the "double-minded." Spiritual discernment is the ability to perceive and understand God's will and work within the world and within the lives of His children. It helps us to see the blessings that surround us and to tap into God's bigger plan even when we're in a valley or are in the midst of trials. The double-minded are individuals that interpret the world, their purpose in the world, and their life situations differently — through a mixture of wisdom gained from years of physical observation of the world with some spiritual insight sprinkled in. Instead of using God's Word as the measure of their circumstances, they try to pick and choose the parts that fit their own agenda and look to human interpretation just as often or more than the spiritual. In contrast, James and Jesus both teach that for success during trials and blessings in life, our hearts must be ready and fully committed to the maintenance of spiritual perspective and discernment — not a subjective and faulty combination of godly and worldly wisdom.

James's doubter is stuck in a turbulent storm because he has *some* understanding of the spiritual, but he's reluctant to fully commit. The observations and "insights" that he's gained from the world tell him to go in a different direction, and he has decided to give this equal weight to the word of the Lord. Even though he knows that God is in control, the doubter turns to sinful and worldly avenues contrary to God in order to cope with what he finds difficult to comprehend or hard to endure. Perhaps he partially believes God but not with the "really big stuff." Maybe he prays for strength to endure but does not actually believe in what he is saying so he searches for a substitute. Or possibly he speaks the "right" Christian words and presents the proper appearance, but behind it all he is acting just the opposite because he dislikes the discomfort involved with endurance. Whatever the case may be, because this kind of mindset is so divergent from true discernment, what he fails to see is that the turbulent sea in which he is caught is of his own making. He is in fact creating turmoil and disorder by trying to straddle the fence between committed faith and worldly intuition. The danger is clear so it's no wonder that James sends these forceful warnings.

The Lord calls his people to walk by faith and not by sight (2 Cor 5:7). This takes a real commitment from God's people and is a skill that must be honed and intentionally pursued in the midst of trials. Otherwise, what will result is the doubt storm described above. Ironically, trials are the best places for this skill to be exercised, which is another reason why we should allow our trials to have their full effect.

One of the best examples that we have of this truth is the Apostle Paul. He told the Corinthian church:

Five times I received at the hands of the Jews the forty lashes less one. Three times I was beaten with rods. Once I was stoned. Three times I was shipwrecked; a night and a day I was adrift at sea; on frequent journeys, in danger from rivers, danger from robbers, danger from my own people, danger from Gentiles, danger in the city, danger in the wilderness, danger at sea, danger from false brothers; in toil and hardship, through many a sleepless night, in hunger and thirst, often without food, in cold and exposure (2 Cor 11:24–27).

If spiritual discernment was gleaned solely through difficult tests and trials, Paul would have possessed the strongest kind of discernment imaginable at the end of this period of time in his life! Yet, we find out this was not the case. Despite all he endured, he still had not fully learned how to discern spiritual meaning from his challenges. Instead, it appears his trials had had the opposite effect and caused him to be prideful. We know this because of what he records in the very next chapter. In a profoundly humble statement of self-reflection, made possible only with spiritual wisdom from above, Paul wrote that even after all these circumstances, a "thorn of flesh" had been given to him in order to prevent him from becoming conceited (2 Cor 12:7). Whatever this "thorn" was, it was a deep valley for him, a trial unlike anything he had faced before. Perhaps in all that he had experienced before he had found ways to still rely on his own abilities to a certain extent. Regardless, this trial was different. This "thorn" brought him to his knees, and he realized that the only way it would be overcome was by God. He cried out and pled with God multiple times to remove it from him, but to no avail. This affliction was proof that even with having overcome so many previous obstacles, Paul could still stumble backward into short-term thinking. He engaged in the pursuit of relief rather than seeking the fortitude to discern spiritual meaning and a God-honoring path forward. Where he had triumphed once before under persecution, Paul was now stagnant in the turbulent sea.

Finally, the Lord responded to Paul, saying, *"My grace is sufficient for you, for my power is made perfect in weakness"* (2 Cor 12:9). Ever receptive to the Lord's instructions, Paul concluded the matter with one of his most famous statements: *"I will boast all the more gladly in my weaknesses, so that the power of Christ may rest on me"* (2 Cor 12:9). It takes real, experiential spiritual discernment to comprehend that the power of God is honed and brought to completion through trials. When we are weak, we are more open to accepting help and direction from the Lord. Circumstances humble us and they cause us to see our limitations. Some bring us to our knees. If we, like Paul, can reach the point of a full commitment to using spiritual discernment to perceive God's will in a trial, we become powerful! The strength does not come from ourselves, but through a mentality that brings us closer to our Creator, the all-powerful God.

James, too, wants us to know that while God is not always the source of our trials, He can make His children stronger through them. It is during these critical moments that we have an opportunity to intentionally draw closer to Him, allowing his "power to be made perfect" in our weakness. This in turn opens our spiritual eyes wider and we will see that no matter how difficult life may become, God is in control. If we stay under His wing, we will be right where we need to be, allowing us to say, *"Have mercy on me, O God, have mercy, for in You my soul takes refuge. In the shadow of Your wings I will take shelter until the danger has passed"* (Ps 57:1).

Paul learned these lessons on spiritual discernment, surrender, and contentment in the end and it was in no small part due to his "thorn" moment. Years later, he spoke of his growth to the Philippian church, saying,

> ... **I have learned** *in whatever situation I am to be content. I know how to be brought low, and I know how to abound. In any and every circumstance, I have learned the secret of facing*

plenty and hunger, abundance and need. I can do all things through him who strengthens me (Phil 4:11–13).

The secret Paul learned was in cultivating spiritual discernment — moving past reacting to our trials from a physical motive and searching for the opportunities for spiritual growth. With a mindset like that, every circumstance becomes an opportunity for spiritual growth because it is a chance to move through life in a peaceful, content, and God-honoring manner which in turn causes us to grow in our spirituality and discernment. Because of this, Paul was ultimately able to see his challenges as a process in which he grew and learned and was enabled to better focus on his blessings, arriving at a state of contentment regardless of circumstance. He was even able to see past his prison bars and chains to the actual will of God for the church: *"Now I want you to know, brethren, that my circumstances have turned out for the greater progress of the gospel"* (Phil 1:12). It is a blessing beyond measure to have the peace, contentment, and joy that comes from spiritual discernment. This skill is critical to spiritual resiliency and endurance in the faith.

III. COMMITTING TO THE LORD

Returning to our verses in James, we can see how it takes commitment to do as James commands and look to God for strength and discernment, resisting the temptation to lean on our own understanding. In his own way, James is mirroring the lessons Paul spoke of by using an imperative to call attention to the need to turn to God for wisdom and a proper perspective of the world. If we do not develop the ability to use spiritual discernment and fully commit, we will be tossed from side to side through life and buffeted by difficulties without an anchor to hold us safe.

James's last imperative in this section is, *"that person **must not suppose** that he will receive anything from the Lord."* This indicates that we ourselves can hinder the spiritual growth process and limit God's hand in our lives. It is not God's will that this should happen, but it is a definite possibility when hearts have not been prepared to receive truth.

I want to leave you with a passage from Proverbs 16. In it, we see how Christians can become more spiritually discerning, avoiding the peril of self-created chaos seas.

> ***Commit*** *your work to the LORD, and your plans will be established. The LORD has made everything for its **purpose**, even the wicked for the day of trouble ... How much better to get wisdom than gold! To **get understanding** is to be chosen rather than silver ... The **wise** of heart is called **discerning** ... (Prov 16:3–4,16, 21a).*

First, you must "commit" to the Lord. Pledge your allegiance to Jesus Christ, not just as your Savior, but also as your King. View your family, your home, your resources, your work, and your plans as an extension of His grace, to be used for His glory. You are a steward of your King and all that you possess has been entrusted to your keeping with the ultimate purpose of bringing Him glory. Commit to the idea that everything you do and all that you have will be used to further His will on earth.

Second, always be mindful of God's purpose. So much of our frustration in life happens when our own expectations are not met, or when people fail to live up to our standards. We can react in anger, rebelliousness, and judgment, railing against what is unfair in our own eyes while trying alternative means to accomplish what we want ... or, we can turn our focus to the Lord. Rather than create a storm of double-mindedness, ask yourself the following questions: "What is God's purpose in all of this? How can I react in a way that honors Him? What am I learning about God right now, in this season?" Remaining concentrated on God and the bigger picture will keep you anchored under the shadow of His wing.

Third, "get understanding." Proverbs 12:15 says, *"The way of a fool is right in his own eyes, but a wise man listens to advice."* If you do not have a spiritual mentor, you are missing out on one of the most amazing blessings that God Himself has mandated. There is a special type of growth that can only happen when we're vulnerable, open, and honest with another person. It is a growth that only takes place when our pride is rooted out of secrecy and removed through exposure and accountability. If you're simultaneously operating on the premise that God will provide you with a path forward and refusing to seek guidance from one of His giants in the faith, your heart is not in a place of preparedness for truth. Don't be afraid of submitting to the direction of someone who has been where you are. It just might be the tool you've been waiting for.

Lastly, develop your ability to exercise spiritual discernment by filling your heart with godly wisdom. Proverbs 2 makes a powerful case for why a person should seek wisdom. The wise of heart can take a blessing from God and can cause it to grow exponentially. Seek God's wisdom through His Word and also by observing how faithful Christians apply such wisdom in their own daily living. If you seek wisdom, it will always be found! Commit your heart and mind to God and you will find peace, even when others are tossed about in the storm.

SPIRITUAL FORMATION SECTION

God has a purpose for everything. If we commit to a life of spiritual discernment, we will be able to see the blessings that surround us more clearly, as well as the blessing of growth that comes with trials and God's ultimate will for us. What are your fears? What are the areas in your life that you have not committed to the Lord? Are you committed to perceiving and understanding the will and work of God, or are you simply just observing and being tossed side to side? Are you asking and seeking direction, or just assuming it will come?

CHAPTER 5

HUMILITY: PERFECTLY BALANCED BEFORE GOD

JAMES 1:9–11

Imperative 6: Boast in Elevation/Humbling

INTRODUCTION

The Lord is the great equalizer. He alone should be the hope and source of strength for our heart, mind, and soul, regardless of our social standing and background. In addition to this, the Lord should also be our "boast." We tend to think of boasting or exaltation as something bad or prideful, but actually that is just what James is commanding us to do in his sixth imperative: *"Let the lowly brother boast."* Far from being a statement of arrogance, boasting in this context gives glory to God and allows all of His children, regardless of whether they are wealthy or poor, to meet in the same, perfectly balanced place called humility.

I. THE LORD, THE GREAT EQUALIZER

Refreshing our memory of verse 2, we recall that James commanded us to "consider" it joy when we go through various trials because they have the potential to make us stronger spiritually, depending on how we choose to respond to them. James continued in verse 3 by commanding us to "allow" steadfastness and endurance to work without hindering the process. Then, in the previous chapter, we saw James build on these spiritual truths by bringing in spiritual discernment. All of these elements are pointing to the single fact that our inner being can and should be used to thoughtfully and intentionally respond to the circumstances of life. Watch how James applies that principle in the familiar dynamic of poverty and wealth.

James begins in verses 9–10 by saying,

> Let the lowly brother **boast in his elevation**, but the rich brother in **humbling**, because like a flower of the grass he will pass away.

Lowly brethren, here, are meant to be understood as those who have very little in terms of material possessions, social standing, and voice. Speaking to the lowly brethren first, James tells them that while they are enduring the trials in life that come with not possessing as much as others, there is still a reason to be joyful.

Due to the world's superficial standard of success, it is possible for our lack of possessions and status to cause us to feel inferior. If all we are doing is simply observing things with our physical eyes and through our human nature, the "glitter and gold" in society easily gives the impression of success and happiness. If we are not exercising spiritual discernment, wealth (or the lack thereof) can cause us to fall into the trap of seeing ourselves as equivalent to our possessions: more (or better) if we have more; less (or valueless) if we have less.

But if we're using spiritual discernment, we are able to see past the superficial and know that our true value comes not from what we own, but from our status in the Lord as His image-bearers. All people, regardless of their status and income, have the intrinsic value of having been created in the image of God (Gen 1:27). James recognized that the lowly brethren did not view themselves in this way. As we saw in chapter 1, James has a tremendous passion for the poor and lowly of this world and was not content to leave them in a place of low esteem or shame so he commands them to lift their countenance because they have been "elevated." This elevation or "exaltation," as some translations say, is what happens when a soul has found its way back to God. This is a joy and self-confidence that can be found amidst all trials. It is not based on the world's goods or systems of measurement. It is an elevation that does not refer to a promotion or the climbing of some social ladder. It is spiritual in nature: a state of being where a soul returns to the warm glow of the Lord's presence and knows its worth in Him — the way the Lord always intended from the beginning before sin destroyed our soul's countenance. Let me expound on that for a moment.

In Genesis 4:6–7, the Lord asked Cain, *"Why are you angry? And why has your countenance fallen? If you do well, will not your countenance be lifted up?"* It is important to note that this took place after Cain's sacrifice had been rejected by God due to disobedience but before Cain killed his brother,

Abel, out of jealousy. Abel's sacrifice HAD been accepted by God; Hebrews 11:4 tells us that this was because it was a sacrifice of faith. It was a result of belief, trust, and obedience to the Lord and His instructions regarding the proper type of sacrifice to make: all necessary components of true faith. Cain's sacrifice was not of faith, and it was rejected. We know that God gave specific direction for the kind of sacrifice he would accept (blood of a firstborn animal), but Cain offered him the fruit of his garden. The problem was not whether or not Cain's offering was fully ripened, or plentiful enough; the issue was that he gave according to what *he* thought was good, and not as the Lord had instructed. His sacrifice was one of "sight," or human effort (2 Cor 5:7), and it implied that Cain believed he knew better than the Lord what was right and holy. It symbolized the clash that still exists between God's offer of salvation by faith in His Son's blood and what is frequently man's rejection of it, insisting he can "do it himself."

What God told Cain that day was absolutely powerful, even for us today! As with salvation itself, when humans propose to tackle life through their own efforts, or with their own interpretations and value systems, the result is one of "sight," and not faith. When we measure something — be it humanity, actions, abilities, or resources — by anything other than what God considers good and has outlined as acceptable, our faces will always end up "fallen." We will always come up short of God's intended blessing. Our faces may fall out of anger and frustration, embarrassment from being rejected, or maybe even because we lack self-worth, but none of these are what God desires for His special creation. As He said to Cain, if we do well (i.e., operate in faith), our countenance will be "lifted up." He wants this for us, and He wants all of mankind to have a view of self that is based on what He deems good and well.

I am reminded of the prophet Jeremiah who told the nation of Israel,

> *Thus says the LORD: 'Let not the wise man boast in his wisdom, let not the mighty man boast in his might, let not the rich man boast in his riches,* **but let him who boasts boast in this, that he understands and knows me, that I am the LORD** *who practices steadfast love, justice, and righteousness in the earth. For in these things I delight,' declares the LORD (Jer 9:23–24).*

A faithful child of God has no reason to suffer with an unhealthy self-esteem because a faithful child of God is, by God's own standard, doing well just by being His and obeying Him. If our face has fallen, this should be an indication that we have either allowed the world's twisted standards and expectations to warp our thinking or, we are in an angry state toward God because of our own sin and pride. Our sense of self and self-esteem should flow from our Creator and when it does, our countenance will naturally be lifted up!

But to the lowly brethren in the church who may be struggling with feeling like you are not worth as much as the next person, James is making sure you know that this self-image issue is of no small concern. If it was unimportant, he would not have drawn attention to it and then commanded us to boast in our elevation as God's children. As Jeremiah prophetically and authoritatively spoke, this is not a sinful boast, but rather an accurate and bold confidence in your true identity in the Lord. James does not encourage us to brag of our own rights and abilities but instead calls us to celebrate them in the Lord knowing that He sustains us all. Through a healthy relationship with our Maker and the use of spiritual discernment, we know who we are and can live confidently with the identity and purpose that God declared good (1 Tim 4:4–5). Nobody can take that identity and position of favor away from us because of something so transitory as money or belongings. Those are useful tools that can be used to the glory of God, but they too were created by Him and were never meant to be used to disparage anyone. What an overwhelming feeling of joy this is, knowing that in the eyes of God, we are His special children and that we are on the right path to be with Him someday in heaven. We can boast of this, for it stems from the love of God itself, lifting our chins by His mercy and care.

But James doesn't just address the lowly brethren; he has a message for the rich as well, and it's the same one: "boast." How can the same principle be applied to such different demographics? Grammatically, yes, the command to "boast" in the Lord is being applied to both groups of people here. Yet, it actually means different things to each one. Notice the descriptors for each: one is going up and the other is coming down ("elevate" vs. "humble"). The word boast is *kauchaomai*. Within this word is the smaller one, "*auchen*," which means "neck." The image is that of a neck which moves the head in various directions.

The poor, or the "lowly," sometimes suffer from having their head bowed low, eyes to the ground, feeling unable or unworthy to look others in the eye. To them, the Lord says to lift up your countenance — to have your neck move the head UP to a state that is not arrogant, but healthy and confident.

While the rich also participate in the identity and joy of their value in Christ, they are instructed to focus on an additional area because due to their circumstances and the difference in power, they have extra responsibility to avoid sin or shame. In some ways, their wealth requires them to be held accountable in more ways than those without it. Because of the increase in temptation that is involved with material wealth, the rich all too often raise their countenances over others in haughtiness. (*"As for the rich in this present age, charge them not to be haughty, nor to set their hopes on the uncertainty of riches"* 1 Tim 6:17). To them, James says boast not just in their salvation, but in the humbling moments of their lives as well — moments which help to hit a spiritual reset button and lower the face from a place of self-importance to one that is eye-to-eye with their fellow man. The neck moves the head DOWN this time. When we are humbled, we receive spiritual clarity regarding who is actually in control and who deserves the admiration and recognition ... and it isn't us, no matter how large our bank account may be. Just as a proper understanding of how valuable the lowly are in Christ, it also keeps the wealthy from falling into the trap of being prideful and self-serving. In both instances, contentment and blessing are found by re-focusing their identity based on Christ, putting aside external factors like income or status.

One must come up and one must come down, but they both meet at the same point of humility before the Lord and security in their proper place as His children. This perfectly balanced view of ourselves is what Paul calls "sober judgment" in Romans 12: *"I say to everyone among you not to think of himself more highly than he ought to think, but to think with* *sober judgment"* (verse 3). In other words, "Don't look at things in the same way that the world does; shape your mind and heart to view the world and yourself as God views things and as He views you. Be spiritually discerning and don't think of yourself more highly than you ought ... Don't think of yourselves too lowly, either, but see yourself in truth as the spirit that you are, created in the image of God. View yourselves in that perfectly balanced, confident, and humble state."

Going back to the imagery in James, both the rich and the lowly have to adjust their head and neck. One must be elevated in value and the other must come down in humbleness, but both must meet in equality. That equal place of spiritual contentment, confidence, and health is called humility. Humility is not low self-esteem; humility is a healthy sense of peaceful self-identity that comes from the Lord, and it is only possible when we see the world through the eyes of spiritual discernment. The lowly brethren can be confident yet humble before the Lord because they know that their sense of self-worth does not come from possessions. The wealthy can also be in this confident yet humble state of peace when they realize that their wealth is not their own and they are not in control; they are simply stewards of God's possessions that must be used to honor Him and His will.

II. SPIRITUAL DISCERNMENT = TRUE SPIRITUAL SUCCESS

James powerfully reinforces this teaching on unity among God's people and the need for spiritual discernment to arrive there by bringing in a well-placed reference to another great equalizer: time. James does this through a reference to the prophet Isaiah. Look at the similarity between this section of Scripture and Isaiah 40:6–8:

> A voice says, "Cry out!" And I asked, "What should I cry out?" "All flesh is like grass, and all its glory like the flowers of the field. The grass withers, the flowers fall when the breath of the LORD blows on them; indeed, the people are grass. The grass withers and the flowers fall, but the word of our God stands forever.

Both of these passages bring to mind the brevity of life and the impartiality of the effects of time. Isaiah argues that time and God's will have ultimate control and no person of any status or income can change the inevitable; therefore, all are the same in their place of dependence. James points out that since external circumstance is not what instills worth, all are the same in what gives them value. Both are emphasizing that there is a place of unity to be had, and this place is the only one that truly satisfies.

Without spiritual discernment, we're left with the illusion that a person's value hinges on their possessions, or lack of them. That kind of thinking destroys unity and raises barriers within the church family. These verses teach us that there is another way to understand the world and our standing therein. At the end of the day, we're all equal and all subject to the Lord; no amount, or deficit, of possessions can change that.

Our days on earth are all coming to an end. That's not an attempt to sadden or depress us with futility; rather, it is just the reality of our human condition. This was not God's intention, but a consequence of sin (Gen 2:17).

Flowers are perfect illustrations of our lives because although their life span is shorter than ours, we share many similarities with them. Flowers are born, they are nourished, they grow, they have great beauty for a while, their beauty begins to fade, and then they die. Although the individual flower passes, more take their place, and on and on it goes. It's the same for a human being. As much as it may pain us to consider, we will die and life will go on; more people will be born, time will pass, and soon, we become just a set of memories to a small, select number of people — one of the millions of citizens that have walked the earth and accomplished good and bad in their lifetime. Some may be remembered more than others or by larger amounts of people, but none are immortal and none can prevent their passing and the overshadowing of those who come after them. Like the flowers that surround us, our lives have cycles that cannot be avoided. When we remember this, truly there is no cause to think ourselves better than anyone else.

Another mistake many makes is to spend their lifetime in worldly pursuits, whether in an attempt to gain them out of dissatisfaction and anger towards the hand they've been dealt, or through efforts to keep what they have and stay in the privileged lifestyle they've led. Both ignore the fact that they are mortal and headed towards a very real spiritual destination. Every being who has ever lived is on an eternal spiritual path. Every being who has ever lived will exist for eternity after their death, but not all will live for eternity in the presence of God, the Creator. Luxuries and comforts can be wonderful, but destructive. Lowly circumstances can cause us to feel valueless. Both can hinder our ability to cultivate spiritual discernment or, even worse, make us unfruitful for Christ (Matt 13:22). James will have a little more to say about this personal responsibility later. Putting all this together, what James is truly saying is that anything that moves our head and neck into a confident and humble state before the Lord ought to bring us joy.

Does this sound familiar? It should. James hinted at it when he began his entire book with, *"Count it all joy when you fall into various trials."* James would know better than anyone else how this could play out in someone's life. While his brother was alive, he didn't believe or support Him. It wasn't until Jesus was crucified and resurrected that James finally came to faith in Him. A moment of extreme pain for his family and himself was the catalyst for turning his life in an entirely new and abundant direction. That is why he is especially qualified to exhort us to rejoice and be glad in the trials of life, even if they cause us distress or pain, because anything that works to turn our focus and attention on the Lord is a real blessing!

After all, we are here for only a short time; but unlike the flower, we have more life to live in the presence of Almighty God after this life is over. As Jesus says in Luke 12:15, *"One's life does not consist in the abundance of his possessions."* This world and its contents are not the end goal. Our life does not consist of or even attain value in the abundance of possessions, but in accepting Christ's work on the cross ... walking closely with Him in the surety that we will be in the presence of God for all eternity ... growing in our ability to see the world through spiritual eyes ... developing our relationship with God, and mirroring Him to the world around us ...

that is true spiritual life and spiritual success! Count it all joy when something causes us to remember that!

SPIRITUAL FORMATION SECTION

Read 1 Timothy 6:17–19:

> *As for the rich in this present age, charge them not to be haughty, nor to set their hopes on the uncertainty of riches, but on God, who richly provides us with everything to enjoy. They are to do good, to be rich in good works, to be generous and ready to share, thus storing up treasure for themselves as a good foundation for the future, **so that they may take hold of that which is truly life.***

Have you truly lived? Paul makes a clear distinction between the physical life and the true spiritual life. The opportunity to do what Paul describes as "storing up treasure" by living for the Lord and building a good foundation for the future is an incredible blessing for a Christian, especially when difficult moments arrive, because it helps keep the challenges we experience in perspective. When we're busy preparing for eternity, it helps our earthly valleys seem brief and temporary. On a scale of 1–10, where would you say your spiritual discernment ability is? What do you think it would take to improve that ability? Choose one of the examples of how to attain discernment described in chapter 4 and commit yourself to apply it in your own life.

CHAPTER 6

BLESSED

INTRODUCTION

Although James 1:12 has no imperative within it, this verse acts as a summary to the previous commands regarding patient endurance and spiritual discernment. By focusing closely on the meaning of endurance and steadfastness illustrated here, we can have a better understanding of how to grow in these virtues.

I. #BLESSED

Many of the newer translations of the English Bible render James 1:12 as, *"Blessed is the man who remains steadfast under trial ... ."* The New American Standard (NAS) says, *"Blessed is a man who perseveres under trial"* and the King James Version (KJV) says, *"Blessed is the man that endureth temptation"* Notice the three different words used in these translations: "steadfast, persevere, and endure." The original Greek word literally means to "bear up under," which is more of a description of what we are doing when we are pressing forward in the midst of trials.

The original meaning invokes the image of a person under some type of weight, moving forward despite being loaded under their burden. Some trials are heavy and others are light, but they are all burdens that must be carried. This verse cries out, "Brethren, blessed is the one who is carrying the weight of trials but is still persevering and not giving up!" The blessing he is describing is not in the trial itself, but in the fact that if the person endures and perseveres, they will have gained something that they did not have before, when they arrive on the other side.

The trials of life are common to all mankind. Christians go through trials, just like the rest of the world, but with some significant differences. First, the Master that we are serving is unlike any other! Jesus famously told His disciples,

> *Come to me, all who labor and are heavy laden, and I will give you rest. Take my yoke upon you, and learn from me, for I am gentle and lowly in heart, and you will find rest for your souls. For my yoke is easy, and my burden is light (Matt 11:28–30).*

At this moment in time when Jesus said these words, the towns that Jesus was visiting to tell them the good news of the Kingdom of God, were all bound and weighed with burdens that they could no longer endure. These burdens were created by the Pharisees and other religious leaders of that day. Jesus said that they, *"tie up heavy burdens, hard to bear, and lay them on people's shoulders, but they themselves are not willing to move them with their finger"* (Matt 23:4). Like them, Jesus invites us to take on His yoke and serve Him.

Unlike the ridiculous boxes and structures of man, His burden light and He is a Master that is meek and lowly in heart, giving us rest and nourishment. Our burdens that we carry in life can, at times, be overwhelming, but under the name of Christ we have a support network like no other! Not only do we have strength and support from the Lord, but we also have fellow brothers and sisters in the faith who stand ready to help.

Second, we have a cloud of witnesses that surrounds us, which gives us courage and endurance. Hebrews 12:1 says, *"Therefore, since we are surrounded by so great a cloud of witnesses, let us also lay aside every weight, and sin which clings so closely, and let us run with endurance the race that is set before us."* The thought of our brethren cheering us on as we go through our own trials is a wonderfully comforting one. The thought of one day becoming one of those cheering voices, cheering on our children and grandchildren is also incredibly strengthening. Although it takes a degree of vulnerability, our children and grandchildren must know about all the triumphs and hardships of life and how God was present through it all. This is the unique *story of redemption* that the cloud is proclaiming to us who are living. Our Christian legacy is not one of surrender and defeat. It is one of victory in Jesus!

Lastly, we go through our trials with courage and dignity, knowing that we have become co-suffers with Christ Jesus. Paul told the Roman church,

> *The Spirit himself bears witness with our spirit that we are children of God, and if children, then heirs — heirs of God and fellow heirs with Christ, **provided we suffer with him** in order that we may also be glorified with him (Rom 8:16–17).*

Blessed is the one who endures because they are enduring their trials while serving a Master that is unlike any other, they are being cheered on by a vast cloud of faithful brethren who endured long before us, and they are persevering in their suffering like Jesus, making them co-heirs of glory!

II. THE REASON FOR BLESSING!

Returning to verse 12, take note of what James says awaits the one who runs with endurance: *"... when he has stood the test he will receive the **crown of life** ... ."* Christians run their race of life with a purpose! This physical world and the life that we live in it is much like a proving ground for the soul. We are not called to live as "mere humans," who are guided by the flesh (1 Cor 3:3); instead, we are called to a more noble way of life. This fundamental principle of the Christian life is the basis of Jesus's teaching in the Sermon on the Mount, where he famously listed all the "blessed" statements and showed how each reaped its own reward. It's no wonder then why James mirrors this pattern; both he and his brother speak of the caliber of a Christian life that does not act like the rest of the world. It surprises the world! It is not a life that is substandard, but one that sets the standard, modeled after a living and powerful God and fueled by trust in Him. In this context, to receive a blessing from the Lord means that a person has conducted themselves in a way that brings honor to the Lord.

This passage is so encouraging because it tells us that without a doubt, we will experience trials, but in the end, it will all be worth it! For making it through the proving ground, we will receive the crown of life eternal in the presence of the Lord! This passage is only the beginning! James is about to open the floodgates of knowledge, giving us tools on how to persevere and more importantly, giving us insight into the role that we are playing within God's broader story of redemption. Verse 12 is the perfect capstone to the previous imperatives. In short, James is saying that the road is not always an easy one, but you are not alone and your pain and suffering have meaning because it is contributing toward your spiritual development.

SPIRITUAL FORMATION SECTION

Do not give up! I know that life can be difficult, but thinking of our challenges as weights that are making us stronger can help keep our trials in perspective. Think about those who went through the same ups and downs of life and stayed faithful until the end. Take a moment to reflect on the life of someone you consider to be a giant in the faith, past or present. If they're still with us, spend some time with them and ask them about their life. Take note of each struggle that they endured. On your own, place a weight value on the burdens that they persevered through. Chart their life on a time line and write down the length of time that they carried the burden. Add weight on top of weight if they carried more during a certain length of time. This will serve as a visual demonstration of how a spiritual giant in the faith is made in this proving ground and equipping life!

CHAPTER 7

DO NOT BLAME GOD

JAMES 1:13–15

Imperative 7: Let No One Say

INTRODUCTION

Verses 13–15 contain our seventh imperative from James. Here, James is imploring us to avoid the temptation of blaming God for our sin and avoid using blame as a means of avoiding personal responsibility for the consequences of our sin. We will also see that the temptation to sin attacks three distinct weaknesses in mankind: the lust of the eyes, the lust of the flesh, and the pride of life. These verses help us better understand the nature of sin and what we can do to fight against it.

I. "LET NO ONE SAY"

Having just capped his discussion on trials with verse 12, James now switches gears and speaks about temptations. This is the other side to the testing of our faith that greatly differs from what comes with the trials and the tests that the Lord allows us to go through in order to grow. Sometimes our faith can be tested in the darker arena of temptation. Interestingly, the word for "test" in places such as Hebrews 11:17 and 2 Corinthians 13:5, in its original language, is the same word that James is using here when he writes "temptation." Whether the word refers to a test or a temptation is determined by the context of the verse. Both have the potential to result in positive outcomes and a greater equipping of our faith, but they are vastly different in appearance and in how they are to be treated. Tests and trials are either sent by God or are things that we experience in the natural course of life and we do not have a choice in the matter. We are instructed to react to them with patience and endurance. Temptations, however, are not from God. These are tests of faith that apply pressure to our weaknesses and all too often have their origin from our adversary. It is not God's will for a temptation to work upon us until we give in to the desire and turn from what is right. He has given us the means to overcome them but the choice is ours.

In verses 13 and 14, James says,

Let no one say when he is tempted, "I am being tempted by God," for God cannot be tempted with evil, and he himself tempts no one. But each person is tempted when he is lured and enticed by his own desire.

The imperative is in verse 13: *"Let no one say I am tempted by God."* James commands Christians everywhere, when they are tempted to sin or are suffering the consequences of a sin, not to blame it on God because God is not in the business of causing His own people to trip and fall. The Lord will never instigate someone to do the very thing that He hates. These are strong words from James about taking personal responsibility for our actions.

Although they are powerfully worded, they're also comforting. There is great comfort in his openness about the human experience. Trials, tests, and temptations are all part of our journey and James does not hide that from his readers. He has gone through such things himself! He's very clear with the fact that it is not a question of *if* you will go through them, but rather *when*. His book is unapologetically real regarding the Christian's struggles with trials and with sin. We do not have to hide our battles with sin from the Lord and pretend like they do not exist; every believer will experience it. The Lord is fully aware that life here on Earth is not only challenging, but also filled with temptation and failure. Even Christ experienced temptation while in the form of man (Heb 4:15). Temptation to sin is all around us and unavoidable. After all, sin is the very reason why Jesus came to Earth: to defeat the works of our enemy (1 John 3:8). If it were possible to achieve sinless perfection, there would have been no need for Jesus to save us. That does not mean that we should not strengthen our resolve to understand temptation and protect ourselves from it.

We can't begin to wrap our minds around temptation and sin without first going to the start of the Bible. It was in this beginning that Satan learned three ways man was especially susceptible to sin, and he has been using them to his advantage ever since.

II. "IN THE BEGINNING ..."

In the beginning of the early days of creation, Satan sought to destroy the perfect peace that God had established by tempting Adam and Eve to sin. Satan desired to reintroduce chaos back into the earth and the means by which he sought to do so was through temptation. To be more specific, Satan desires to tempt mankind into disobeying God's instructions for how we are to use the gifts of creation, including our free will. Immediately following the creation, the Lord told mankind to be fruitful and multiply and subdue the earth, but in the course of exercising authority over the creation, they were not permitted to eat of the Tree of the Knowledge of Good and Evil. It was here that Satan saw an opportunity. He asked Eve, *"Did God actually say, 'You shall not eat of any tree in the garden'?"* (Gen 3:1). Eve responded to him saying, *"We may eat of the fruit of the trees in the garden, but God said, 'You shall not eat of the fruit of the tree that is in the midst of the garden, neither shall you touch it, lest you die.'"*

It's easy to miss, but there's an error in what Eve said. Remember, Eve was not the one who received the command; Adam was, in Genesis 1:15–17, which took place before Eve was created. She received the command from Adam, but if you compare God's original ordinance to what she repeated to Satan, you'll see that something has been added. She said, "Neither shall you touch it." Now, we do not know if this part was added by Adam to give a little "extra" layer of warning regarding the tree's fruit, or how this embellishment came about, but regardless of the source, it worked against them (as does anything man tries to "add" to God's words). Once persuaded, as soon as Eve touched the fruit and saw that she wasn't killed instantly, she must have become more emboldened to step further into her sinful decision. The seemingly small weakness was exploited, and it would not be the last time that our adversary would employ this tactic.

This is the origin story of sin and the downfall of mankind and notice that it all began with temptation — the same kind of temptation James is warning about in our verses. In Genesis 3:6, we see Satan's use of the three components of temptation.

> So when the woman **saw that the tree was good for food,** and that it was a **delight to the eyes,** and that the tree was to be **desired to make one wise,** she took of its fruit and ate, and she also gave some to her husband who was with her, and he ate.

First, the fruit was a "delight to the eyes." Delight is from the Hebrew word *avach,* which means "to lean into," implying there is a kind of pull involved with it. The fruit was so mesmerizing in Eve's eyes that the more she looked at it, the more it caused her to lean in towards the tree; the closer she came to the fruit, the harder it was to escape. She felt the draw of its attraction. Second, the fruit was "good for food," which represents the lust and desires of the human body or flesh. And finally, the fruit was coveted by Eve because it promised "to make one wise"— in other words, in exchange for disobedience, she believed she would gain the wisdom to be like and perhaps even equal to God himself. This was the pride of life at work because that is what pride does: it convinces us that we can rival or replace God Himself.

The lust of the eyes, the lust of the flesh, and the pride of life are Satan's weapons and by using them together, he put Eve in a situation where her own desires would lead her to an opening to sin. Satan has long understood that when these three parts to temptation are met with an opportunity, that is the moment when mankind is most vulnerable to sin. Therefore, this cannot be overstated: *the closer we get to the opportunity to sin, the harder it is to resist!*

Luke 4 is the next place that we see Satan employ these three temptation tactics, but this time he's targeting the Son of God, "the second Adam" (1 Cor 15:45–49). Because Jesus was fully human, Satan saw an opportunity. Jesus was capable of feeling the same pull and desires as Adam and Eve, so Satan decided to attack in the same manner that caused the fall of man earlier.

After forty days of traveling in the wilderness, Jesus was hungry. Satan presented Jesus with an offer. He said, *"If you are the Son of God, command this stone to become bread."* He wanted Jesus to abuse His power for personal comfort and thus satisfy the **lust of the flesh**. Satan thought that because Jesus had a human body, He would be susceptible to this weakness in his flesh. Jesus rejected Him by quoting Scripture, *"It is written, Man shall not live by bread alone."*

Next, Satan took Jesus up on a high point and

> **showed** Him all the kingdoms of the world in a moment of time, and said to Him, 'To you I will give all this authority **and their glory** ... If you, then, will worship me, it will all be yours.

Here, Satan tempted Jesus with the **lust of the eyes** by visually presenting what he thought would be appealing enough to cause Christ to sin. But Jesus again countered with Scripture and said, *"It is written, 'You shall worship the LORD your God, and Him only shall you serve.'"*

Finally, Satan tempted Jesus with the **pride of life** by taking Jesus to the pinnacle of the temple and saying,

> *If you are the Son of God, throw yourself down; for it is written, "He will commend His angels concerning you, to guard you ... on their hands they will bear you up, lest you strike your foot against a stone."*

If Christ had obeyed and thrown Himself from that height, He would have forced His Father to protect him, thereby arrogantly demonstrating that He could manipulate God — a thought that only the most prideful heart could even conjure. Jesus simply responded with more Scripture: *"It is written, you shall not tempt the Lord your God."*

After failing to bait Jesus, Luke 4:13 says that Satan, *"departed from him until an opportune time."* Our enemy will not rest from presenting opportunities for us to sin. Even when Jesus defeated him in this encounter, he began working through the lives of others to try and hinder Jesus's work. To drive the point home even further and demonstrate just how persistent Satan is, Luke goes on to tell us that Satan even asked God personally for Jesus's disciples. He asked to sift each of them "like wheat" (Luke 22:31). In those days, wheat was vigorously tossed about to separate the wheat from the chaff. The wind would blow away the lighter chaff, leaving the heavier wheat to fall to the ground and be collected. Satan's "winds" are the opportunities he presents for us to sin. These are temptations that separate the true and committed followers of God from those who are prideful and self-serving and easily carried away. When

Satan asked to "sift" the disciples, it was his intent for them to fail, revealing what kind of disciples Jesus surrounded Himself with and how they reacted under pressure. Sadly, they would end up carried away by fear, doubt, and self-preservation, accomplishing Satan's goal. Yet, like James, the apostles would recover from their failures and rise again as bold, committed followers of God, never to waver again! Satan may try his best, but God will always be the victor.

These stories can encourage us by illustrating that it is possible to overcome temptation and not sin. Even if we have wavered or fallen, they inspire us to get back up and keep moving forward. James's words are also helpful in revealing details of how Satan uses his tactics in a variety of ways. A forewarned person is a prepared person; understanding the danger will equip us to recognize and react when such situations appear in our own lives. To quote Paul, we are not ignorant of the Devil's devices (2 Cor 2:11). Even John reminds us of Satan's arsenal when he admonishes,

> Do not love the world or anything in the world. If anyone loves the world, the love of the Father is not in him. For all that is in the world — **the desires of the flesh, the desires of the eyes, and the pride of life** — is not from the Father but from the world. The world is passing away along with its desires, but whoever does the will of God remains forever (1 John 2:15–17).

Having looked at Satan's opportunities for sin and how our own desires make us susceptible to them, let's bring all of this context into what James says next regarding sin.

III. AN UNHEALTHY UNION

> *But each person is tempted when he is lured and enticed by his*
> *own desire. **Then desire when it has conceived gives birth***
> ***to sin**, and sin when it is fully grown brings forth death (Jas*
> *1:13–15).*

Just as the origin story of sin from Genesis 3 illustrated how universal sin entered the world, James is explaining the source of our own personal sin. He says our desire, when coupled with opportunity, brings forth sin at the point at which we give in, forming an unhealthy union between the two. I will say it again: when opportunity for sin and our desires join together in an unhealthy union, sin is conceived. And sin, when it is fully grown or developed (or when we have nurtured and cared for it and caused it to increase), becomes overwhelming and destructive, to the point of spiritual death.

As humans living in a fleshly body in the earthly world, we are plagued by our weaknesses and the desires of our old way of life, but that does not mean that we have to give in to those temptations. Our temptation is only one-half of the unhealthy union. Recall that the other parent of sin is the opportunity itself. Remove the opportunity and you remove the hold that sin can have. Paul says in 1 Corinthians 10:13,

> *No temptation has overtaken you that is not common to man.*
> *God is faithful, and **he will not let you be tempted beyond***
> ***your ability**, but with the temptation, **he will also provide***
> ***the way of escape**, that you may be able to endure it.*

Escape from what you might ask? Escape from the opportunity! It is for this very reason that Ephesians 4:27 also says, *"Give **no opportunity** to the devil."* There will always be a way to get away and flee temptation; God will not allow Satan to work on us beyond our ability to escape from him. But it is vitally important to remember the downfall of man in Genesis 3! Remember that the "way of escape" from the temptation to sin becomes more and more difficult the nearer we get to it. The closer we put ourselves to the opportunity to sin, the more likely that we will give in to that temptation. I like to think of the story of Joseph in captivity in Egypt. At one point, his master's wife attempted to seduce him; she even grabbed a hold of his shirt in the process. Jacob took escaping from temptation quite seriously; he turned and ran away so quickly that his shirt tore and she was left standing alone with a piece of his sleeve! This may seem comical in a way, but in reality, sin is so very devastating that we should all flee from it — literally, if need be.

Do not forget: Opportunity + Desire = Sin. It is often quicker and most effective to concentrate on neutralizing the opportunity portion of the equation. Each of us has particular weaknesses and sins that we are susceptible to and must constantly keep in check. If we know that we are especially vulnerable to a weakness of the flesh, then we must do what we can to remove any opportunity possible that relates to it so that we do not sin. Be mindful of the fact that weaknesses change over time, as well. The weaknesses and sins we struggle with in our youth may not be the same that we struggle with in adulthood. As Christians, we must stay aware and grow stronger against the weaknesses of the flesh and its temptations because that is what brings about the holiness we are called to pursue.

IV. COMBATING TEMPTATION

As James has illustrated, sin occurs when we yield to temptations, whether external or internal. External temptations come from others and from our surroundings. Internal temptations are personal weaknesses that we give into that may not even be visible or known to anyone else. To combat sin, we need to be cognizant of both. And regardless of the source of temptation, we have some effective devices to utilize as we seek to remain firmly committed to God.

First, create distance between yourself and the opportunity to sin by "putting on" Christ for all to see. Look at Romans 13:13–14:

> Let us behave properly as in the day, not in carousing and drunkenness, not in sexual promiscuity and sensuality, not in strife and jealousy. **But put on the Lord Jesus Christ** and make no provision for the flesh in regard to its lusts.

"Putting on" Christ, or being "clothed" with Him means that we radiate the personality and character of Christ to the point that Jesus becomes clearly seen in us — almost as though He was a part of the very clothes we wear! By doing this, we will "make no provision for the flesh," creating space between us and worldly behavior. If you have a clearly visible testimony and reputation for following God's ways, you will attract people of similar mentality and purpose. Your status as a true believer will encourage any who are serious about their faith to engage with you. As a result, there will be less exposure to sinful temptation and more support for godly choices. Your light will also give those lost in the sea of chaos a way back to safety.

Another way of looking at this strategy is through accountability. It is incredibly difficult to act in a way that dishonors God when everyone knows that you are a believer, just as it is much harder to lie when you know the people around you are aware of the truth. There is something about "wearing" Jesus that helps give you that extra motivation to bypass Satan's pitfalls. We represent the Lord and our behavior should mirror that truth. In no way would a true believer ever wish to disparage his Savior or somehow reflect badly upon Him. Reminding ourselves of this dynamic in some way can be the key to successfully withstanding temptation.

Accountability also provides a secondary method of avoiding sin. If we have a close Christian friend, often that relationship can assist us in fighting temptation. It is a valuable bond indeed when we have someone who understands our weaknesses and will encourage us in standing strong against them. I have heard of Christians who, recognizing they were being tempted, called upon their friends for help and thereby avoided something they would later regret.

A second strategy to combat sin is to renew and refocus our mind daily. Ephesians 4:22–23 talks of this.

> *Put off your old self,* which belongs to your former manner of life and is corrupt through deceitful desires, and to be *renewed in the spirit of your minds*, and to put on the new self, created after the likeness of God in true *righteousness and holiness.*

It is amazing what happens when we begin the day in meditation and prayer. Starting the day with a spirit of humility and gratitude to the Lord for the blessings of life, expressing to Him our appreciation for the ways in which the day will bring chances for us to do His will and take care of our responsibilities, is an excellent way of filling your mind with God. As Paul says above, we need to renew our minds and mold it in the image of God, who is righteousness and holy. This is especially important when we are in our workplaces because not everyone that we meet will respect the Lord. Sometimes the world has a way of bringing our renewed minds down, so find moments throughout the day to pause and pray. When we fill our minds with good things, it leaves little room for thoughts and actions that lead to sin. When the flesh is pulling fiercely and the desire to sin is growing, invite the Lord into the situation through prayer. You'll find this to be one of the most powerful weapons that we have. No wonder our hearts and minds are to pray without ceasing!

Along the same lines, memorization of Scripture also renews our minds in Him. Remember how effective it was for Jesus in deterring Satan in the desert! God's Word is mightier than any temptation and it can help a great deal if we build an arsenal of verses to strengthen us during tempting situations. When our minds are filled with God and His Word, we close the window of opportunity for sin.

Finally, remember that pride can easily fool us into thinking that our life is our own to use freely as we please, living to satisfy fleshly wants and desires. This kind of approach operates under the assumption that we know how to direct our steps better than our Creator does. Paul alludes to those who fell prey to this kind of thinking in Romans 1:21,

> For **although they knew God, they did not honor him as God** or give thanks to him, but they became futile in their thinking, and their foolish hearts were darkened.

Honoring God means honoring Him as the Creator. This means living life to the fullest, but under His guidance and for His glory. A life of sin, selfishness, and pride can often present itself in such a way that it seems appealing at first, but the wise who live for God will avoid the snares of death that lurk underneath (Prov 13:14–15). James 1:13–15 is all about taking personal responsibility for our actions and finding ways to fortify our hearts and minds against temptation. As every voice cheering in the cloud of witnesses can attest to, it is a lifelong journey, but one that is possible!

SPIRITUAL FORMATION SECTION

What are your sins? Honestly, now: what do you struggle with in secret? What seas of chaos have you created? Has secrecy kept these sins alive? Bring your sin out into the open by finding a person that you trust and sharing with them the challenges that you face. Find someone who is willing to be as open with you as you are with them. Discuss your struggles and brainstorm ways to keep each other accountable in the battle. This kind of vulnerability forges powerful bonds. As God did in the early days of creation, defeat the darkness and chaos by inviting the *"light of the knowledge of the glory of God in the face of Jesus Christ"* (2 Cor 4:1–6).

CHAPTER 8

SELF-DECEPTION

JAMES 1:16–18

Imperative 8: Do not be Deceived

INTRODUCTION

The first chapter of James has primarily consisted of his guidance regarding the trials of life and the temptations that we experience along the way and how to protect the heart, mind, soul, and strength from sin. In this section, verses 16–18, James gives us our eighth imperative command. This imperative will serve as a conclusion to all that has come before. James brings in several interesting arguments to illustrate that there are two paths in life. One wanders aimlessly away from the Lord, the other leads to the Lord, and we get to decide for ourselves which one we will take. This section serves as James's version of Joshua's famous line to the nation of Israel: *"Choose you this day whom you will serve"* (Josh 24:15).

I. "DO NOT BE DECEIVED"

Do not be deceived, my beloved brothers (Jas 1:16).

Our imperative is found in the phrase, "Do not be deceived." The word "deception" used here is the Greek word, *planao*, which is where we get our modern word, "planet." The planets were once thought to be wandering and roaming bodies in the sky. What a vivid way to describe someone who has been deceived: roaming away from the truth and wandering off the path of righteousness. The deceived are just like this, wearing self-imposed blinders and ignoring any truth they may encounter. For them, the truth stands in the way of their own personal desires. That is what self-deception is: the act of fooling ourselves, or allowing ourselves to be misled, so that we then proceed to remove any moral "obstacle" standing in the way of what we want, pretending it doesn't exist. Yet, we know that flouting truth and pursuing our own fleshly desires always results in sin, pain, and destruction in the end. That is why self-deception can be considered the precursor to self-inflicted heartache.

In this context, self-deception occurs when a person knows the truth but has rationalized their immoral actions by putting a biblical twist on their behavior. It appears that there were individuals who were not only being tempted and failing, but who were also attempting to justify their sin and make excuses for it by blaming the circumstances on God. They were rationalizing their behavior by shifting the blame for their actions, saying that it was the Lord who had either caused them to sin, or had permitted them to sin. They were submitting to temptation and feeding the desires of their flesh, all the while saying that the Lord approved of this.

This is a clear form of self-deception. God will never put someone in a position where they would do the very thing that brought about the need for Him to sacrifice His Son. As we discussed earlier, temptation is from Satan, and it is designed to cause a Christian to fall. Rationalizing, justifying, and blaming are not ways in which the Lord wants us to deal with our sin. On the contrary, these behaviors are simply ways of deceiving ourselves by hardening our hearts to the truth. Proverbs 28:13–14 tells us,

> *Whoever **conceals his transgressions** will not prosper, but he who confesses and forsakes them will obtain mercy. Blessed is the one who fears the LORD always, but whoever **hardens his heart** will fall into calamity.*

One of the absolute worst things that a Christian can do before the Lord is attempt to conceal or make light of sin. For the believer, hardening our hearts to the sin in our lives is unquestionably dangerous because God's grace is intimately connected to our reception of that grace. You cannot receive what you do not need. When we harden our hearts and refuse to admit our desperate need for the Lord and His mercy, we are voluntarily rejecting the forgiving sacrifice of Jesus because in essence, we are denying the very need for His sacrifice. Any attempt to decrease, downplay, or shift the blame of our sin is an indirect cheapening of the sacrifice of Jesus.

The Lord will not fail to show mercy to those who cry out to Him for help and will rescue those who are open with Him about their sin, but to those who wish to make excuses and who are prideful about their sin, there no longer remains a sacrifice for them. Hebrews 10:26 speaks on precisely this issue: "For if we go on sinning deliberately after receiving the knowledge of the truth, there no longer remains a sacrifice for sins." The free gift of God's grace is such an incredible blessing, it has unfortunately attempted to be abused by the self-deceived. The deliberate sin referenced in Hebrews occurs when someone intentionally abuses God's mercy and the propitiatory sacrifice of Jesus by sinning with the mindset that God's grace will cover them anyway, regardless of how much evil they commit. This is self-deception! To this, Paul would say,

> *What shall we say then? Are we to continue in sin that grace may abound? By no means! How can we who died to sin still live in it?... Do you not know that if you present yourselves to anyone as obedient slaves, you are slaves of the one whom you obey, either of sin, which leads to death, or of obedience, which leads to righteousness? (Rom 6:1–2, 16)*

The choice whether to abuse the gift of grace and live for sin and the flesh or humbly obey the Lord is entirely up to us. It dictates whether we choose to receive the gift of grace or reject it outright. Self-deception is a choice! The Lord wants us to scrape away all the lies that the world tries to convince us to believe, remove the layers of self-deception, and rise up as His true image-bearers by taking personal responsibility for our actions and decision. When we are humble and under the shadow of His wing and walking *"in the light as He is in the light, we have fellowship with one another, and the blood of Jesus His Son cleanses us from all sin"* (1 John 1:7). On the other hand, if we deceive ourselves and make light of sin or *"say we have not sinned, we make him a liar, and his word is not in us"* (1 John 1:10). The choice is ours, but so is the consequence of that choice! As James says, "do not be deceived."

II. GOD DOES NOT CHANGE

> *Every good* **gift** *and every perfect* **gift** *is from above, coming down from the Father of lights with whom there is no variation or shadow due to change (Jas 1:17).*

God cannot be the source of temptation because only good flows from God. Anyone who says that it was God who put the opportunity to sin in front of them has obviously deceived themselves. This is James's imperative message for verse 17. Notice the two occurrences of the word "gift" in this verse. Although they appear the same in our English translation, in their original Greek form, there are actually two different words that carry slightly different meanings. In my opinion, The New American Standard Version (NASV) is the best at capturing the subtle difference. Notice the way it renders the verse: *"Every* **good thing given** *and every* **perfect gift** *is from above, coming down from the Father of lights, with whom there is no variation or shifting shadow."* Again, it's subtle, but James is saying that the very act of giving good things, as well as everything that is just plain good, comes from God! Said another way, every single act of goodness that you see in the world today comes from the same source within us: God. At our core, we all have the capacity for good!

Every single being on this earth has goodness and the

capacity to be good within them because we have been created in God's image. All have His "goodness thumbprint" upon our heart, mind, and soul —even those that do not believe in God. When James brings up God's goodness in us during his discussion of temptation and sin, he is saying, "God is the ultimate Father, and He would absolutely never do something that would cause His children to stumble. God has only — and will only — give good things to His creation, and that will never change. So, for those who want to blame God for their behavior, own up to your mistakes and take responsibility!"

James's emphasis on God as a good Father is a truth he no doubt heard Jesus speak of many times over. One of the best characteristics of his goodness is that it does not change; God Himself does not change! As His children, we need stability and someone whose constancy we can completely trust without reservation. Hear Jesus's own words about the Father:

> Ask, and it will be given to you; seek, and you will find; knock, and it will be opened to you. For everyone who asks receives, and the one who seeks, finds and to the one who knocks, it will be opened. Or which one of you, if his son asks him for bread, will give him a stone? Or if he asks for a fish, will give him a serpent? If you then, who are evil, know how to give good gifts to your children, how much more will your Father who is in heaven give good things to those who ask him! (Matt 7:7–11)

Even the Psalmist said, "The LORD is like a Father to His children, tender and compassionate to those who fear Him." (Ps 103:13). It is an impossibility to even think that God would be the author of anything so negative as sin in His children's lives when He is good and desires only good for them. The best part about that is that this characteristic of God will never go away: *"Forever, O LORD, your word is firmly fixed in the heavens. Your faithfulness endures to all generations; you have established the earth, and it stands fast"* (Ps 119: 89–90).

I love the planetary imagery used in this Psalm. God's Word is firmly fixed, planted, and immovable in the heavens. Speaking of the heavens, watch this! Remember the Greek word *planao,* or wandering planets, we discussed earlier in verse 16? It has a connection here in verse 17. James writes that God is the giver of every good thing and every perfect gift; in Him "there is no variation or shadow due to change." Unlike the deceived, who wander about like the planets, God doesn't change. His light doesn't change or move or cast different shadows due to movement. The word "variation" here in verse 17 is another Grecian word that alludes to the idea of an orbit. The variation of the orbits and shadows formed from light are constantly shifting in perspective because of the rotation of the Earth. From where we stand, the brightest light of all is the sun, and even the sun seems to move throughout the day, rising and setting in different locations and casting shadows here and there depending upon the time. But God is the ultimate Father and source of light, and His light never changes. We can only speculate as to why he chose to make this play on words, but the point is clear: God is unchanging! Choose Him!

III. GOD'S PEOPLE: THE FIRST FRUITS OF HIS CREATION

Of his own will he brought us forth by the word of truth, that we should be a kind of first fruits of his creatures (Jas 1:18).

James has made it a point to stress that everything good and everything good to be given, all have God's "goodness thumbprint" on them. The world has a way of adding unnecessary layers on top of this simple truth, but in difficult moments those layers are pushed away and goodness has a way of rising to the top. We see it all the time on shared posts on social media. Stories of two people, from different walks of life, coming together in a moment of panic and crisis. Simple acts of kindness that were done for a stranger, acts that changed their life. In verse 18, James points at a critical truth: what God desires most is a special people unto Himself ... ones who are not tossed from side to side in a doubt storm ... who are not fearful or anxious during trials ... and who are not self-deceived wanderers. He desires a genuine people, born not from the world but from His very Word!

James tells us that God "brought us forth" by His Word of Truth so that we would be a "kind of first-fruits of His creation." The expression, "to be brought forth," is a reference to birth. The KJV captures this by saying, "He begat us," but I also like the New International Version (NIV) which reads, *"He chose to give us birth through the word of truth, that we might be a kind of first-fruits of all he created."* This reference to our spiritual birth fits snugly with the previous one about God's Fatherhood of light, because James is explaining more perfectly the nature of God's Fatherhood. Not only is He the source of all life, but He is specifically the Father of a new creation of people, born of water and Spirit (John 3:5).

James isn't the only one to describe our spiritual birth in this manner. Colossians 1:13–14 and 2:12 elaborate on how we came into existence as new Christians and what that new birth means to the Lord.

> *He has rescued us from the dominion of darkness and brought us into the kingdom of His beloved Son, in whom we have redemption, the forgiveness of sins … buried with Him in baptism, in which you were also raised with Him through faith in the powerful working of God, who raised Him from the dead.*

Combining these metaphors from James and Paul, we get a powerful image of what salvation looks like through the eyes of God. First, there's a people lost in darkness, wandering and stumbling in the dark (Isa 59:9–10). Then, a gospel call of salvation is sent forth, and we turn our attention to the sound. The gospel call tells us what to do and where to go for help! People begin to turn to the one calling, turning to the Lord for help, ready to receive the gift of salvation in Jesus. As Paul says in Colossians, the people are then buried with Jesus in baptism (2:12). In one act of solidarity with Jesus, we go through the same death, burial, and resurrection as Jesus Himself (Rom 6:4). Through this process, they go through the act of putting their old way of life to death, being raised by God into a new state of forgiveness, the forgiveness of sins. As they rise from the water of baptism, they are summoned forth out of darkness and into the light by the Father of Light and are called to live a new life for God. What appears in the light of the Father is a new person, born from the Word of Truth, created to be a kind of first-fruits of the creation!

It should be noted that this new birth is the contrasting alternative to the birth that James described earlier in verse 15: *"Desire when it has conceived gives birth to sin, and sin when it is fully grown brings forth death."* It's as though James is concluding this entire discussion of temptation and our response to the trials of life by saying, "All of life can be reduced to two choices: a birth of sin that leads to death, or a birth in the Lord which leads to a new and called out life in Jesus. Choose you this day!"

The choice we make will be reflected in the actions that flow afterward. The choice we make will also demonstrate to the world who we really serve, either ourselves or the Lord. The question is, "Whose will are we honoring? Ours or God's?" James tells us very clearly that God's will and intention for His people are that we would be a new creation in Jesus Christ. Whether we, as Christians, will honor this is entirely up to us, but remember: the decisions that we make now will impact our spiritual trajectory and destination.

This verse really comes to life when you consider the idea of choice. God *chose*! Let that sink in for a minute. God *chose* to create a special people, the "first-fruits of His creation." He *chose* to do this of His own will. He made the decision to go forward with creating us, knowing what it would cost Him. I love that James includes this truth here, after a long section that deals with the struggles of life and our shortcomings — almost as a way of pleading, "Choose wisely, but please, choose God because He chose you."

Sin and disobedience to the Lord bring feelings of shame

and regret. Sometimes those feelings of shame and regret can completely swallow us whole to the point where we feel unloved and unworthy. I know James understood this first-hand, so I appreciate that subtle reminder. It's his way of pointing out that God already knew His creation would wander away and He knew that in order to fix that wandering, He would have to endure the most excruciating pain, both physical and spiritual. Despite all that, He chose to do it anyway. He chose to move forward and give us life. So now, James pleads with us to choose God. Don't minimize your sin; don't make excuses for your sin. Do not deceive yourself. Choose God. He will never leave you. He will never abandon you. He is firmly planted and fixed; choose God!

Spiritual Formation Section

God gave us life. He saw our lives from their beginning to their end. He saw our mistakes, our triumphs, our shouts of praise and our regrets. He viewed our lives in their entirety, errors and all. Despite all of this, of His own freewill He brought us forth and gave us life. It is humbling to see what God did to make us His special "first-fruits people." The presentation of the first fruits in the Law of Moses was a big celebration where no work was to be done and honor and glory were to be given to God (Num 28:26). Here are some questions related to this to reflect on: Have you used this precious life to serve Him and honor Him? What parts have you retained and kept back for yourself? Are you the very best of the creation, demonstrating to others what a relationship with the true and living God is like?

CHAPTER 9

THE FIRST-FRUITS OF THE CREATION—REVISITED

JAMES 1:18

Of his own will he brought us forth by the
word of truth, that we should be a kind of
first fruits of his creatures.

INTRODUCTION

All too often we as Christians focus on our actions, emphasizing good works and overlooking the reasons why we do them. Some may say that the "why" is easy: "Because God says so!" That is a valid point, but the Lord has never required His children follow Him blindly. In fact, the faith that we have in Him is not a blind faith at all; it is based on reason and sound judgment. No less reasonable is the motivation for our service to Him. Oftentimes, it is directly connected to who we are. This correlation can be found all throughout the Scriptures and James 1:18 is a prime example. This short but powerful verse tells us what the Lord's purpose is for His children, intentions that serve as both their identity and their motivation to follow His will.

His intention is for His special people "to be the first-fruits of His creation."

The reference to a new "first-fruits" creation is actually part of a much larger story of redemption. The Redemption Story is important because it reminds us that we are participants, not spectators, in the events included in it. It invites us into the story, helping us to feel as though we are part of something bigger than ourselves. I want to invite you into a deeper understanding of the "first-fruits" reference here in verse 18, but to really explore its significance, I am first going to tell you the Redemption Story itself. By the end of the story, it will be clear that what James is referring to is nothing less than the total remaking of creation through a partnership between the Lord and His first-fruits children.

I. "IN THE BEGINNING"

In the beginning, God created the heavens and the earth. The earth was without form and void, and darkness was over the face of the deep. And the Spirit of God was hovering over the face of the waters (Gen 1:1–2).

In this beautiful opening scene of the Bible, we see a powerful image described. The physical world is in complete *chaos and darkness*. But then there is hope. In this scene, the Spirit of God is nestled between the divine plan of God and the sea of chaos. In the midst of all that chaos and darkness is the Spirit of God. The Spirit of God is serving as the divine connection between God who is Spirit and this physical world. It's a powerful image! From there, the Lord begins to remake the creation layer by layer. Removing the chaos and darkness from the world and filling it up with order and peace through each spoken word breathed out.

> *Then God said, "Let us make man in our image, after our likeness …" then the LORD God formed the man of dust from the ground and breathed into his nostrils the breath of life, and the man became a living creature (Gen 1:26; 2:7).*

The next major scene in this powerful Redemption Story is when the Lord forms man and breathes life into him, extending a strand of existence to this lifeless form. In this scene, mankind comes to represent a smaller version of the first two verses of the Bible: the perfect mixture of Spirit and a body made from this physical world. Imagine God, cradling this being made of dust, breathing His breath of life into him, and the very first thing that this newly created being sees is the face of God. The potential is limitless; the relationship is limitless. The union between God and Man is declared "very good." The intimacy of this moment shows how close God desires to be to us!

Then, this mixture of Spirit and the physical world, this living being called Adam, was given a charge by God in Genesis 1:28:

> *God blessed them and said to them, "Be fruitful and multiply and fill the earth and subdue it, and have dominion over the fish of the sea and over the birds of the heavens and over every living thing that moves on the earth."*

God allowed mankind to take over. He handed the responsibility for continuing the great work He'd started, over to mankind, a work that would honor Him through creation itself and man's stewardship of it. He gave all of his excellent creation to Adam and Eve to fully enjoy and manage, with but one exception: not to eat of a particular tree.

The tree represented choice. Without the ability to choose goes free will. Free will, however, is crucial to being created in the image of God. Up until this point, it had been God who declared what was good and what was very good, but now mankind sought to decide this for themselves and replace God. Rather than devote themselves to their role of stewards of God's earth, Adam and Eve chose to abandon God and His instructions altogether and use the creation for their own selfish desires:

> So when the woman saw that the tree was good for food, and that it was a delight to the eyes, and that the tree was to be desired to make one wise, she took of its fruit and ate, and she also gave some to her husband who was with her, and he ate (Gen 3:6).

With this one act, sin entered the world and things could no longer remain as they were before. Where there was a closeness with the Lord at one time, now there was separation. Where there was life, now there was spiritual death.

II. PARALLELS TO THE CREATION

You would think that the story ended there since even today mankind battles with sin and spiritual death, but that's only two pages into it. The rest of the Story of Redemption lies in what God did to bring mankind back from the chaos of sin and into the state and relationship of peace He'd always intended. Scripture tells us exactly where to look, and what God did to make this happen in Romans 5:1: *"We have peace with God through our Lord Jesus Christ."* The central point in this Story is Jesus, so that is where we look next.

The creation of the world is a unique event with words and phrases specific to it, things like: "creation," "be fruitful and multiply," "subdue and fill the earth," "chaos and darkness," "In the beginning," and "the Spirit of Life." In a powerful statement by the early writers, these words and phrases would be reimagined through the life and work of Jesus. John 1:1–5 says,

> **In the beginning** was the Word, and the Word was with God, and the Word was God. He was in the beginning with God. **All things were made through Him**, and without Him was not anything made that was made. In Him was life, and the life was the light of men. The **light shines in the darkness**, and the darkness has not overcome it.

Notice the description of how all things were made in the beginning through God and how the light (a clear reference to God's opening statement in Genesis 1:3, *"Let there be light."*), continues to shine through Jesus. It is important to really consider the parallels between these words and phrases because in them are glimpses of how the early Church understood themselves and the work of Jesus Christ. 2 Corinthians 4:6 states, *"For God, who said, '**Let light shine out of darkness**,' has shone in our hearts to give the **light** of the knowledge of the glory of God **in the face of Jesus Christ**."* The world had descended back into such a place of darkness and chaos all over again that it desperately needed another *"Let* *there be light"* moment. So, God did precisely that. He said, "Let there be light in the face of Jesus Christ," and sent His Son to earth as Savior.

The next significant moment in the creation was the formation and fall of mankind, so naturally the early Church would have understood the work of Jesus in this way as well. Look at how Jesus as Adam's counterpart is discussed in Romans 5:12, and 18–19:

> *Therefore, just as sin came into the world through one man, and death through sin, and so death spread to all men because all sinned ... As one trespass led to condemnation for all men, so one act of righteousness leads to justification and life for all men. For as by the one man's disobedience, the many were made sinners, so by the one man's obedience, the many will be made righteousness.*

Where, in the first creation, mankind failed to honor the Lord in the Garden of Eden and ever afterward, Jesus succeeded!

But at this point, sin had saturated the world. So, the Lord designed a new special place where people would come out of darkness and chaos and sin and He called it the Kingdom of God. Its residents would be a new people, born of God:

> To all who did receive Him, who believed in His name, he gave the right to become children of God, who were born, not of blood, nor of the will of the flesh, nor of the will of man, but of God (John 1:12–13).

In further describing this new Kingdom of God, James

says that they were born through God's word of truth to be a type of first fruits, called out of all His creation. Just like Adam and Eve were a product of the Spirit and the physical world, when we are "born again," we unify our physicality with God's spirituality through the indwelling of the Holy Spirit. Jesus addressed this in John 3:5–6 when He said, "Truly, truly, I tell you: no one can enter the kingdom of God unless he is born of water and the Spirit. Flesh is born of flesh, but spirit is born of the Spirit." Notice his reference to "water" and "Spirit." These allusions are like little book-marks within the overall Redemption Story and are there to help us piece together the big picture. By connecting water and Spirit here to the same words used in Genesis 1:1–2 describing the Spirit of God and the deep waters, the Scrip-tures are continuing this theme of new creation, a new "Let there be light" moment. The difference being that this new light results in a Christian being *created after the likeness of God in true righteousness and holiness* (Eph 4:24).

The Lord truly had a new Genesis in mind through Jesus the Christ! No wonder Matthew 1:1 in Greek says, "Book of Genesis of Jesus Christ, Son of David, Son of Abraham." The work of Jesus was a reconciliation and a restoration of God's original Genesis intention, made whole again through His Son's sacrifice. From the decay would rise a new first-fruit people, born of water and Spirit. Born of God!

III. BEING TRUE TO OUR MISSION

The work, life, and sacrifice of Christ were meant to fix what had been broken in the Garden. So God re-made His creation through Christ, but on an even better, spiritual level than the world had seen up to that point! Jesus became a "new

Adam," creating new children in the true likeness and image of God, children who reflect the righteousness and holiness of God and who were brought to new spiritual life through the Spirit. What the Lord accomplished through Jesus Christ was nothing less than the recreation of the world. But here's the challenging part about it. Just as He delegated responsibility to the first humans to be fruitful and multiply, filling the earth, God has given us as Christians the same charge — but on a much greater and more spiritual scale!

In Colossians 1:10, in what is one of the strongest comparisons between the old creation of Genesis and the new creation in Christ, the church, Paul states, *"Walk in a manner worthy of the Lord, fully pleasing to him: **bearing fruit in every good work** and **increasing** in the knowledge of God."* The phrase "bearing fruit and increasing" is the New Testament charge, "Christians, your responsibility to the Lord, having been given spiritual and eternal life in Jesus, is to go out into the World and fill the earth, being fruitful and multiplying."

This is why we were given life! This is why we were made in Jesus as a new creation in the true likeness and image of God: so that we might go out into the world and be fruitful and multiply, but on the next spiritual level. Our purpose is to cover the earth with redemption by going into *"**all the world** and preach[ing] the gospel to every creature"* (Mark 16:15). Jesus told His apostles in Acts that they would receive power when the Holy Spirit came upon them and that they were to become His witnesses in Jerusalem, all of Judea and Samaria and to the ends of the earth (Acts 1:8). God's intention is that He would have a people not bound by physical territory, but who would fill the entire earth as a living and spiritual Kingdom, and who would remove the seas of chaos and drive out the darkness.

As the first fruits of the creation, we must first seek to honor God as the Creator, and then honor His intention to have a people who would reflect His goodness and His holiness to the rest of the world. We are a special people — the church, the body of Christ, the Kingdom of God — and we are to shine as lights in a world taken over by darkness. One of the ways in which we do that is by being devoted to God's will and showing those in need of a Savior a better way of life in the light of the gospel:

*By grace you have been saved through faith. And this is not your own doing; it is the gift of God, not a result of works, so that no one may boast. For we are his workmanship, **created in Christ Jesus for good works**, which God prepared before-hand, that we should walk in them (Eph 2:8–10).*

"Good works" are actions that bear fruit so that others can "taste and see" how good the Lord is (Ps 34:8). As spiritually recreated people, our good works and the fruit that we produce look and taste like God Himself. Paul calls this the fruit of the Spirit and lists them as love, joy, peace, patience, kindness, goodness, faithfulness, gentleness, and self-control (Gal 5:22–23). We were "created" or as James says, "brought forth" (birthed), for this reason.

We must push ourselves daily to be devoted to God in holiness because of His amazing grace! We bring goodness into this lost world, not because we're forced to, but in partnership with our loving Father, knowing that *"faith works through love"* (Gal 5:6). Of course, this is a daily process within ourselves, but as the first-fruits of God's new creation, we have forgiveness in Jesus. When we take the darkness still in us and bring it to light through confession (1 John 1:5–10), we draw closer to the light. One day at a time, one step at a time. This is how we change the world!

SPIRITUAL FORMATION SECTION

Telling the story of redemption is important because it invites us to not just be spectators, but to also participate. What is your role within the story? What are the special contributions that you, as the first fruits of the new creation, bring to your part of the world? How does this truth give new meaning to your pain, suffering, triumphs, and desires?

CHAPTER 10

THE FIRST-FRUITS: A REFLECTION OF GOD

JAMES 1:19–20

Imperative 9: Let Every Person Be

INTRODUCTION

In the previous chapter, we closed with James's declaration that we were birthed ("brought forth") through the Word of Truth for the purpose of being the first fruits of His creation. We also saw that God's intention has always been that He would have a special people, molded and shaped by his righteousness, who would go out into the world and reshape the creation by reflecting His goodness to the rest of the world. James elaborates on this in the most amazing way with his ninth imperative.

I. LET EVERY PERSON BE — VS. 19

Before we dive into the specific imperative contained in verse 19, there are two issues that need to be addressed. First, it is important to know that most modern translations begin this verse by saying, *"Know this/take note of this/under-stand this, beloved brethren, everyone should be quick to listen, slow to speak, and slow to anger."* I would like to offer a word of caution here for those whose translations do use the word "should." "Should" implies a choice, or a suggestion of a good idea — as in, "You could do this or that, but you *should* do this because it is better." But as we're beginning to understand, this is an imperative and thus the force of this verse is more than a suggestion; it is a command!

Second, nearly every modern English translation renders the beginning of verse 19 as a form of "Know this." The KJV, on the other hand, starts verse 19 by saying, *"Wherefore, my beloved brethren ... ."* It's a very subtle difference, but it signif-icantly impacts how we understand the verse. The first version prepares the reader for what is about to be said, pointing them forward into the coming text. The KJV version does the opposite. There are manuscript-related reasons for this difference, but I believe that the use of the word, "wherefore," is perfectly appropriate given the flow of James's arguments and how verses 19 and 20 build upon what has just been outlined in the previous sections. "Wherefore" is somewhat of a dated word and not one that we use often today, but it actually means, "Because of," or "On account of this reason, then ..." I had an English teacher whose pet peeve was the line, "Wherefore art thou, Romeo?" from William Shakespeare's play, *Romeo and Juliet.* Actors depict the line in a searching manner, as if Juliet is wondering where Romeo is hiding. "Wherefore," my teacher would say, "Is not a question of where, but why."

Keeping this in mind, when we read verse 19, it becomes clear that James is about to give a command on how we should treat one another but he's stressing that the reason for this command has been provided in the previous verse. As we know, in verse 18, he explained that the Body of Christ can be more perfectly understood as the first fruits of God's creation and that our lives ought to reflect this status. James, having reminded us of this as a way of "setting the stage" and explaining our role in the world, then reveals the ninth imperative.

The command is in the expression, *"Let every person be quick to hear, slow to speak, slow to anger."* He is commanding Christians to set the standard in how we listen and respond to our fellow man, knowing that we are new creatures in Christ Jesus and representative of the very best of creation. This command is a formula for how to live up to our position as God's representatives on earth. I believe that the phrasing of this formula hints at what is at the heart of God's first-fruits people: love!

Look at the description of love from 1 Corinthians 13 and see how closely it mirrors the three parts to James's imperative:

> *Love is **patient** and kind; love does not envy or boast; it is **not arrogant or rude**. It **does not insist on its own way**; it **is not irritable** or resentful; it does not rejoice at wrongdoing but rejoices with the truth. Love bears all things, believes all things, hopes all things, **endures all things** (5–7).*

Being "quick to hear" is, at its core, the characteristic of a person who does not insist on their own way. Rather, this person is more concerned with hearing the facts and listening to another's point of view. Being "slow to speak" is a characteristic of a person who is not rude or irritable, but courteous, even in the middle of a disagreement. And lastly, being "slow to anger" is patience, the ability to endure all things. This formula that James is giving us for righteous living is basically love in action!

As we all know, it is far easier to destroy and tear down than it is to preserve and protect; the latter requires special attention and maturity of character. If we are going to live in such a way as to honor our special place as God's first fruits of creation, we will need to pay particular attention to this imperative from James. We will have to be deliberate and intentional in how we interact with others, especially when disagreements arise.

II. QUICK TO LISTEN, SLOW TO SPEAK, SLOW TO ANGER = A PRACTICAL EXPRESSION OF LOVE

James gives us a practical expression of love made up of three guiding principles: quick to listen, slow to speak, and slow to anger. I believe the best form of listening is active listening. Active listening is the type of listening that seeks to understand. This skill is critical, especially in moments of disagreement when we are not naturally in a listening frame of mind. In heated moments, people are very often a posture of defense, which actually works against the Christian. When you are defensive, your focus is on preserving your perceived sense of safety. Very often this involves seeking ways to dominate others and their viewpoint, before you are hurt or your position defeated. As Christians, we are called to consider each person greater than our own selves and to respect others as beings made in God's image. It is so important to have the ability to set aside our personal feelings in order to really feel and see what the other person is trying to explain to us. This is an expression of love toward your fellow image-bearer.

In Matthew 13:13 Jesus said, *"That is why I use these parables, for they look, but they don't really see. They hear, but they don't really listen or understand."* The parables of Jesus required the listener to listen *with the intent* to understand. The Pharisees could not understand the parables of Jesus because they didn't want to listen to understand, they listened solely for the purpose of entrapping Jesus. They only heard what served their harmful purposes. Jesus knew this, so He openly presented His truths and scattered the seed of the Word in story form, with meanings that were clear only to those who were truly listening. In this way, only the hearts that were in the right place received the Word and went on to change the world.

When we listen to each other, especially in moments of disagreement, we need to have the same type of heart Jesus describes — one that wishes to understand — so that we can enter into the conversation or disagreement with respect and empathy for the other's perspective. Christians should be masters of empathy! As the writer of Hebrews said, *"Remember those who are in prison, **as though in prison with them**, and those who are mistreated, since you also are in the body"* (13:3). We can't arrive at that level of compassion if our own voice and self-concern drowns everything out. Active listening within the Church demonstrates to our brethren that we value them as people and co-laborers in the new creation in Jesus. (Take note of this, as well: it breaks down barriers with non-believers, too. Wouldn't you be more open to someone's message if they first tried to understand your situation with empathy and respect?)

Once we have actively listened to our brother or sister in

Christ, it is our turn to present our thoughts in the manner James has called "slow to speak." Said another way, we are to be deliberate and intentional about our words. All through the Bible, wisdom and careful speaking are equated with each other. Proverbs 17:27–28 reads, *"Whoever restrains his words has knowledge, and he who has a cool spirit is a man of understanding. Even a fool who keeps silent is considered wise; when he closes his lips, he is deemed intelligent."* A wise person knows that it is best not to speak when angry. A person who speaks from a "cool spirit" and with restraint, like the Proverb says, is a person who is filled with maturity, knowledge, and insight.

Think of the last time you argued with someone. What happened to your heartbeat? Your hands and palms? How was your breathing rate? When the body experiences anger, blood begins pumping faster to the major organs and the brain temporarily "turns off" the part of itself responsible for rational thinking. In moments of anger, the body thinks that it is in danger, so our fight or flight response kicks in. In the moment, we are not thinking rationally or logically; we're responding from a place of fear and self-protection! That is why it is so easy to say things in the heat of the moment that we come to regret later when we can think more clearly. This is also the reason why the severity and sometimes the embarrassment of what we said and did while angry doesn't occur to us until after the fact, once our body has returned to normal. By telling us to be "slow to speak," James gives excellent advice to slow down the conversation, especially when it is a disagreement and has the potential to turn to anger. He commands us to pause our responses long enough to consider all the facts of the matter and until we have full understanding of the situation and the other person's point of view. By slowing our response, we are now in a place where we can accomplish the final part of his formula: to be slow to anger.

Being slow to anger and frustration is the definition of patience, and look at that: now we've come full circle with where this all began in James 1:2! We know that one of the blessings of going through trials is that it will create patience in us. Patience, then, will help us to be more long-suffering with others. The more our trials push and pull us apart, the more we can handle when individuals attempt to push and pull us in an ungodly direction through conflict. It's amazing how being knocked down by life and by life's trials can help us to be more patient with others and with ourselves. Giants in the faith are distinctly known as possessing a calming presence and this is a direct result of the trials they have weathered.

This patience allows for real communication to take place and for truths to be reached in a sincere and effective way. It lends credence to the Christian's words and distinguishes him or her as someone of intelligence and compassion. Every time we determine to be quick to hear, slow to speak, and slow to anger, our obedience becomes an intentional expression of love for our fellow man and love for our brethren in Christ. Not only does this work wonders for the impact of our message, it also pleases our Father in heaven at the same time. Through spiritual discernment, we understand that we are not here to add more chaos to the creation. Instead, we're here to re-make it according to the wisdom and will of God. James's formula is a powerful guide to navigating challenging conversations so that we always respond in a way that honors our Lord.

III. GOD'S EXPECTATION OF HIS FIRST-FRUITS CREATION: REPLACE CHAOS BY PRODUCING HIS RIGHTEOUSNESS

> *... the anger of man does not produce the righteousness of God.*
> *(Jas 1:20).*

James next explains that it is vitally important that we interact with each other in this manner because responding in anger is a fleshly response and cannot produce the righteousness of God. Paul taught the same spiritual truth through his example of fruit and how fruit is grown. He says in Galatians 6:6–8,

> *Let the one who is taught the word share all good things with the one who teaches. Do not be deceived: God is not mocked, for whatever one sows, that will he also reap. For **the one who sows to his own flesh** will from the flesh reap corruption, **but the one who sows to the Spirit** will from the Spirit reap eternal life.*

Our duty, as the first fruits of the new creation in Jesus, is to continue to sow the seeds of the fruit of the Spirit so that new spiritual growth can occur. This is what James calls, *"the righteousness of God"* and what he refers to later as a harvest of righteousness. The sum of our Christian existence is to glorify God through our actions and in so doing, we will radiate His goodness and righteousness to the world around us and bring the lost out of darkness. As James alluded to earlier through his use of the word "chose" in James 1:18, it has always been God's ultimate plan for this to take place. Ephesians 2:10 echoes this truth, saying, *"We are his workmanship, created in Christ Jesus for good works, which God prepared beforehand, that we should walk in them."*

It was God's eternal purpose to have a people "conformed" or molded after the very image of His Son and for this divinely-conformed and spiritually-changed people to produce righteous actions and words that would flow from an enlightened heart. Fleshly, emotion-driven responses and actions do not bring forth the conditions where the righteousness of God can grow. Only behaviors rooted in the Spirit can do so. We are daily caretakers of spiritual seeds of righteousness that are meant to be shared with others to bring them to the Lord and push out the darkness in the world.

We never know the eternal impact a small act of God's goodness can have in someone else's life! Fruit is meant to multiply through the seeds it produces. May the Lord give the increase! (1 Cor 3:6)

SPIRITUAL FORMATION SECTION

Who knew that our school teachers were actually teaching spiritual truths when they told us to count to 20 before we respond to someone in anger! The flesh and the Spirit are always at odds with one another. We can only feed one at a time so the question is, "Which one have you fed more?" Do you see yourself as a person who brings chaos into the world by acting according to the flesh, or have you advanced God's spiritual intention of restoring peace to the creation?

CHAPTER 11

HEARTS READY TO RECEIVE

JAMES 1:21

Imperative 10: Receive

INTRODUCTION

The tenth imperative from James is going to challenge us to continue to work on our spiritual and inner being. God's people must have the humility to yield in order to receive direction from the Lord. In this chapter, we're also going to see how James masterfully humbles his readers and prepares them for the correction that he's going to bring in his second chapter. When it comes to God's Word, meekness and humility must be what guide the heart because if changes need to be made, changes must be made. What's at stake is nothing less than God's will and desire to rebuild the creation and restore peace.

I. "SET ASIDE ..."

Therefore, having set aside all filthiness and the remains of rampant wickedness, receive with meekness the implanted Word ...

Before we get into the depth of James's instructions here, there are two connections in this verse that will appear again in the upcoming chapter — two aspects that could be easy to miss but should be noted in order to understand the flow into James chapter 2.

The first has to do with James's curious use of the word "filthiness." What is missed in our English translations is that this word is the same as the phrase "shabby or dirty or vile" in James 2:2. This is absolutely critical to understand because what James is doing is masterfully turning his readers' attention to their own spiritual shabbiness first, humbling their hearts to receive his correction.

It seems that James's early readers had forgotten their own humble roots and were making their brethren stand apart or sit on the ground because of what they were wearing (Jas 2:1–4). For a man who dedicated one-fourth of his book to the proper treatment of the poor, James is understandably upset by this discrimination. The problem for him was that Christians were looking at the outward appearance of a person to determine worth or inclusivity. Material wealth is a big factor in how a person dresses and even in their level of hygiene. By separating those who were shabby or dirty, they were essentially excluding the poor from their midst.

James takes a moment to remind these Christians that

before they were saved and made clean, they had filthiness of the soul which is far worse. He is preparing their minds for the coming chapter where he will address and correct their behavior. He wants them to think of a time when their soul (of much more important than the body) was filthy with the residue from sin and instead of pushing them away, the Lord cleansed them and brought them close.

The second connection to chapter 2 is the phrase, "rampant wickedness." The NASV translation, from my perspective, does the best in capturing the original word and thought by rendering this expression as the "remains of wickedness." The original Greek word is *periseian* which can be defined as a residue or film. The brethren of that day refused to allow those with filthy or shabby clothes to sit on the best seats in the house. Perhaps it was because they were concerned for the appearance of the furniture, but James says that they were having the "shabby-clothed" brethren stand or just sit on the ground. I view his double use of this word as James asking them, "Remember when you had filthiness of the soul and even a residue of wickedness on you? Do you remember when the Lord washed you? Why are you treating your brethren with disrespect when Jesus never treated you in such a way?" He continues to expound on their spiritual stains and defilement in verse 27, saying, *"Religion that is* **'undefiled'** *before God is this ... visit the orphans and widows in their tribulation and to keep oneself* '*unstained*' *from the world."*

His words are a call for humility and meekness. Somewhere along the lines, the early Church had forgotten where they came from and were showing favoritism amongst their assembly. Somehow, they had lost their deep sense of gratitude to the Lord and their awareness of their own desperate need for spiritual cleansing. They stopped being spiritually discerning and began treating each other as the world would, according to appearance and possessions, rather than seeing each other as equals created in the image of God. They had become more concerned with the cleanliness of their couches than the cleanliness of the soul. James is pulling them back to a time when their souls were filthy, the residue of wickedness staining their inner selves, in the hopes that this reminder would bring them to humility again before the Lord and reveal the error in how they were treating their brethren. He calls them to remember their humble spiritual origins so that they can receive the Word that he is preparing for them.

II. "RECEIVE WITH HUMILITY ..."

This is the tenth imperative from James: the command to receive. When reading this verse, it may seem at first that he is speaking of other Scriptures written beforehand. That is certainly appropriate to do, but actually, James is specifically referring to the words that he is giving them at that moment. We know this because after he calls them to receive his words with humility, he tells them to not only be hearers of the word but doers as well — in other words, he is building them up and preparing them to receive the sharp correction that is coming and he expects them to put it into action. That is why the connections between this verse and James 2 have to be highlighted and cannot be missed. James is telling the church, "I'm about to give you some very heavy correction and if you hear these words of correction with a haughty or prideful heart, then they will not be able to penetrate the hardness of your heart and the words will not take root. When you hear these words of correction, have enough humility to receive the correction and act upon it. Don't just hear the Word spoken, make the corrections that are necessary and be doers of the Word also."

James describes the Word as "implanted." This word only occurs once in the New Testament, and it refers to germination. Why would James use such a unique word to describe the Word of God? It's not just a coincidence; every word James wrote was deliberate and intentional, guided by the Holy Spirit. There is a very significant reason he calls the Word "implanted."

Remember that in verse 18, James spoke about God's first-fruits people and His intention for them to sow spiritual seeds to create a spiritual harvest. The reference to germination in the word "implant," in this verse brings this spiritual harvest principle back into the conversation. Nothing kills the growth of the seed of the Word quicker than the prideful attitude of an earthly-minded person. In order for the harvest process to work the way it should, Christians must be humble and yielding to God, ready to receive and carry out His will. For the seed of the Word of the Lord to grow and produce fruit in our lives, we have to water and nourish it daily and that process begins with humility. As the Hebrews writer says, *"The word of God is alive and active. Sharper than any double-edged sword, it penetrates even to dividing soul and spirit, joints and marrow; it judges the thoughts and attitudes of the heart."* But in order for this to happen, we have to have our hearts open and receptive to the Word of Truth. A heart that is full of pride cannot be filled with anything else. We must empty ourselves in order to be filled. A body that is hungry and thirsty is empty of food and water. Jesus says, empty yourselves of earthly pride and *"hunger and thirst for righteousness"* and you will *"be filled"* (Matt 5:6). As Proverbs 7:1–3 says, the Word should be so close to our hearts, that it sinks down and carves its letters onto our hearts. Only then will the streams of life flow as they should, keeping us on the right path (Prov 4:23–27).

III. SHOWING HUMILITY TOWARD THE WORD

So, how do we fulfill this command to receive the Word through humility and personal surrender? Here are a few methods to nurture humility toward the Word. First, we can start by asking ourselves some weighty questions. On a personal level, how much of our lives do we entrust to the Word? How much of our actions do we surrender to the Word? Do we do what we want to do with our lives or do we use the Word to inform our behavior? Do we devote a portion of our personal time to the study of the Word? Our personal actions tell a story about the God we serve. If our Bible sits on a table all week, or remains unopened for the majority of our lives, the story that we are telling to the world around us is that we don't find God helpful or necessary when it comes to our Christian formation. We're implying that we're capable of creating our own form of spirituality apart from God's guidance.

A second way that we can show humility toward the Word is by inviting it into our family. As the heads of our households, we're used to guiding the family and being seen as leaders but there is something powerful about Grandpa and Grandma and Mom and Dad attributing that leadership to the Lord. In our family Bible reading time recently, I read from Matthew 3:11 where John the Baptist says, "He who is coming after me is mightier than I, whose sandals I am not worthy to carry." Speaking the words, "I am not worthy," out loud before my wife and children brought me instantly to tears. The most precious treasures I have were sitting right in front of me, and I could not help but be overcome with my unworthiness. Despite all my mistakes, God still blessed me with this wonderful family. The tears rolled down my face and confused my children. My tears became an opportunity to invite God into our midst in a very real way and pass on my faith to them.

Inviting the Word into our families takes deep humility because doing so is an acknowledgment that the Word of God is more authoritative than we are and that we all must yield to the guidance within it! One of the most potent expressions of humility is when the Word of God is read by parents or grandparents. That act alone sends a powerful statement to everyone that you feel the Word is important and must be heard. This applies to the dynamic of marriage as well as the raising of a family. Other than the Lord, our spouses know us better than anyone else on the planet. Bringing a routine Bible study into a marriage causes both husband and wife to set aside their wills and surrender equally before the Lord. Like James says, that takes humility!

Lastly, and perhaps the most difficult way of all to show humility to the Word, is by publicly associating ourselves with it. This means bringing the Word of God into our public persona. Christians are expected to have a public faith in the Lord. I know that many of us were taught not to discuss religion with friends because it is impolite, but that runs contrary to God's expectation for the church. If He views us as His representatives on earth, then that means

His expectation is that His first fruits of the creation are going to tell the world around them about Him. How can we tell the world about Him if we hide what we know and believe? Right actions will demonstrate God's righteousness, but at some point, the world around us will have to be told the Word of Truth so that they can know what they have to do to be saved. Otherwise, how will they know? How will we reach "the corners of the earth" if we don't start with the people around us? We have to move our faith and our knowledge outside of the walls of our churches and into the world!

SPIRITUAL FORMATION SECTION

"Receive with meekness the implanted Word." What are some areas where you still need to surrender to the guidance of the Word on a personal level? What are some ways in which you can invite the Word into your family? Into your public persona? What are you allowing to sit in the best seat of your heart instead of the Lord?

CHAPTER 12

THE WORD BECOMES ACTION

JAMES 1:22–24

Imperative 11: Be Doers

INTRODUCTION

We have finally arrived at one of the most famous and widely quoted passages in the book of James. Out of all the commands that we've read so far, this is one of the most challenging because it requires nothing less than a total, 100% fully committed life to God. In many ways, this passage is a reinforcement to the call that James made in verses 5–8. In this chapter, we're not only going to examine the passage, we are also going to discuss how it is put into action in the lives of two different people in Luke 18 and 19. By the end of the discussion, we will be better equipped to fully commit to the redeemed, new creation life!

I. IMPERATIVE 11: BE DOERS OF THE WORD, AND NOT HEARERS ONLY

James 1:22–24 is an explanation from James on how to arrive at the level of spirituality God intends for every Christian: a place of testimony through a lifestyle that sets the standard in behavior and outreach. This place is not intended for our own glory, but so that the world may come to a better understanding of who God is and see His glory through our modeled actions. The eleventh imperative is the command to put the Word into action. That makes it easy to understand, but difficult to carry out. But it is the only way to achieve the standard of living that is worthy of being called the "first-fruits of the Creation."

Fulfilling God's intention for His people takes more than just casual obedience and more than just a partial commitment. James commands us to commit every single facet of our lives to God. This is a lifelong dedication that requires both humility and surrender. As we're about to see from Luke 18 and 19, the state of the heart makes all the difference in the world!

II. LUKE 18 AND 19: A CASE STUDY OF THE 11TH COMMAND

In Luke chapters 18 and 19, there is a powerful example of what can happen when a person is fully committed to not only receiving the Word, but also allowing the Word to alter their identity and behavior. In chapter 18, there is an unnamed, young wealthy ruler who approaches Jesus with an honest and sincere question. He asks,

"Good teacher, what must I do to inherit eternal life?" "Why do you call me good?" Jesus answered. "No one is good—except God alone. You know the commandments: 'You shall not commit adultery, you shall not murder, you shall not steal, you shall not give false testimony, honor your father and mother.'" "All these I have kept since I was a boy," [the ruler] said (18–28).

It is obvious that the young man knew who Jesus was and that he had a familiarity with His teachings, but I wonder what was stirring in his heart that pushed him to talk to Jesus and ask this question about salvation. Most likely, something inside of him just didn't feel at peace. I say that because if he had truly believed he was on the right path, he wouldn't have felt the need to approach Jesus and inquire after something more.

I love Jesus's response: "What about the commandments? If you're keeping the commandments, then why exactly are you here?" Now, Jesus already knew what was going on in the young ruler's heart, and He knew why the young man was there. But it seems almost as if Jesus wanted the young man to examine his own heart and admit for himself why he was there. Jesus's response was His way of encouraging the man towards a sharper scrutiny of his life and beliefs: "If you're really on the right track, why are you here? Why are you so restless?"

Deep down inside, the young ruler knew that there was something he was missing, some deeper spiritual truth that he hadn't grasped or claimed. That is why he was still searching. Then, at that moment, Jesus says, "You're right. You are still missing something. Sell everything you have and give to the poor, and you will have treasure in heaven.

Then come, follow me." The Bible tells us that when the ruler heard this, he became very sad *"because he was very wealthy"* (verse 23).

It is important for us to understand what happened in that moment. Jesus was not teaching a new, sweeping commandment against material possessions that now all potential citizens of His Kingdom must follow. We know for a fact that both rich and poor reside in the Kingdom of God. Jesus is not speaking against being rich. Instead, His response was an honest answer to someone who had asked an honest and sincere question, and it showed His deity at work. The ruler wanted Jesus to look into his life and tell him what needed to be done in order to arrive in God's presence (salvation). Jesus, infinite in His knowledge, recognized that this man had something spiritually hindering him from eternal life. Jesus knew that the young ruler, would not be able live a fully committed life to God because his possessions sat in the best seat of his heart instead of God. Perhaps Jesus saw that in a few years' time, Christianity would become so unpopular that a believer would not be permitted to do business in Rome, a trial that the young man would fail out of fear and a desire to retain his financial status. Jesus looked into this man's future and saw that his possessions were going to be his downfall in some way. They would be the stumbling block that would prevent him from fully committing to God. Indeed, to save this man, Jesus told him exactly what he needed to hear in order to be saved: remove the obstacle that was either currently holding him back, or would do so in the future.

Sadly, the Bible tells us that the young ruler heard this Word of God, but he walked away sorrowful and unchanged **because** he was very wealthy — he thought it too great a sacrifice to be made. We pray that he made the necessary changes later but at least in this interaction, he was unwilling to do so. His question and conversation with Christ even hampered the morale of Jesus's own disciples because they began to ask, "Then who can be saved?" (Luke 18:26).

Jesus answers their question through a conversation with a different wealthy person. In the very next chapter, He travels to Jericho, where he comes face to face with Zacchaeus, another man with both riches and questions. Luke 19:1–9 reads,

> *Jesus entered Jericho and was passing through. A man was there by the name of Zacchaeus; he was a chief tax collector and was wealthy. He wanted to see who Jesus was, but because he was short, he could not see over the crowd. So he ran ahead and climbed a sycamore-fig tree to see him, since Jesus was coming that way. When Jesus reached the spot, he looked up and said to him, "**Zacchaeus, come down immediately. I must stay at your house today.**"*

Why do you think Jesus selected this town for His destination, and within that town, this particular road underneath that particular tree? Remember, Jesus's disciples were still disturbed by what they had seen with the young ruler earlier, so I believe this was Jesus's answer to their question of who could be saved: someone who yields their will to God's Word.

Luke continues in verses 6–10,

> *So he came down at once and welcomed him gladly. All the people saw this and began to mutter, "He has gone to be the*

guest of a sinner." But Zacchaeus stood up and said to the Lord, "Look, Lord! Here and now I give half of my possessions to the poor, and if I have cheated anybody out of anything, I will pay back four times the amount." Jesus said to him, "Today salvation has come to this house, because this man, too, is a son of Abraham. For the Son of Man came to seek and to save the lost."

"Today, salvation has come to this house!" Here is the salvation that the rich young ruler had sought after. But why did it come now, and not before? What was so different between these two men? Both had status, wealth, and many possessions, and both wanted salvation. But when they heard the Word, one walked away unchanged, saddened by the cost, while the other rejoiced and received it in obedience. They both had stumbling blocks before them, but only one had the humility and the heart to do something about it. For the rich young ruler, his barrier was his commitment to his possessions and how he allowed his possessions to dictate his life. For Zacchaeus, it was the wealth that he had accumulated by defrauding people through his job as a tax collector. One responded well, gladly receiving Jesus's words, and the other did not. One came to salvation, the other to sorrow.

This is the heart of James's 11th command. He is not asking us to select the parts of God's Word that pertain to us and then casually act on some of it, here and there. No, he is commanding us to spend all the days of our lives putting it into consistent practice. That's a rough and humbling process that demands our own personal stumbling blocks be removed, but the result is that we will become more and more like God.

Our stumbling blocks are simply remnants of our stubborn will that do not wish to change, pieces of an old way of life that was supposed to have been buried in baptism, never to return. But what happens when we attempt to go forth and try and live the Christian life with these obstacles left untouched and unaddressed? What happens when we carry the attitude of the rich young ruler into our first fruits, new creation life? James answers that question next.

II. "DO NOT BE DECEIVED"

But be doers of the word, and not hearers only, ***deceiving yourselves****.*

When we come across something challenging in the Scriptures and we read it but choose not to put it into practice, that is another form of self-deception. We deceive ourselves when we believe we can be effective Christians through some subjective blend of God's will and our own — that we don't necessarily have to mold completely to the image of God, just some parts of it, and we can still please Him. Nothing could be further from the truth. In fact, part of our baptismal commitment to the Lord that we made when we received the gift of salvation stipulated that we would live for God's will and not our own. 1 Corinthians 6:19 says clearly,

Or do you not know that your body is a temple of the Holy Spirit within you, whom you have from God? ***You are not your own****, for you were bought with a price. So glorify God in your body.*

Romans 6:17–18 is in agreement:

But thanks be to God that, though you once were slaves to sin, you wholeheartedly obeyed the form of teaching to which **you were committed.** *You have been set free from sin and have become* **slaves to righteousness.**

Without commitment, a Christian is a spectator in the new creation transformation, not a participant — a "hearer" but not a "doer." We "see" (know) what God's will is and what He desires to do through us, but we're unwilling to "do" (undergo) the transformation that is necessary to push forward on this charge. We were never intended to be observers of God's amazing plan. He blessed us with the incredible task of putting His Word into action so that the world could take notice and come to know God ... not so that we can join the world!

The thought of a Christian enjoying the blessings of salvation and God's grace without any subsequent involvement or effort, and with no fruit being produced in their life, should be repulsive to a true believer and is, in reality, self-deception. To those who are saved but produce no fruit, Jesus said,

I am the true vine, and my Father is the gardener. He cuts off every branch in me that bears no fruit, while every branch that does bear fruit he prunes so that it will be even more fruitful (John 15:1–2).

If we are producing very little good fruit, then that is a sign that we are not fully connected to Jesus and invested in advancing His will for us as His first-fruit people, which is why Jesus says that these branches will be cut off to nurture the health of the tree. Jesus explains what He means in verses 5–8,

I am the vine; you are the branches. If you remain in me and I in you, you will bear much fruit; apart from me, you can do nothing. If you do not remain in me, you are like a branch that is thrown away and withers; such branches are picked up, thrown into the fire and burned. If you remain in me and my words remain in you, ask whatever you wish, and it will be done for you. This is to my Father's glory, that you bear much fruit, showing yourselves to be my disciples.

Our fruit is not meant to earn our right to be connected to the vine, our fruit is the *result* of being *nourished* by it! A fruit tree that is in season is hard to resist! Our fruit is meant to bring people in and invite them to be nourished with us by joining Jesus and His Kingdom! A branch that receives nourishment from the tree and yet produces no fruit is at odds with God's intention and design for the tree. Jesus famously said in the Sermon on the Mount, *"You are the light of the world. A city set on a hill cannot be hidden"* (Matt 5:14). Jesus used many metaphors to describe the same intention: His desire for His followers to draw people out of the world. Proverbs 20:27 says, *"The spirit of man is the lamp of the LORD, searching all his innermost parts."* This works both ways. Our spirit reveals to the Lord our true motives, but it also originates ideas which then become fruit. Send forth fruit; be that light on the hill that cannot be ignored; be the lamp of God and shine a way for people out of darkness. You have all the nourishment that you need from Jesus, the vine!

When a person is fully committed to not only receiving

the Word but also to allowing it to alter their spirit and identity, the actions that flow become real-time examples of the goodness of God. It cannot be stressed enough that our fruit (actions) are not to earn our salvation; rather, they are meant to give the world a taste of God's righteousness and draw people to Him. We are replacing the chaos of the world with newness of spirit. This requires us to understand what God's intention is for us as His first-fruit people AND it requires action. With a committed heart and spiritual fruit, the possibilities of new spiritual growth are limitless!

SPIRITUAL FORMATION SECTION

Are you the young ruler, or the man up the tree? Envision yourself standing before Jesus. In your mind's eye, ask Him, "Lord, what do I still need to give up in order to be the person that you want me to be?" Write down what Jesus replies, and commit to the change it requires.

CHAPTER 13

THE FIRST FRUITS IN ACTION

JAMES 1:25–27

INTRODUCTION

The Bible begins with God's vision of a faultless, peaceful, and inhabited world being realized through His hand of creation. He made everything to His own standard, including mankind, created in His image to be loved and to enjoy a relationship with their Maker. Sadly, the world was corrupted and mankind departed from God's vision of perfection, harmony, and relationship. But that didn't change God's ultimate desire: a peaceful relationship with mankind, and a place to enjoy that connection. Because of this, God set forth a chain of redemptive events that would slowly bring healing to the broken relationship: a redemptive plan that would be accomplished in the birth, life, death, and resurrection of Jesus Christ! Although there are no imperatives or commands in this section of James, these verses provide invaluable insight into God's dealings with and expectations for His people, past and present — and not just any people, but His first fruits, New Kingdom and Covenant people. To better understand verses 25–27, let's return to the beginning of the story.

I. BLESSEDNESS IS PUTTING THE WORD IN ACTION

The family line, the land Jesus would inhabit, and even the nation into which He would be born did not in exist when God decided *how* He would redeem mankind. In fact, nothing existed, not even the foundation of the world itself (Eph 1:4). In His omniscience prior to the creation, God saw the future and knew what was to come if He moved forward with creating His special image-bearing people. He knew that they would fall short and would one day be in need of a Redeemer, something only He could be. Imagine the tremendous love that God had for mankind, to have continued as intended, knowing what it would cost Him. Once sin came into the world, the Lord set His plan in motion — His plan to redeem mankind. He had to start from scratch and usher in each specific element along a very particular timeline. His plan would end with the death of His Son, but before then, an incalculable number of events, people, places, and spans of time had to be woven together. Yet, He was willing.

He started with Abraham, then Isaac and Jacob, and their descendants. To each one, He gave His vision for the future. Eventually, however, His people were enslaved in Egypt, where they remained persecuted and without a national identity. Honoring the covenant that He had made with Abraham and with an eye toward the birth of Jesus over a thousand years later, God called Moses to bring the children of Israel out of slavery and lead them to Mount

Sinai. It was here that God made them a nation and gave them a set of laws, specific to that time in history, that would advance them beyond all the other nations around them. God's plan to redeem and restore the world was advanced there, but only in part. The plan was only getting started! God began with one person, then a family, and now a nation, but remember, His sights were always on the world! (Gen 22:18)

God continued to work through the nation of Israel until the right moment and time when His Son could be born (Gal 4:4). Up until that point, there had been numerous references and prophecies hinting at what God had in mind, but the record was not complete and the world was not ready to know the fullness of His plan (1 Pet 1:11–12). Finally, when Jesus Christ came, He brought what mankind desperately needed. Jesus brought salvation and along with that, He filled in the shadows of the Law of Moses with the fullness of God's intention, character, and will. Jesus ushered in a new era — God's final vision for the world. Along with that vision, Jesus also established the means by which the Lord would bring new spiritual growth to a sin-decayed world: The church. As the church, we are the first fruits ... we are a city set on a hill ... we are the reflection of His light to the World. The church, comprised of individuals molded and shaped by God's goodness and character, would collectively form His hands and heart in this world. Jesus brought all of God's redemptive work together like a tapestry and clothed the church, sending her forth to continue in His footsteps.

With that framework in mind, let's read verse 25:

But the one who looks into the perfect law, the law of liberty, and perseveres, being no hearer who forgets, but a doer who acts, he will be blessed in his doing.

I want to highlight James's expression, *"the perfect law, the law of liberty."* When we hear the word "perfect," our minds tend to think about something flawless or something that has no error or fault in it. Although we can say that without hesitation about the Word of God, the word "perfect" here is *teleios*, which carries a different meaning. This word signifies "completion." I love how James describes the Law of Liberty in this way, as something finished and whole. He is reinforcing the wonderful thread that runs throughout the Scriptures — the fact that God had been working toward mankind's redemption since the very beginning and it all culminated in Jesus and the New Covenant. Paul elaborates on this in Romans 10:4. The ESV translation of Romans 10:4 reads, *"Christ is the **end** of the Law for righteousness to everyone who believes."* The word "end" is *teleios*, which again, speaks to bringing all things to completion. The NIV gets a little closer to *teleios* by translating the verse as, *"Christ is the **culmination** of the law."* By calling Christ's sacrifice the "end," or the "culmination," Paul is underscoring that Jesus brought the fulfillment of all that had come before and if a person is to be declared righteous before God, it could only be done through Him and no one else.

Some read *"the perfect law, the law of liberty"* and are tempted to interpret it to mean there is a new blended system in place. Others read this and hear a works-based, righteousness-earning system of salvation, but that is also not what James is saying. Instead, this phrase outlines the distinctiveness of the law of Jesus from that of Moses. It's a title that differentiates the old law from the new and is a description of God's new guidance for His people.

That's not to say that the old law did not have a purpose in God's plan of redemption. In fact, it served a crucial role. It revealed more of God's righteous character and standard to the nation of Israel at a time when nations had no concept of holiness and a standard for the fair treatment of all people. The Law of Moses also highlighted man's immense need for atonement in light of God's standard of righteousness. The old laws were instrumental in establishing mankind's understanding of sin and the penalty for it, the holiness of God, and sanctification in light of that holiness. Despite these blessings, the law was limited in providing true remission of sins. Atonement, or the covering for sin, could be made through animal sacrifices and the shedding of their blood, but that's not the same as remission of sins. Remission of sins occurs when our sin debt is paid in full, something the blood of bulls and goats could not do (Heb 10:4).

The blood of animals was used because the precious gift of life is contained within blood; God allowed for the life of the animal to be used to cover the sins of mankind (Lev 17:11), a metaphor for the later sacrifice of Jesus Christ. Unlike the death of Jesus, however, an animal sacrifice was unable to remit payment for sin and produce true forgiveness as it was not a "like for like" sacrifice. The life of an animal was not the same thing as the life that was within a person who sinned. We were created separate and higher than the animal kingdom, having been created in the image of God with the capacity for the indwelling of the Holy Spirit.

In addition, we were created with the free will of choice.

Our sin was a result of choice, but an animal lacks the ability to choose right from wrong in the same way that we do. The only sacrifice that could cover mankind's sin was one that possessed the same characteristics and attributes as they did. It had to have been tested and yet able to arrive absolutely sinless and perfect on the other side of death. Thus, Jesus took on the form of man, complete with the same free will. He was tested in every way and remained without fault or sin. Then, He voluntarily gave His life on our behalf as payment for the remission of our sins! For the first time in mankind's history, people could be once again reconciled or reconnected to God in the way He'd always intended (Rom 5:1,10; 2 Cor 5:18).

The Law of Righteousness, or the Law of Christ, also opened the floodgates of salvation to all people worldwide and made it available to any who would call out to God (Rom 10:12). Paul referred to the Story of Redemption as "the mystery," a plan realized in Christ and given to the church to proclaim across the world! (Eph 3:1–11)

This "perfect law that gives freedom," was made possible over the course of millennia, from generations and empires, through languages and lands, out of joy and pain, not the least of which was the very blood of Jesus Christ! James pulls from that deep and rich Story of Redemption and invites his readers into it. He urges them, "Continue carrying on and persevering because you are part of that story! Don't just hear the words and mentally acknowledge their truth, let the words sink deeply into your heart and have them produce new growth!"

With the immense amount of love, patience, and planning that God had to do in order to truly liberate us from sin and cause us to be considered justified in His sight, how could we not want to spend our entire lives in service and gratitude to Him? It is profoundly difficult to ignore God's will and guidance when we learn more about what He did for us. James's guidance to be doers of the Word is not just a command for obedience, it's an invitation to add your own strand to the redemptive work tapestry! What an incredible thing it is to know that we are a part of God's massive plan and that everything that we do to participate in that story and advance God's desire to rebuild will be called blessed! You are so important to what He is doing in the world. Don't ever forget that!

II. WORTHLESS RELIGION

A Christian must always be aware of the role that they play within God's Story of Redemption. Not only does this honor God, but the actions that flow from a heart fully committed to God's mission form a life full of meaning and spiritual impact. Sadly, as we saw in the previous chapter, self-deception can creep in, causing people to think that they can receive the benefits of salvation and still avoid living in service to Him. It seems like this was a significant issue among James's readers because he revisits and reinforces his earlier teachings on this idea with a discussion of religion itself.

James 1:26 states, *"If anyone thinks he is religious and does not bridle his tongue but deceives his heart, this person's religion is worthless."* In the eyes of the world, our acts and our message are one and the same; all can come crashing down around us with a single, misplaced word or unrighteous action. No matter how much good we do, everything can be rendered worthless in a single moment if we are not careful.

With one slip of the tongue or one moment of anger, a Christian can destroy their public witness and authenticity and damage someone's idea of God. We've all been there. We have all said and done things that we ended up regretting because we knew that it just wasn't worthy of the name of Christ we wear. It's one of the hardest parts about being the "First-Fruits of God's Creation." Because we have that blessing, we will be under even greater scrutiny from others. But here again, James is teaching something that Jesus already told us.

> *You are the salt of the earth, but if salt has lost its taste, how shall its saltiness be restored? It is no longer good for anything except to be thrown out and trampled under people's feet. You are the light of the world. A city set on a hill cannot be hidden. Nor do people light a lamp and put it under a basket, but on a stand, and it gives light to all in the house. In the same way, let your light shine before others, so that they may see your good works and give glory to your Father who is in heaven (Matt 5:13–16).*

It is a blessing beyond measure to be associated with the Lord and to represent Him by mirroring His goodness to our fellow man. But just as our lives have the ability to break down walls and bring others to Christ through their good fruit, they have equal capacity to cause walls to be erected and people to turn from the Lord through carelessness and lack of wisdom. This is a substantial responsibility placed upon us, and it requires both intention and vigilance to shoulder it properly.

III. THE SUMMARY OF JAMES 1: BE LIKE GOD

Throughout this entire chapter, James has stressed that our conduct should be like the Lord's. We were birthed through the Word, we wear His name, we were bought by the blood of Jesus, and we are part of the Story of Redemption. It goes without saying that we should be like Him in every way, for our own sake and for those watching us. James 1:27 addresses that truth with a spotlight on one area of God's heart that He considers especially noteworthy and important:

> *Religion that is pure and undefiled before God the Father is this: to visit orphans and widows in their affliction, and to keep oneself unstained from the world.*

The phrase, "the widowed and the orphan" is an expression that is repeated within the Bible nearly seventy times. It cannot be stressed enough how great the Lord champions the cause of the widow and the orphan. In fact, in the list of traits found in Psalm 68 that make God worthy of praise, the first one named after the introduction is, *"He is a Father of the fatherless and a protector of the widows."* Jeremiah 49:11 says that He tells the prophet to entrust the widow and the orphan to Him. In Deuteronomy 10:18, He told the children of Israel that He personally was responsible for executing justice for the widow and the orphan. In Exodus 22:22–24, He threatens,

> *You must not mistreat any widow or orphan. If you do mistreat them, and they cry out to Me in distress, I will surely hear their cry. My anger will blaze against you, and I will kill*

you with the sword, and your wives shall become widows and
your children fatherless.

Within the Law of Moses, during every third year, a tithe was to be collected from the entire nation and given to the Levites, the strangers among them, and the widows and the orphans. In ancient Israel, care for the widowed and the orphaned was one of the highest virtues that one could have. This noble pursuit required a special attribute, the trait of being a defender of the defenseless. This is one of the most powerful traits of Almighty God Himself, who stands up for those who have no voice. He is the ultimate Vindicator and the ultimate Judge, but even more than that, He is the ultimate form of compassion.

So, when James proclaims that pure service to the Lord is to care for the widowed and the orphan, he is, at its core, saying: be like God. Plain and simple. Have a heart like Him. A person who has the heart to stand up for the widow and orphan and champion their cause is a person who will also do the same for the rest of their fellow man. James doesn't mean that only the widows and orphans deserve or need care; he instructs us to care for them the same way God does (i.e., to cultivate a heart like the Lord's). With this kind of perspective and compassion in us, we will naturally do the same for our neighbors as well. By mirroring God's timeless attributes and by being molded and shaped by His Word, we can become partners with Him in His great redemptive work, just like He always envisioned.

James 1 is a challenging chapter that invites us to be participants in the Story of Redemption, not just forgetful hearers. This chapter implores us to abandon worldly pride and remain humble under the shadow of His wing. This is critical, especially when the deep valleys of life come. If we remain firmly committed to God and nurture our spiritual nature, seeking to be more like Him, we will constantly be in bloom, no matter what season of life we may be in!

SPIRITUAL FORMATION SECTION

Love the Lord your God and love your neighbor! It's amazing how God's character rises from pages of the Scripture and highlights how truly unchanging God has always been! God's Plan of Redemption invites us to participate in the story and be a part of God's work to bring about new healing to the sin-sick world.

Close your eyes and picture God's will and plan as a massive ball. Who do you see pushing that ball with all their might? Are you? What do you need to let go of in order to free your hands for the push? Are your hands firmly planted on it? Are you pushing in the right direction?

CHAPTER 14

DO NOT BE "IMBALANCED" IN YOUR RELATIONSHIPS

JAMES 2:1–4

Imperative 12: Hold Fast

INTRODUCTION

James closed his first chapter with an appeal for his readers to love God and to love their neighbors as God has. The entire second chapter is dedicated to these two principles, starting with his reactions to the injustices against the poor taking place in the early church.

In Matthew 18, Jesus taught the parable of an unforgiving servant whose master had forgiven him an unpayable debt of 10,000 talents (a form of currency used in biblical times). Initially, the servant begged his master to allow him time to pay the debt even though the amount was insurmountable and could never be repaid. His master, choosing to be gracious and merciful, erased the servant's debt and set him free of any need to repay it. What a gift! The servant was probably overwhelmed by the grace of the master and felt like he had a new lease on life, right? Wrong. Instead, he left his master's presence and immediately began to choke a fellow servant who owed HIM 100 denarii (another form of currency and just a minute fraction of what he himself had owed earlier). When the master found out this had happened, he called the man a wicked servant and said, "I forgave you all that debt because you pleaded with me. Should you not have had mercy on your fellow servant, as I had mercy on you?"

Sadly, the early church receiving James's letters was guilty of this same wickedness. In response, James is going to address this disparity by going back to the basics of faith. When properly understood and lived, faith brings healing and builds strong relationships with God and others. Let's begin this amazing chapter with our 12th imperative from verses 1–4.

I. IMPERATIVE 12: HOLD FAST TO THE FAITH – VS. 1

You will recall that James had already brought up and addressed some of the issues between rich and poor when he spoke regarding their standing before the Lord. The lowly brethren were to "raise their heads" and have a healthy sense of self-confidence in the Lord. The rich were told to avoid haughtiness in their treatment of others, bringing "their head downwards" in equality. As we saw in that passage, one comes up and the other comes down, but the place at which they are to meet is called humility. That perfectly *balanced* and humble state before the Lord is a place we all should aspire to, regardless of how much we have. Those verses were subtle hints regarding an apparent issue that was plaguing the Church. In James 2, this problem is brought out into the open.

Unfortunately, rather than being healthy and balanced before the Lord, the poor and the wealthy were deeply imbalanced and at odds. Partiality and favoritism were being displayed towards the rich, while the poor were being embarrassed by the brethren. James 2:1 begins, *"My brothers, show no partiality as you hold the faith in our Lord Jesus Christ, the Lord of glory."* The title "the Lord of Glory" would have immediately stood out to James's readers and caught their attention. In the Hebrew mind, the word "glory," or *kabod,* carried the meaning of "weight" or "weightiness" and was related to God Himself. At the dedication of the temple in 2 Chronicles, the priests were unable to stand in the chamber containing the presence of God because His "glory" or weight, filled the temple (5:14). It's noteworthy that James begins his conversation on partiality and imbalanced relationships by using a word that directly relates to the One whose glory is the weightiest of all and worthy of all reverence, the Lord of Glory. God is the only one who determines what is important and what is not, what is to be revered or considered weighty and what is to be disdained. In light of His glory, no one can stand before the weight of God. All have sinned and fallen short. True value comes from what is connected to Him and nothing else.

When it comes to justice, impartiality, and the poor, the Scriptures are clear where the Lord stands, and the church absolutely would have known about it. No doubt they were aware of the fact that God *"shows no partiality to princes, nor regards the rich more than the poor, for they are all the work of His hands"* (Job 34:19). And without question, they would have been familiar with Leviticus 19:9–14:

When you reap the harvest of your land, you shall not reap your field right up to its edge, neither shall you gather the gleanings after your harvest. And you shall not strip your vineyard bare, neither shall you gather the fallen grapes of your vineyard. You shall leave them for the poor and for the sojourner: I am the LORD your God ... You shall not oppress your neighbor or rob him. The wages of a hired worker shall not remain with you all night until the morning ... You shall do no injustice in court. You shall not be partial to the poor or defer to the great, but in righteousness shall you judge your neighbor.

Notice the similarity between how Leviticus and James connect righteousness and impartiality to God. Righteousness flows from God, and His character demands that His children emulate His divine characteristic of impartiality toward all!

James's message is apparent: "If you wish to hold fast to your faith and run the Christian race with steadfastness, and if you wish to see the Lord face to face, then be like Him in every way. Be like Him not just in the way you love, but also in how you treat the rest of His creation equally. Emulate His righteousness to the world and show them, as the first fruits of the creation, what it means to serve Him and others!"

God is not a partial God, showing favoritism to one over another and neither should we. The first chapter of James was all about being spiritually discerning, using our spiritual eyesight to see past the trials of life and stay focused on the prize of Heaven. Now, he is challenging the church to use that same spiritual eyesight to see past the external and recognize that every person on earth has value because their life is from God.

II. PARTIALITY BASED ON APPEARANCE – VS. 2–4

Lest they feign confusion or ignorance, James proceeds to be explicit in describing just how this partiality was being conducted: by assigning honor and rank to individuals within their assembly based upon appearance and material wealth.

> *For if a man wearing a gold ring and fine clothing comes into your assembly, and a poor man in shabby clothing also comes in, and if you pay attention to the one who wears the fine clothing and say, "You sit here in a good place," while you say to the poor man, "You stand over there," or, "Sit down at my feet," have you not then made distinctions among yourselves and become judges with evil thoughts?*

In chapter 11, when we looked at James's tenth imperative, I mentioned the connection between the word "filthiness" there and the word "shabby" here. It is the same original Greek word in both places. I read this as James's way of preparing his readers for his coming reprimand. Just as the prophet Nathan told King David a parable that softened his heart before he confronted him about his sin, James also recalled their former sin-stained souls to humble and disarm those guilty of partiality prior to his correction. Said another way, I hear his words unfolding along the lines of, "My beloved brethren, the Creator of the universe was gracious to you and has helped you through every trial in your life. He loved you when your soul was filthy and washed you clean in the blood of Jesus Christ. There was no residue left when you were cleaned because you were restored and clothed with the new garments of salvation. Don't you remember this? My brethren, instead of turning around and radiating that grace to others, you have treated your fellow servants in Christ as inferior because you were looking only at the clothing, disregarding the spiritual unity you share. You rejected them because their clothes were not as clean as others, but the Lord, the purest of all pulled you in and clothed you with His precious garment. Why could you not do the same? Where the Lord lifted you up, you have pushed them down. Where the Lord elevated you, you have embarrassed and rejected them."

Imagine their guilt, knowing that they were being like the wicked servant in Jesus's parable. They had been all too eager to receive the gracious cleansing of Jesus's sacrifice, but they were unwilling to show that same compassion to their fellow brothers and sisters in Christ. The Lord had washed their soul, viewing them as clean and whole in His Son, but they refused to do the same for their brethren, choosing instead to treat them in an imbalanced and disgraceful manner. There are three more imperatives in this section that are not on our list because they are not coming from James, they are spoken by the perpetrators. "You sit here," is an imperative, imploring the well-dressed individuals to take the best seat. "You stand or sit over there," are commands being given to the poorest among them. This was no casual misstep by the guilty. This was a command spoken by individuals who had somehow lifted their status within the assembly and felt entitled enough to command their fellow brethren. They were speaking authoritatively like the *shofetim* or "judges" of old. This is why James rebukes them as "evil-thinking" judges in verse 4! When we think of a judge, our 21st-century minds turn toward our own county or district judges, but in the ancient world, the *shofet* were so much more than legal figures, they were to embody the balanced and righteous character of God, impartial like those charged in Leviticus 19.

Justice is a prevalent theme in the Old Testament, like the fair treatment of the poor, widowed, and orphaned. The Lord God has always passionately revealed how greatly He desires that balanced justice be carried out among His people, because He is a just God. This was critical when it came to those of lesser means and status because they were the most vulnerable in the land, having no recourse if justice was perverted. The Law of Moses said in Deuteronomy 16:19,

> *You shall not pervert justice. You shall not show partiality, and you shall not accept a bribe, for a bribe blinds the eyes of the wise and subverts the cause of the righteous.*

The prophet Isaiah also wrote,

> *Learn to do good; seek justice, correct oppression; bring justice to the fatherless, plead the widow's cause ... for I the Lord love justice. I hate robbery and wrong; I will faithfully give them their recompense, and I will make an everlasting covenant with them (1:17; 61:8).*

Regarding the judges, the Lord said,

> *At that time I charged your judges: "Hear the disputes between your brothers, and judge fairly between a man and his brother or a foreign resident. **Show no partiality** in judging; hear both small and great alike. Do not be intimidated by anyone, for judgment belongs to God (Deut 1:16–17).*

In other words, be balanced in how you treat and view others, including those that you do not know. Whether they be great or small, they all deserve fair and equal treatment because you are all equal before God. The shofet spoke authoritatively, but they did so in order to maintain justice and ensure that balance and fair treatment was maintained because the power structures of mankind often lean against the most vulnerable among us.

Lastly, Zechariah expounds,

> *Thus says the Lord of hosts, **Render true judgments**, show kindness and mercy to one another, **do not oppress the widow, the fatherless, the sojourner, or the poor**, and let none of you devise evil against another in your heart (7:9–10).*

Over time, because of the Lord's emphasis on what was right and what was just and because justice was so closely linked with God's own personality, the Israelites also began to emphasize righteous judgment, even creating the Sanhedrin Court. Unfortunately, even those attempts at justice became corrupt and were part of the structures that eventually put Jesus to death. Whatever the motivation was, their behavior was out of step with the Kingdom of God and it was out of step with the very virtues that guided God's people of old, justice, and righteousness.

When understood in this light, you can hear James saying, "You've become the very judges that twisted and perverted justice by showing partiality to citizens based upon their name and status. You have invited that wickedness into the holy and pure assembly of God's people. Rather than set the standard for all the world to see as the first fruits of God's creation, you've become the very thing that you previously despised: judges who show favoritism and are imbalanced and partial. You hinged your decision on who would receive kindness and honor on clothing and by doing so, you revealed that it is not the shabbiness of clothing that is the issue in your assembly, it's the spiritual filthiness that needs to be addressed." In this section, James has strong words again the mistreatment of the poor, and the way that he addresses it is through balance. Holding onto the faith and onto the Lord as tightly as we can will go a long way in making sure that we stay right where we need to be, under the shadow of His wing!

III. IMBALANCED RELATIONSHIPS

It is hard for us to fathom a situation where we would ask a fellow church member to give up their seat and sit on the floor so that another, more prominent member could take their place. Although that may be true, there certainly are other forms of imbalance that still exist and need to be addressed so that we do not fall into the same trap our first-century brethren did.

First, one way that we can be imbalanced today is in the way we love. As God's people, showing love and kindness to all — not just those who love us too — should be one of our strongest forces for good in our mission to bring new spiritual growth to the world. Jesus told us in Matthew 5:43–47,

> You have heard that it was said, "You shall love your neighbor and hate your enemy." But I say to you, Love your enemies and pray for those who persecute you, so that you may be sons of your Father who is in heaven. For he makes his sun rise on the evil and on the good, and sends rain on the just and on the unjust. For if you love those who love you, what reward do you have? **Do not even the tax collectors do the same?** And if you greet only your brothers, **what more are you doing than others?** Do not even the Gentiles do the same? You therefore must be perfect, as your heavenly Father is perfect.

Jesus's expectation is that His people will do more and go further than the world's bare minimum. He expects His people to be guided by the manifold wisdom of God and to show the people of the world a better way of life (Rom 9:1–3). The word "perfect" here in Matthew is identical to the one in James 1:25, meaning "completion." Jesus is teaching that God loves completely, and not just the people who love Him back; He gives both the just and the unjust life-giving rain and other blessings, so we are to love indiscriminately as well.

In this difficult life, people will wrong us; they are going to cheat us, and hurt us, and they are going to do so deliberately, sometimes with great cruelty and malice. Our natural tendency is to keep our circle small, only reaching out to those who treat us with the same level of kindness and respect as we do them. But that is the world's bare-minimum reaction. Christians have the ability to do so much more because our love for others starts with God's love for us and flows through us. How about bringing some balance to the offense by answering the wrongs with a soft word or a kind and unexpected gesture? That does not mean we have to approve of their actions or condone their behavior, nor does it mean we have to allow abuse towards us, but it does mean that we are to care more about a person's soul than the insult.

Second, another way that we can be imbalanced is in our care for the saved over the lost. Churches are comfortable and routine. As a church family, we encourage one another, we call on one another, and we share in worship with one another. Those are the absolute joys of being a Christian, but what about those in our communities that are lost? Our responsibility is not to keep the manifold wisdom of God within the walls of our homes and places of worship, but to send that wisdom out into the world (Eph 3:10). We love our church family, but we should nurture a love in our hearts for the lost too. We ought to have a balanced approach like Paul, who loved the church dearly, but also had a passion for the lost:

> I am speaking the truth in Christ — I am not lying; my conscience bears me witness in the Holy Spirit — that I have great sorrow and unceasing anguish in my heart. For I could wish that I myself were accursed and cut off from Christ for the sake of my brothers, my kinsmen according to the flesh (Rom 9:1-3).

We must have a softened and sorrowful heart for the lost souls of our community, knowing that they will perish without the gospel. We cannot just mentally acknowledge that there are lost souls without doing something about it.

Truth must penetrate our hearts and translate into action. Love for the brethren is absolutely essential, but let us never forget about the ones who are living and dying out in the world without Jesus! Holding fast to the faith in Jesus applies not just to our personal connection to God, it also empowers us to treat others as God has treated us. What an opportunity to show the world a better way of life!

SPIRITUAL FORMATION SECTION

An imbalance happens when people see themselves as being of greater value than others. Why do you think this happens? Where does our understanding of value come from? Where should it come from? What can we do to increase the love that we feel in our hearts for others?

CHAPTER 15

EQUALITY IN CHRIST

JAMES 2:5-7

Imperative 13: Listen!

INTRODUCTION

Our 13th imperative continues the discussion on partiality in the first-century Church. James tells his readers, *"Don't mistreat the poor because God chose them to be rich in faith"* (Jas 2:5). It is overwhelming to think of how the early church started from incredibly humble roots to rise and change the world! One of the ways they accomplished this was through their care for one another. This care ended up changing the world because it was unlike anything the world had ever seen! Brethren who had never met were caring for each other. Collections were being gathered and out of those resources, people were being loved in ways that the Roman state could not and would not do! The world was beginning to taste of the fruit of the Lord in the most powerful way. Our imperative is going to nurture that connection, cautioning against overlooking the humble of this world. If the church was going to turn the world upside down, it was going to need everyone, from the least to the greatest!

I. IMPERATIVE 13: "LISTEN!" – VS. 5

The purpose of a church assembly is to gather together as the body of Christ and show reverence to God through worship and prayer, the taking of communion, the preaching and teaching of the Word, and monetary collection for the saints. The assembly was and has always been a divine and special moment where believers can commune one with another and with the Lord. But in the church receiving this letter from James, brethren were bringing shame to that assembly by incorporating several terrible practices of the world — practices that the Lord Himself passionately spoke against. James admonishes them, *"**Listen!** My beloved brethren, has God not chosen the poor in this world to be rich in faith and heirs of the kingdom, which he has promised to those who love Him?"*

The word, "listen," is our imperative. It's obvious from this fact alone that he was passionate about aiding the poor and the lowly and he wanted his readers to understand why. This is a divine passion since even the Lord equates Himself with the care of the poor: *"Whoever is generous to the poor lends to the LORD, and He will repay him for his deed"* (Prov 19:17). Service to the lowly and the poor is serving God because He has always been the champion of the downtrodden and oppressed. He personally has an eye on their needs and an ear for their cries, and anyone who shares this concern blesses the Lord Himself.

To give added weight to his command to listen up and

not mistreat the poor, James gives a very interesting reasoning here: because "God chose the poor in the world to be rich in faith and heirs of the kingdom." The plan that would alter the course of the world and would bring rich goodness into the world would begin with lowly and poor of this world. James, however, is clear: God chose to start there, and He did so for a reason.

In our modern age, it is difficult to really wrap our minds around the deep poverty and extreme conditions that most people experienced at that time. The rich that James writes about were not like those in our society today who are well-to-do. The rich at that time were primarily Roman citizens and strongly connected to the Roman Empire. The number of people who were citizens was a fraction of the population, which meant the bulk of wealth was possessed by very few. The rest suffered immeasurably. Without citizenship status, there were very few (if any) rights. There were no social service programs available to help widows, orphans, or the poor. Without the patronage of an individual, life was exceedingly difficult.

One of the worst parts of living in this society was the corruption. Roman authority was a sword that could be used against anyone who was not a citizen of the Empire. Courts, politicians, and wealthy citizens could secure their positions by robbing what little the people had without the possibility of repercussion.

Roman taxation centers were spread throughout the Empire to raise funds. One such taxation hub was centered in Galilee, which meant that James, John, and Peter would have experienced this hardship firsthand. The Empire even hired contractors from within the conquered population to collect taxes from their people. These tax collectors gained a terrible reputation for lining their own pockets with impunity. The desperation was tremendous. The suffering in the world due to this hardship and cruelty cannot be put into words, but little did the oppressed people of the world know that the Lord God had something planned to bring about massive change — not just in Judea, but the world.

When Jesus began His earthly ministry, He went into the synagogue, took the Isaiah scroll and read aloud,

> *The Spirit of the Lord is upon me, because he has anointed me to proclaim good news to the poor. He has sent me to proclaim liberty to the captives and recovering of sight to the blind, to set at liberty those who are oppressed, to proclaim the year of the Lord's favor (Luke 4:18–21).*

Then he rolled up the scroll, gave it back to the attendant, and sat down. The eyes of all in the synagogue were fixed on him. He announced to them, "Today, this Scripture has been fulfilled in your hearing." He proclaimed that His mission was to bring good news to the poor, release those in captivity and oppression, and heal the blind. He prioritized the very ones who had come last every day of their lives.

Jesus's mission started out as a solo endeavor. He then gathered twelve disciples around Himself (including a tax collector!) and sent them out into the community. Soon after, the message of hope lit up the land like a fire. That message of salvation filled the hearts of the hopeless. The broken-hearted ... the ill ... the widow ... the orphan ... all saw a great light in what was previously pure darkness. When the church was established, the floodgates of salvation were opened and these people became redeemed and valued citizens of the Kingdom of God. They now had more than just a few new friends; they had a church family. For the first time, they were seen as special and loved, being cared for and not living in fear. All because of this new "let there be light" moment. The darkness that had overcome the world and caused humanity's eyes to become dim was being driven out!

These new groups began to connect their local church families with other congregations of God's people. They combined their resources to support other Christians, some they had never met and others they would never have met if not for Jesus. If one group had need and another plenty, they supported each other. Paul recognized this beautiful movement in the church of Macedonia, relating how even though they were in poverty, they begged earnestly for the opportunity to give for the relief of the saints (1 Cor 8:4). For the first time in the history of the world, there was an organization that connected people from all over the world under one name and one God, an organization that cared for their own and others. The city set on the hill, shining as a great unifying light, drawing all to it, was born and it was remarkable! The most astonishing aspect of this explosive growth was that it all started in the humblest of places and with the discarded of society!

II. CHRISTIANITY'S HUMBLE BEGINNINGS

For consider your calling, brothers: not many of you were wise according to worldly standards, not many were powerful, not many were of noble birth. But God chose what is foolish in the world to shame the wise; God chose what is weak in the world to shame the strong; God chose what is low and despised in the

world, even things that are not, to bring to nothing things that
are, so that no human being might boast in the presence of
God (1 Cor 1:26–31).

It was God's plan that Jesus's work would begin with those
of the humblest of circumstances, living completely desti-
tute and completely emptied of His heavenly glory. This was
so it would be clear to the world it was only through God's
power that the amazing church swallowed the world! Jesus
had no earthly wealth, no possessions, and no home. He
worked with individuals who were of humble origin, and
from these unprivileged beginnings the Lord built and
established the most powerful force for good that the world
had ever known and would ever know!

Rome had the wealth, the power, the prestige, the
scholars and the philosophers, the architects and the
schools of learning. Their citizens completely dominated the
land and they possessed every luxury possible. They fought
with all their might to suppress the good news of hope and
unity Jesus Christ brought, and yet, Rome was the one that
fell. Rome was utterly destroyed, and the church lived on
and grew. Putting all this together then, James reminds
them, "I beg you brethren, do not dishonor the poor because
the poor changed the world. God's plan began with the
lowly and through His power, He chose to lift them up,
connect them together and create a new and diverse
community of people. These people, bound together in love,
are going to reach into the world and lift the faces of the
broken and hurting. To dishonor them is to dishonor God
and His purpose for the church. He is the voice for the voiceless. The rich and politically-connected Roman elite oppress
you and drag you into court and they blaspheme the honor-

able name of Jesus, so please do not bring their way of life into the precious assembly of God. Don't bring their understanding of what is valuable into the body of Christ. The two are not remotely alike."

I have often wondered if James's mind went further back than most when considering where this all began. If he returned back to their childhood, perhaps recounting their own deep poverty and humble upbringing. I wonder if James thought of his siblings and parents when he said, "God chose the poor of this world." Either way, this was deeply personal for him and rightly so!

III. WHAT DOES THIS MEAN FOR THE CHURCH TODAY?

There is nothing wrong with possessions. Many wealthy people have been effective Christians in the past and many are today. But material belongings come with a big caveat: don't let them define who you are, or define how you view other living beings. Death is the great equalizer of us all. When we emerge on the other side, everyone will stand equal before God with no distinction of any kind. The only factor that will separate one from another when we are standing before God will be whether we were the Lord's first fruits people or not. So, while we are on the earth, *"set your minds on things above, not on earthly things"* (Col 3:2).

God specifically chose the weak to show His strength. 1 Corinthians 1:27–29 is so powerful because it's a passage that acknowledges how weak we really are. In the Lord's special community of people, the church, the first fruits of His creation, we have our faults and weaknesses and we have made mistakes along the way. We have hurt people and we have been hurt. Our bodies ache and we are riddled with daily trials and tribulations. Despite our weaknesses, we can still smile and we still have hope because of the precious love of God and the love of our church family. Only God could design something so powerful and lasting. The fact that such beautiful and godly fruits of the Spirit can be displayed in humans who are weak and frail is just a testament to how good and how mighty God is!

As you read the words on this page, in your mind's eye and heart, feel the embrace of these humble brethren. You are a product of their fierce love for one another and the boldness of their faith. In moments of weakness and doubt, remember them and what they accomplished in the Lord and know that the same Lord that empowered them to turn the world upside down is the Lord that is reigning today! 2 Peter 1:3–9 says,

> *His divine power has granted to us all things that pertain to life and godliness, through the knowledge of him who called us to his own glory and excellence, by which he has granted to us his precious and very great promises, so that through them you may become partakers of the divine nature, having escaped from the corruption that is in the world because of sinful desire. For this very reason, make every effort to supplement your faith with virtue, and virtue with knowledge, and knowledge with self-control, and self-control with steadfastness, and steadfastness with godliness, and godliness with brotherly affection, and brotherly affection with love. For if these qualities are yours and are **increasing**, they **keep you from being ineffective or unfruitful** in the knowledge of our Lord Jesus Christ. For whoever lacks these qualities is so nearsighted that*

he is blind, having forgotten that he was cleansed from his former sins.

Every one of us came from humble spiritual beginnings in the Lord. Regardless of our earthly status or possessions, all of us were stained with sin and in need of redemption. We all were equally received into the love of God when we escaped the corruption of sin and became partakers of God when we were saved. Every one of us, equally, was then charged with fiercely pursuing these divine virtues so that we would become fruitful and multiply in our knowledge and ability in Jesus. As Peter says here and as James boldly proclaims, never forget where we came from, when we deserved spiritual death, but Jesus embraced us. To God be all the glory!

SPIRITUAL FORMATION SECTION

Jesus said, *"By this all people will know that you are My disciples, if you have love for one another"* (John 13:35). In what ways can God's special gifted love appear in our lives? What are some ways we can love that will cause others to give God the glory?

CHAPTER 16

THE ROYAL LAW

JAMES 2:8–11

INTRODUCTION

We have liberty in Christ Jesus! When His light shone into the darkness and He set the captives free, He ushered in a new era of grace and mercy. Now, God's people were free to radiate the love of God outward, having had their hearts molded and shaped by the grace of God! Still, as we saw, that doesn't mean that we are without fault. In this section, James continues to give us guidance on how to treat others as God desires. This is another section that has no imperative, but it is vital to gaining a robust understanding of the Lord's intention for His people. In addition to that, this section of Scripture also provides a more perfect understanding of the Royal Law or, as we know it today, "The Golden Rule."

I. THE ROYAL LAW — VS. 8

If you really fulfill the royal law according to the Scripture,
'You shall love your neighbor as yourself,' you are doing well
(Jas 2:8).

What is the "royal law" that James mentions here? Why is it
"royal"? I want to add context to this reference, but to do it
correctly, we are going to have to take the long way around,
back to the contrast between the Law of Moses and the Law
of the Lord.

Christianity was the substance hidden in the shadows in
the Old Testament's Law of Moses. What took place under
the Law of Moses was meant to give mankind a glimpse into
what was to come, but the fullness of God's plan would not
be fully revealed until Jesus Christ and the church era: "... *the*
*law has but a **shadow** of the good things to come instead of the*
***true form** of these realities*" (Heb 10:1). A shadow resembles
the form but it lacks the detail of the element it is casting; it
is not actually the substance itself (person, object, etc.).
Righteousness, holiness, love, peace, sacrifice, atonement,
and justification—all of these things were present under the
Law of Moses, but only in part. The Lord introduced these
principles to the Israelites through festival days, food purity
laws, the priesthood, the tabernacle, animal sacrifices, and
so much more. True righteousness, holiness, love, peace,
sacrifice, atonement, and justification would not be ***experi-***
entially and personally known until Jesus. Remember
teleios from James 1:25. The Law of Christ was the fullness —
the completion — the realization of God's plan for redemption. No more shadows, the true form had arrived!

One of the most pronounced differences between the Law of Moses and the Law of Christ is the level to which they reveal the mind of God. The Law of Moses was written at a time when the Lord was introducing aspects of His holiness and character to a newly formed people. At the risk of oversimplifying the wonderfully diverse Hebrew Scriptures, the Law of Moses primarily served as a detailed, instruction-based guide on how to *do* holiness, but it rarely opened the eyes of the reader to deeper, spiritual truths.

It's understandable why the Lord would go this route because at this phase in their development, the Lord saw the new nation of Israel as a child. The Lord told the prophet Hosea in Hosea 11:1–4, *"When Israel was a child, I loved him, and out of Egypt I called my son ... It was I who taught Ephraim to walk; I took them up by their arms ... I bent down to them and fed them."* When we were children, how many of our parents said, "I don't owe you an explanation, just do as you're told"? Developmentally, the world and the nation of Israel were not ready for the fullness of God's revelation, so they received the "do's and don'ts" laws which served as a type of guardian and protector for the people. When Jesus came, He came to open the spiritual truths behind these laws. Jesus, and the subsequent New Testament Scriptures, revealed God's mind behind the shadows of the Old Testament. What an amazing time it must have been to learn about the intention and meaning behind the well-known rules from God Himself! When Jesus taught, He taught from the position of Originator and not as a commentator or student of the Law. This teaching style amazed the people because they had never heard this type of authoritative instruction before (Matt 7:29).

Although it is true that the Israelites did not have the

completed revelation from God and did not have deeper spiritual teachings like the New Testament, every now and then there were moments of insight from God concerning the reasoning behind the instructions. Every now and then there were moments when God would give the Israelites a little glimpse into the "why" of the commandments. One of these glimpses is found in Leviticus 19. As I said, we're taking the long way around, but stay with me! We're going to put *ALL* of this together in a moment.

II. LEVITICUS 19: A GLIMPSE INTO WHAT WAS TO COME!

There is an expression in the Hebrew Scriptures that is extremely rare. It's the phrase, "Speak to *ALL* the children of Israel." Rarely were all the people called to hear a word from the Lord collectively as a nation. When this happened, you can be sure that what was about to be said was something of tremendous significance and far-reaching importance. One of those times took place in Leviticus 19: *"And the LORD spoke to Moses, saying, "Speak to all the congregation of the people of Israel and say to them, 'You shall be holy, **for I the LORD your God am holy**"*(vs. 1–2).

Don't miss the significance of what just happened here. The Lord is binding Himself to His people, and the binding agent that the Lord designed to accomplish this was **holiness** — not just any standard of holiness, but His unchanging holiness. From that moment forward, the people of Israel were called to live a life of holiness. Why? Because the God they were to represent is holy. In the book of Leviticus alone, there are ten times that the Lord commanded a certain law to be obeyed and gave the reason as, "I am the LORD." In other words, the nation and the Lord were bound together. The nation's conduct, their way of life, and their understanding of godliness, all came as a direct result of being tied together with the Lord God in holiness.

Leviticus 19 speaks about holiness in a way that is very unique to the rest of the Law of Moses. It was a foretaste of the Lord's ultimate goal: a holy, spiritually-conscious people reflecting Him to the world around them. Israel was being given a peek into a truth that would later be revealed to all: that they were more than just the objects they possessed or the groups they formed, they were spiritual beings created by a perfect and spiritual God, bound together with Him in holiness. This chapter is particularly important because it is here, too, that the Lord informs the people that not only are they spiritual beings, but what they do physically is also of spiritual significance.

For example, in Leviticus 19:8, the Lord tells them, *"Everyone who eats it shall bear his iniquity, because he has profaned what is holy to the LORD, and that person shall be cut off from his people."* The Hebrew word for "person" is *nephesh,* the same word for "soul." The spiritual nature of the person presenting the offering is being connected with the act itself. For the first time, the Lord told His people that eternal consequences could occur from the physical actions they were performing. When spiritually-conscious decisions informed their actions, those physical actions bound them together with their Spiritual God!

Leviticus 19:18 contains a summary that might sound familiar to you: "... *You shall love your neighbor as yourself: I am the LORD."* This is a royalty command because it sums up the discussion on spirituality and holiness. God provided His people with an encapsulation of everything to do with

His holiness, their own spiritual nature, and their actions in the world — *"Love your neighbor as yourself."* This phrase previewed what God had always wanted, a people who would love Him with all their heart, mind, and soul and show that love toward their fellow man. They would do this because they would know the truth about who they were: spiritual beings! They would follow through on the commandments of the Lord because by doing so, their physical actions, having been spiritually discerned, would become the way to be bound together with God in holiness.

Many years later, Jesus would add another layer of depth to this teaching in Matthew 22:

> *And he said to him, "You shall love the Lord your God with all your heart and with all your soul and with all your mind. This is the great and first commandment. And a second is like it: You shall love your neighbor as yourself. On these two commandments depend all the Law and the Prophets"* *(37–40).*

For the first time, Jesus introduced the concept of the fundamental interconnectedness of the Law of Moses. When reduced to its most fundamental and basic truths, its principles all have the same root: love! This is why it would come to be known as "the Royal Law." From this one source, all of the rest of the teachings of God flowed outward. As you can see, although there was a different covenant in place, God's intention for His people was still the same: love! He wanted them to love like Him, from that spiritual place within, to send their sacrifices to Him in love with all their heart, and to care for one another from that place of love. He was training them for what was to come in Jesus.

Turning our attention back to James, it appears that rather than honoring this deep spiritual principle, the early church tried to abuse its meaning.

III. MISUSING THE ROYAL LAW

*If you really fulfill the **royal law** according to the Scripture, 'You shall love your neighbor as yourself,' you are doing well. But if you show **partiality**, you are committing sin and are convicted by the law as transgressors. For whoever keeps the whole law but fails in one point has become guilty of all of it. For he who said, 'Do not commit adultery,' also said, 'Do not murder.' If you do not commit adultery but do murder, you have become a transgressor of the law" (Jas 2: 8–11).*

Reading this, it seems that the guilty fully believed it was possible to show partiality while at the same time claim to be fulfilling this Royal Law. They must have attempted to justify themselves because James adds the conditional statement, "If" at the beginning of his guidance. Again, as we saw earlier, hiding and shifting blame is the fastest path toward self-deception, which is why James addresses their behavior in such a direct manner. One has to wonder how exactly they argued their case. Perhaps they said something to the effect of, "I'm giving the chief seats to the wealthy because if I walked into an assembly, I would want the chief seat too. Doesn't the Royal Law say to do unto others as you would have them do unto you? Isn't giving them the best seats a way of showing them love? I certainly would like to be shown love like that." Of course, that's hypothetical, but it's entirely feasible. What is not hypothetical, though, is from this text we get the sense that they were shielding their behavior by misusing Scripture. Whether they knew it or not, they were pitting one law of the Lord against another law!

To answer their misuse and misunderstanding, James references two of the Ten Commandments in the Law of Moses, the law against adultery and the law against murder. This has caused some to infer that James is attaching the Ten Commandments to all believers in the Christian era. This idea is why we had to take the long way through Leviticus to come here. What James is actually doing is demonstrating their error by simply using adultery and murder as examples of their flawed logic. These two crimes were punishable by death under the Law of Moses. James writes, "You would never, ever say that a murderer is right with God just because he didn't commit adultery, nor would you say that an adulterer was right with God because he'd never killed anyone." The authority of God's law works in unison. If your interpretation of it causes another part of it to be nullified, then it's not a valid interpretation. In like manner, James tells them, "You can't excuse your behavior of showing partiality by claiming that you're fulfilling the Royal Law because not only does this violate the equality of God's statutes, it goes against the deeply-rooted spiritual intention behind the law."

God intended for this special law of loving our neighbors to be the framework by which His people would affect change in the world and affirm the holiness of God and their role in Him. To use that law for anything other than its intended purpose, ESPECIALLY to twist it until it dishonors a fellow brother or sister in Christ, was to make them guilty of the entire thing! Sadly, the early church had some work to do regarding these truths. They had brought the old way of life in with them. They allowed the worldly culture of the day to influence their behavior.

IV. ANTIDOTE FOR PARTIALITY: UNDERSTAND THE SIGNIFICANCE OF LOVING YOUR NEIGHBOR

Loving God and loving others are tied together, just like the Lord and His people are bound together in holiness. This was God's heart from the very beginning when He created mankind in His image. Sin has a way of clouding the way we understand the world around us and how we view people. The early church's establishment and growth was a wonderful time of healing because people were beginning to see themselves in a healthy way, the way God had always intended. When we view others and view ourselves with spiritual discernment, we can avoid the traps that our first-century brethren fell into, traps of division, partiality, and disrespect.

All those years ago, when He said, *"You shall love your neighbor as yourself: I am the LORD,"* the Lord was teaching His people that their actions are tied to Him. The way we treat others hinges on the depth of connection that we have with Him. The two are inseparable. As we saw in the book of Leviticus and in this portion of the book of James, God's wish for His people to see others and the world in a spiritu-ally meaningful way has remained unchanged. As His special first-fruits people, our responsibility is to see like He sees. We have to yearn for this spiritual sight like the Psalmist, who said, *"Open my eyes, that I may behold wondrous things out of your law"* (119:18). When we stop seeing others according to what divides us and start seeing each other as precious souls who have been given a singular chance to live for His glory and service, then we will know that our eyes have been opened and we are living according to the virtues that God set forth in the Royal Law. This is also how the world will know we are connected to God, by the love we radiate to others (John 13:35). This is the heart of all of the teachings of God which is why James calls it royal!

SPIRITUAL FORMATION SECTION

In this chapter, we saw that what happens in our daily lives is connected to God on a spiritual level. This was what God envisioned: a spiritually discerning people who could understand that and have their love for Him shape their heart so that they would turn around and bless the world around them. For this reason, unity and harmony with others is tied to our relationship with God, and vice versa. When one suffers, it impacts the other. Paul says in Romans 15:5, *"May the God of endurance and encouragement grant you to live in such **harmony with one another**, **in accord** with **Christ Jesus**."* Is there harmony in your life? Has contention with others taken a toll on your relationship with God? Have you loved your neighbor in a way that honors God? Or have you been angry at God and blamed Him? Has this taken a toll on your relationships with your church family? Your spouse?

CHAPTER 17

PERFECT LOVE CASTS OUT ALL FEAR

JAMES 2:12–13

Imperatives 14–15: Speak and Act

INTRODUCTION

Our 14th and 15th imperatives are in the commands to *"speak and act as those who will be judged under the Law of Liberty."* There are multiple ways to interpret this charge, but I'm going to propose that instead of just ordering us to act right without explanation, what James is really saying is that there is something about the Law of Liberty and the coming Judgment Day that should inform the way we treat other people right now. I'll give you a hint. Although Judgment Day is a day usually associated with fear, what James is speaking about is not fear; it has something to do with mercy! James is going to make a case for speaking and acting in a way that honors God instead of causing division, using anticipated love and mercy as powerful motivators! Let's explore that together!

I. IMPERATIVES 14 & 15: "SPEAK AND ACT"

In the earlier verses, James brought to the surface two abusive situations in the church. First, the poor of the congregation were being disrespected and discriminated against when they were commanded to sit on the floor or stand, giving up their seats for the wealthy. Then (as if that wasn't bad enough) those guilty of this went on to disrespect the Scripture by misapplying the Royal Law in an attempt to provide themselves with cover. Without reservation, James confronted them about their attempt to speak authoritatively like the judges of old, while abandoning the values of justice and righteousness that guided the judges in their work! Now, through imperatives 14 and 15, James is providing a further solution to these issues that were fracturing their unity.

Let's begin with verse 12, which reads, *"Speak and act as those who are to be judged under the law of liberty."* The imperatives are in James's commands to the brethren who had lost their way to "speak" and to "act." He's commanding them to change their behavior in the here and now, by having it guided by a future judgment. As I mentioned, the temptation is to read judgment and immediately think fear. Fear is not a good motivator because, although it may produce actions, the rote, mechanical actions lack the agreement of the heart. This is absolutely contrary to God's desire for a heart change before action (Hos 6), so obviously that cannot be James's intention. To get the fullness of what James is saying, we need to start first with the reference to the "law of liberty" and let that inform how we read his reference to judgment.

When the world was ready, our Lord was born on this

earth and with His birth came a message of liberation and freedom that the world desperately needed. He came to bring good news to all who were in darkness and spiritual captivity. With this new era came incredible amounts of new knowledge. The mystery of salvation was now fully revealed (Col 1:26). God's people were ready to receive the deeper truths regarding God's vision for the whole world.

His people were also ready to move past the restrictions and prohibitions of Moses's Law and enjoy the new law, the Law of Liberty, which was now found in Christ Jesus. When you read the Law of Moses and compare it to the Law of Christ, there's a big difference isn't there? Where did the dates, times, and places go? Where did the weights, measurements, and protocols go? Where did the food restrictions, holy days, and locations for worship go? The new Law of Liberty in Jesus, uniquely focuses on heart transformation, starting first with the special form of gifted love that the Lord showed through Jesus's sacrifice. In the Law of Liberty, the focus is on heart transformation which leads to being holy, rather than provide instructions on how to *do* holiness using measurements, dates, times, places, weights, and quantities. Don't misunderstand, the Law of Moses served a purpose. Its purpose was to serve as a *"guardian until Christ came...but now that faith has come, we are no longer under a guardian"* (Gal 3:24–25). The Law of Moses introduced new concepts of holiness, boundaries, and sin (Rom 7:7–13), but those restrictions and prohibitions only further highlighted mankind's desperate need for a Savior!

On the other hand, Jesus, the Christ and Savior of the world, ushered in the age of the spiritually-discerning children of God: special people whose actions flowed from a heart and mind personally and experientially shaped by God's gifted love and sacrifice. These were liberated people, free to move past the stone tablets because their redeemed hearts would serve as living tablets (2 Cor 3:2–3)!

This change was prophesied back in Jeremiah 31:33–34,

> *This is the covenant I will make with the people of Israel after that time," declares the LORD. "I will put my law in their minds and write it on their hearts. I will be their God, and they will be my people. And no longer shall each one **teach** his neighbor and each his brother, saying, "**Know** the LORD," for they shall all know me, from the least of them to the greatest, declares the LORD. For I will forgive their iniquity, and I will remember their sin no more.*

Jeremiah's "new covenant" people would no longer need to be taught what God had done and why they should love the Lord because they would have experienced God for themselves. The word "know" here is *yadah*, which means experiential and personal knowledge. And what does Jeremiah say concerning what they would experience? He clearly defines it as "forgiveness of sins." The New Covenant people would be able to move past the rule-following phase and be liberated to go and show the world what it means to receive the grace of God personally! All too often, people went through the motions, following instruction, but their heart was far from Him (Isa 29:13). In this New Covenant of liberty, God's people would now exercise their faith out of an overflow of love for Him (Gal 5:6).

II. MERCY TRIUMPHS OVER JUDGMENT

The Law of Liberty brings tremendous freedom and opportunity for us to go out and show the world what God's grace means to us and what it is to enjoy the blessings that are in Christ Jesus. This is what James has in mind when he calls the Law of Christ the "Law of Freedom." I think that there is a temptation to stop here and just read James 2:12 as a call to simply live in a manner that is worthy of the liberty we have in Jesus. There is nothing wrong with that thought, especially since Paul himself makes that case in Galatians 5:13–16, but again, remember that James is connecting the anticipated judgment under Law of Liberty as *positive motivation* for our words and deeds now, in the present. What positive motivation could come from being judged on Judgment Day under the Law of Liberty? For the answer, James gives us a hint on where to look in verse 13, with his three references to mercy!

> **Speak and act** as those who are to be **judged** under the law of liberty. **For judgment** is without mercy to one who has shown no mercy. Mercy triumphs over judgment. (Jas 2:12–13).

One of the most liberating parts of the new Law of Liberty that Jesus brought was the liberation from living in fear. Not just fear of death, but also of the fear of the Judgment Day. Jesus took the fear of the unknowns of the Judgment Day out of our relationship with God and replaced it with love. And yet, despite that loud and clear statement, so many of us fear the Day of Judgment because we believe that this day is going to be a day where we will be weighed according to how much we did against how much we did wrong. This is a fundamental misunderstanding of this day because it removes the love and grace of God and hinges our salvation on our own works. The fact that Jesus came to offer Himself as a sacrifice in the first place should tell us all that *IF* we have to be weighed (good deeds and bad deeds), we can know for certain that we would all fail. Otherwise, what need would there have been for Jesus? If we could just try hard enough to make sure that we produced enough good deeds and followed enough rules, to outweigh our mistakes, then theoretically, one could bypass Jesus and force God to let us into His eternal presence. The road to the Judgement Seat of God, for those who are His children, under the Law of Liberty, does not end in fear, it ends in mercy! When that is properly understood, it is life-changing! Let's begin to put these pieces together: Law of Liberty, Judgment Day, mercy, and speak/act as those who will be judged under these.

In Isaiah 53, the prophecy concerning the coming Messiah, we are told that the Messiah's death would do three things: provide a propitiation for us, credit righteousness to us, and justify us before God. Starting with propitiation, which simply means a sacrifice that satisfies or appeases God's wrath because of sin, Isaiah says,

> But he was pierced for our transgressions; he was crushed for
> our iniquities; upon him was the chastisement that brought us
> peace, and with his wounds we are healed (vs. 5).

The sacrifice of Jesus would be a propitiation because the wrath that was supposed to come upon us for our sin would instead fall on Him and satisfy God.

Later, John would say it this way in 1 John 2:2,

My little children, I am writing these things to you so that you may not sin. But if anyone does sin, we have an advocate with the Father, Jesus Christ the righteous.

Paul addressed it in the book of Romans by declaring,

We are justified freely by His grace through redemption that is in Christ Jesus. Whom God put forward as a propitiation by His blood, to be received by faith (3:24–25).

Sin had incurred the wrath of our holy God, and there was no way for mankind to fully appease that on their own, no matter how many rules they kept or good deeds they produced. Sin leads to death! Jesus's death upon the cross was the means by which peace was brought to our relationship with the Father because it was the perfect *like for like* sacrifice that we needed, given voluntarily on our behalf. This was the propitiatory element of Jesus's sacrifice.

Second, Isaiah foretold that the sacrifice of the Messiah would credit righteousness to us; or, said another way, the sacrifice of Jesus would allow us to be considered righteous before God, despite our sin and failings. This was not a righteousness that we earned, but a righteousness from Jesus. Isaiah 53:11 declares,

*Out of the anguish of his soul he shall see and be satisfied; by his knowledge shall the righteous one, my servant, **make many to be accounted righteous**, and he shall bear their iniquities.*

Again, in Romans, Paul makes the following distinctions:

> This **righteousness from God comes through faith** in Jesus Christ to all who believe (3:22); Righteousness is credited to us (4:22); Because of one man's trespass, death reigned through that one man, much more will those who receive the abundance of grace and the **free gift of righteousness** reign in life through the one man Jesus Christ (5:17).

This was one of the purposes for God sending His Son to earth and allow Him to be a propitiation for our sins: so that those who pledged their allegiance to Him in true faith could be counted as righteous before Him. Isaiah 61:10 paints a beautiful picture of this transformation saying:

> I will greatly rejoice in the LORD; my soul shall exult in my God, for he has clothed me with the garments of salvation; he has **covered me with the robe of righteousness.**

Lastly, the sacrifice of Jesus was given in order to justify us. This one is essential to understanding our James passage. To this point, Isaiah writes,

> Yet it was the will of the LORD to crush him; he has put him to grief; when his soul makes an **offering for guilt** ... he poured out his soul to death and was numbered with the transgressors; yet he bore the sin of many and makes intercession for the transgressors (53:10, 12).

Having nothing in our possession that is truly ours, the only thing of value that we own is our soul/life. Without a sacrifice, or "offering for guilt," the debt that our sin created with God could only be paid by forfeiting our life (Rom 6:23). God, not wanting that for us, provided for us a "like for like" sacrifice. He took someone with a body like ours, with the same ability to choose as us, and with the same temptations as us, yet without sin, and allowed Him to die in our place. This payment for sin, on our behalf, is the part of the good news of the gospel that liberates us from fear of death and more importantly, fear of the Judgment Day.

Since Judgment Day is the day when full payment will have to be paid, and we know that Jesus's sacrifice already paid that debt, and there is no reason to doubt that it will still be in full effect on that day, then we can fully anticipate that we will be shown mercy! Justification means that payment has been remitted and because it has been paid, we will not be asked to pay on that day!

I've heard it said that justification is "just as if I had never sinned," but that's not quite accurate. The sacrifice of Jesus didn't go back and prevent anyone from committing their sins, it paid the price for sins committed so we won't have to on the Day of Judgment. Saying, "Just as if I had never sinned," implies that there was no cost to our actions. There was indeed a great cost, but Jesus paid that price so that it would not "be counted against" us (2 Cor 5:18–19).

III. WHAT CAN WE EXPECT ON JUDGMENT DAY?

When James commands us to speak and act now, in the present, as those who will be judged (future) under this Law of Liberty, he's not saying that to invoke obedience out of fear, he's giving us positive motivation! He is commanding us to let the anticipation of future mercy, undeserved mercy, and grace that is found in the Law of Liberty for God's first fruits people, to overflow in our speech and actions! Let that be our motivation for treating others with grace, kindness, love, and compassion!

On the Day of Judgment, every secret and hidden thing will be brought out and into the open (1 Cor 4:5). We will all — equally and without exception — confess and give an account of what we have done (Rom 14:10–12). When the entirety of our lives, every word, fault, and mistake, is revealed in the presence of the utter and absolute holiness of God, every single person who has ever lived will fully understand the severity and disgust of their actions. The sheer contrast between the ugliness of our lives and the infinite perfection of God Himself will ensure that there will be no boasting there. Even what we consider our "good deeds" will appear as filthy rags when held up in comparison to His glory and majesty (Isa 64:6). There will be nothing in our lives that we will be able to put before God to make a case for our own righteousness apart from Jesus. Despite how high others elevated us in life and despite how highly we thought of ourselves and despite our possessions or status, no one will be able to stand taller or raise themselves over another in the presence of God. In the face of such immense righteousness, holiness, and glory, our tongues will ONLY be confessing that the Lord's majesty alone is great and there is none like Him! Surrounded by his glory and in the presence of His legions of angels, every single one of us will realize how deserving we are of death! It will be clear, beyond measure, that we do not belong in the presence of such radiance and purity!

At that moment — the moment of utter and complete

desperation — the *sentencing* or the *true* purpose of the Judgment Day, will begin.

> *When the Son of Man comes in his glory, and all the angels with him, then he will sit on his glorious throne. Before him will be gathered all the nations, and he will separate people one from another as a shepherd separates the sheep from the goats. And he will place the sheep on his right, but the goats on the left. Then the King will say to those on his right, "Come, you who are blessed by my Father, inherit the kingdom prepared for you from the foundation of the world ..." Then he will say to those on his left, "Depart from me, you cursed, into the eternal fire prepared for the devil and his angels ..." And these will go away into eternal punishment, but the righteous into eternal life (Matt 25:31–34, 41, 46).*

Really stop and think about what Jesus just said. If all mankind kneeling before God is equally deserving of death because of sin, why will some receive punishment and others not? Why are some called "sheep" and others "goats"?

Acts 2:38 is a verse that is quoted often but over the years has lost its full meaning and understanding because of the way the newer translations have rendered it. In the New King James Version, it says, "And Peter said to them,

> *Repent and be baptized every one of you in the name of Jesus Christ for the **remission of your sins**, and you will receive the gift of the Holy Spirit.*

Remission, or remitting payment, is a legal term which carries the idea of a discharge of debt (think of the Parable of the Unforgiving Debtor in Matt 18:21–35). Remission has been made for our sin through Christ's death. A legal pardon has been granted to us for our sin because payment has been made on our behalf. This means that on Judgment Day, the day designated for payment to be made for sin to God, the "sheep" (saved believers) will not have to pay with their lives because their sin debt will not be held or counted against them.

The gift of salvation and the sacrifice of Jesus included a propitiation for our sin. This means that when it is time to receive what should be coming to us, the sheep will not receive an eternal punishment because theirs was already placed on Jesus at the cross. They chose to obey the gospel, placed their trust in the promise that Jesus made regarding their sin not being counted against them, and the way they lived reflected that blessed trust when they lived in obedience to Jesus the King! They appeared as sheep not because they hadn't sinned before God, but because the sacrifice of Jesus was credited to them and they were counted as righteous before Him.

> *More than that, I count all things as loss compared to the surpassing excellence of knowing Christ Jesus my Lord, for whom I have lost all things. I consider them rubbish, that I may gain Christ and be found in Him, not having my own righteousness from the Law, but that which is through faith in Christ, the righteousness from God on the basis of faith (Phil 3:8–9).*

I am in tears as I write this! Imagine what that is going to feel like! Imagine being bent over and kneeling before God in total humiliation, in awe of His weight, glory, and majesty. With all of our sin and shame exposed before all and before the Righteous Judge, we will kneel. Imagine that feeling of hopelessness as the sentencing begins. Then, just at the moment when we feel as if we are about to be cast out of God's sight for our shameful sin and separated from Him forever, all of a sudden, we begin to look around. We realize that instead of being on the left of the Lord, we are on His right, in the place of honor. We begin to see faces that we recognize. Faces of our dear brothers and sisters in Christ that we had not seen in many years. Brethren who had long passed away.

"Lord God, why am I here? I do not deserve to be here in Your presence. I have failed You so many times."

"Yes," says the Lord, "but I loved you enough to die for you and you believed Me, you trusted Me, and you followed Me, all the days of your life. You made mistakes along the way, but my Son paid in full. Well done, my faithful servant, well done."

In that moment, the full weight of God's grace and mercy will be felt by all of us who are on that side. None of us will have even an inkling that we deserve or earned this reward. When we begin to separate to the right and are escorted to the most magnificent place we have ever seen, I believe we're going to erupt in tears of relief and gratitude to God. That's why Revelation 21:4 says that on that day, God is going to wipe away our tears. In my mind, I envision a beautiful scene where the Lord wipes our tears away and says, "Didn't I tell you that you would receive mercy? Well done, my good and faithful servant. You believed Me and lived a life of gratitude for this gift that you had not seen and out of the overflow of love for Me, you served Me all of the days of your life. Enter into My rest! Come and see what I have prepared for you!"

III. THEREFORE

Now we can understand why James wrote what he did. In essence he told the early church, "We are going to be shown extraordinary mercy and grace on the Day of Judgment, so *therefore*, 'speak and act' in way that is worthy of the mercy you will receive under the Law of Liberty in Jesus, and *demonstrate* to God that your heart is profoundly grateful for the mercy you will be shown that day by treating others with love and respect. If we cannot show mercy in this life, then we have voluntarily chosen to forfeit the blessing of Jesus's sacrifice and have chosen to be judged by our own merit."

The freewill to choose was so important to God, He chose to grant us that precious gift knowing what it would cost Him. God is all-powerful and no soul can be snatched out of the hand of God (John 10:28–29), but as James's warning suggests, we can voluntarily choose to turn from God. The moment we stop acting out of overwhelming gratitude for the mercy we will be shown on the Day of Judgment and cease being merciful to our fellow man, that's the moment when we tell the Lord, "I want to be judged like the goats. I do not want a propitiation sacrifice for me. I don't want the robe of righteousness and I don't want payment for my sins to be remitted by the blood of Jesus. I want to receive exactly what I have earned on my own."

This ungrateful response to the death of Jesus is what the Hebrews writer addresses saying,

If we deliberately keep on sinning after we have received the
knowledge of the truth, no sacrifice for sins is left, but only a
fearful expectation of judgment and of raging fire that will
consume the enemies of God (10:26–27).

All sin is deliberate, but this crime takes place when a person voluntarily rejects or lives in a manner that is equivalent to "crucifying once again the Son of God to their own harm and holding Him up to contempt" (Heb 6:6). Our actions flow from the thoughts and intentions of the heart/spirit — that's part of our image-bearing, free will ability to choose.

Out of the heart flow all sorts of actions (Mark 7:21–23), and each of those actions tells a story to the Lord and to the world around us about what we treasure the most (Matt 6:21). The heart that values what God has done, treating the Kingdom of God like a treasure worth sacrificing everything for (Matt 13:44), is a heart that is firmly planted under the shadow of God's wing. This heart has removed all pride and is humble unto God. The Lord will receive this heart with open arms. What we choose to treasure is up to us, but there is only one way to the Father and that is through Jesus (John 14:6). We cannot create our own way, on our terms, in the manner that we desire. There is grace and peace through Jesus (John 1:17), so choose Jesus!

As those who have been shown this tremendous mercy, grace, and peace, we decide for ourselves whether we wish to accept the free gift of Jesus's sacrifice. The gift is freely available, but it must be received in the way that the Lord has dictated. His gift comes with a responsibility to bring good works into the world (Eph 2:10) and to follow the teachings of Jesus through love (John 14:15; Gal 5:6). The decision to receive salvation is demonstrated by how we "speak and act" here on earth. The fruit we bear does not earn the mercy we will be shown, but comes about *because of* the mercy we will be shown. To the Christians who were mistreating one another, James warns, "speak and act" in a manner that reflects the deep gratitude Jesus is owed for all He has done. If a Christian's actions and words do not reflect this, then it calls into question the state of their soul. The Lord cherished the lowly of this world, and in like manner, He has called us, His people, to do the same.

SPIRITUAL FORMATION SECTION

When you have a moment of quiet and are able to reflect, close your eyes and enter into a conversation with Jesus. This conversation is not a prayer, but a time where you imagine Christ speaking back to you. Imagine that He is on the cross. You are surrounded by the other disciples and Mary. Ask Jesus, "Lord, have I lived in a way that honors what you are doing right now?" What is His response?

CHAPTER 18

THE GOLDEN RULE'S COUSIN

JAMES 2:14–17

INTRODUCTION

In this chapter, we will discuss a principle that spans the entirety of the Scriptures and is fundamental to a relationship with God. James 2:14–17 shows us what happens when there is a break in that principle. As we're going to see, concern for our brethren should not just be in the mind alone, but also in heart. This will not only forge strong connections, but it will also compel us to action! This is the kind of connection that treats others as God has treated us!

I. "THE GOLDEN RULE'S COUSIN"

What good is it, my brothers, if someone says he has faith but does not have works? Can that faith save him? If a brother or sister is poorly clothed and lacking in daily food, and one of you says to them, "Go in peace, be warmed and be filled," without giving them the things needed for the body, what good

is that? So also faith by itself, if it does not have works, is dead
(Jas 2:14–17).

James begins this section by asking an extremely important and poignant question, "Can *that* faith save him?" Can the kind of faith that only mentally acknowledges a person is struggling and in need be the kind of sound, saving faith that the Scriptures speak of? Can telling a hungry person, "I hope you figure that out, bless your heart," be the kind of connection that God expects from His people? I know that we can all agree something is wrong with that picture. If a person who has been blessed with the material goods to help others sees their brother or sister in Christ in need and turns them away, James indicates that this is a clear sign there is a spiritual sickness within their heart.

Surprisingly, there are imperatives found in verse 16, but as we saw in James 2:3, James is not the one speaking, it is those who are at fault. In response to the needs of the poorest among them, some were saying with the force of a command, "be warmed and be filled." Again, this change in how the imperatives are used shows his audience the absolute absurdity of what was being done. These believers, knowing full well they had it in their ability to assist, were commanding the hungry and the naked to go fill their bellies and find warmth on their own — an impossible feat. And they were doing it with the same kind of forcefulness that James has been using with his own imperatives! This is in stark contrast to the Lord, who equips when He commands. He gives His people everything they may need to move forward in their lives. We can infer from James's words that he is making a clear distinction between a hollow and disconnected faith (which is no faith at all!) and true, biblical faith that moves to action.

Although not said explicitly, James is pointing to a fundamental principle in the Bible. For simplicity's sake, it is a principle that I'd like to call, "The Golden Rule's Cousin." Let's take the long way around and explore that together.

Every one of us has heard of the Golden Rule: *"Do unto others as you would have them do unto you!"* Having said that, did you know that this divine principle has a second part to it that is so similar, it can easily be seen as a relative? Here's the Golden Rule's Cousin: Do to others **as God** has done to you! What this means is that the Christian walk is like a two-part cycle involving our vertical relationships and our horizontal relationships and the two impact one another.

Although this principle can be a bit hidden in the Scriptures, I assure you, it is absolutely everywhere! I'll give you some examples. Think of the structure and arrangement of the Ten Commandments that the Lord gave to Moses. The first five serve as a foundation in the heart and mind. They formulate the vertical flow. Four pertain to our relationship with God who is the ultimate source of all authority as the Creator. The fifth relates to another aspect of the vertical authority structure: our parents, who are also our creators. We honor them because of their role and authority in our lives. The last five commandments have to do with our horizontal relationships with each other. The first half of the commandments were meant to flow into God's people and inform the horizontal relationships outlined in second.

Looking specifically at the law pertaining to the Sabbath, notice how the principle appears. The Lord commanded the children of Israel to cease all work. Not only were they commanded to rest, but so were their children, servants, animals, and even any strangers who were among them. Everyone was commanded to rest (horizontal/inter-personal, everyday life), and the reason the Lord gave them was because they *"were slaves in Egypt and the LORD your God brought you out of there with a mighty hand"* (verti-cal/gratitude to God) (Deut 5:14–15). What the Lord has done for them vertically was meant to inform how they behaved horizontally! That's the Golden Rule's Cousin: do to others as God has done for you. As I mentioned, the Scrip-ture is filled to the brim with this principle, but I want to narrow our focus now to the church.

II. "HE FIRST LOVED US ..."

"Do to others as God has done for you," is the bedrock of the Christian faith! It is the theme of a people motivated to radiate the love of God outward, fueled by what they have received from the Lord! The Apostle John really drives this point home in 1 John. Watch how he uses the Golden Rule's Cousin: *"Love another* (horizontal) *for love is of God* (verti-cal)" (1 John 4:7); *"We love* (horizontal) *because He first loved us* (vertical)" (1 John 4:19); *"By this we know love, that He laid down His life for us,* (vertical) *and we ought to lay down our lives for the brother* (horizontal)" (1 John 3:16).

This principle is foundational to our faith because it clarifies that the way we respond to the Lord will impact the way we respond to others. The Lord intended to do some-thing so powerful for mankind that this act of love would drive His people to love others. They would become people motivated by love, gratitude, and appreciation and not by compulsion. When this two-part cycle functions the way that it should, the church family can maintain the unity of the Spirit in the bond of peace because they're all of the same heart and mind before God!

As James expressed in our verses for this chapter and as we saw in John 15, it is a sign of spiritual sickness in the vertical part of our relationships when we treat our brethren with a lack of care and compassion. John makes a similar statement in 1 John 3:17, *"If anyone has the world's goods and sees his brother in need, yet closes his heart against him, how does God's love abide in him?"* This is one of the most powerful aspects of the Golden Rule's Cousin principle: the fact that God and His people are connected together. We are to receive the love and blessings from the Lord and have them inform and motivate the way we treat others; when we do not do this, we break the relationship with the Lord. The Hebrews writer says it this way, *"God is not unjust. He will not forget how hard you have worked for Him and how you have shown your love to Him* (vertical) *by caring for other believers* (horizontal)" (6:10). Faith is not just about our vertical relationship with God, it is also about connection outward through action! The type of correlation that occurs only in the mind, void of any action, is a purely superficial one. That is not what the blood of Christ purchased. Our care and compassion for one another could not and is not meant to repay God for our salvation. Our actions towards others are meant to be an extension of our thankfulness for all that He has done for us. This is what a healthy and thriving faith is all about! Do to others as God has done for you!

III. LOVE OF GOD + HEART + MIND = CONNECTION OF EMPATHY

Now that we've seen how important the Golden Rule's Cousin principle is to God and how it is the reason why His people should care for one another, I want to turn our attention to a wonderful passage in Romans 12 that can help nurture the type of connection that is pleasing to God.

> *Rejoice with those who rejoice; weep with those who weep. Be of the same mind toward one another. Do not set your mind on high things, but associate with the lowly. Do not be wise in your own opinion (vs. 15–16).*

The word "mind" here, in the original language, is a special word that is not commonly used. The sense of this word indicates that Paul wanted harmony within the body of Christ to exist not just in the mind, but to flow from both a place of reason and feeling. Another way to think of this special type of unity is empathy. Empathy, forged by the heart and mind, creates unity and mutual care, and compassion for one another. Spiritual empathy is first fueled by the love of God and the heavy price paid for the beloved church.

Unlike sympathy, which only mentally acknowledges that someone is going through difficulty, empathy is the ability to understand what a person is experiencing and why they feel the way that they do. Within a church family, empathy is critical because it builds deep connections between people and pushes them to genuinely support one another. Empathy requires us to be selfless, as the only way to truly feel or experience what someone else is going through is to prioritize them and not ourselves. It causes us to put away our own expectations and reactions and open ourselves to their pain, as they experience it. This enables us to be an authentic, strong source of support for someone caught in a deep valley.

As God's people, we have to be able to rejoice and weep in equal parts with our church family, but without empathy, that can't happen. Hebrews, again, wonderfully demonstrates the type of actions that come when mind and heart move together: "*Remember the prisoners **as if chained with them** — those who are mistreated — since you yourselves are in the body also*" (13:3). God's expectation is that the body of Christ would be unified, not just in mental acknowledgment and thinking, but also in feeling for one another, leading to compassionate care. That is what spiritual empathy is all about: being connected to each other as a church family and putting ourselves in another's position so that we can take turns being strong for one another ... all out of love and appreciation for the Lord and His children.

IV. SEEING JESUS IN OTHERS

It seems that the Christians being addressed by James believed that God-honoring faith could thrive in the same believers who turned away their brethren in need. Either their vertical connection to God was broken due to pride or an ungrateful spirit, or it was broken *because of* the way they chose to treat others. Either way, James calls the condition of their faith "dead." James's word here closely resembles Jesus's in Matthew 25 regarding the hungry, naked, and imprisoned. In that famous passage, Christ preaches that the ones who see His face in the hungry, thirsty, naked, sick, or stranger would be the ones called to the right hand of the throne in a place of honor. He said, *"As you did it to one of the least of these my brothers, you did it to Me"* (25:40).

Jesus, James, Paul, John, and so many others are speaking to us in unison. We must do to others as God has done for us. We must nurture the type of connection between our brethren that is first shaped by the love of God and is then born in the place where the head and heart come together. This empathy connection is what the Lord expects and what He envisioned all along. This is the kind of faith that is pleasing to God!

SPIRITUAL FORMATION SECTION

As we saw in this chapter, the vertical and horizontal relationships that we have are connected to each other. One informs and impacts the other. This is why servant leadership is so effective; these leaders have first learned to serve under others before taking that humility and sense of service and using it to inform the way they lead. Learning to submit to our vertical relationship is essential to thriving in our horizontal relationships. This includes honoring our parents (Eph 6:2), honoring the elders who are over us (1 Thess 5:12), and honoring the Lord as Creator (Rom 1:20–21). The Golden Rule's Cousin teaches us that a heart that struggles with submission is a heart that has deeper spiritual issues. This principle also teaches us that our vertical relationship with God can be impacted by our conduct horizontally. Peter talks about this when he writes about how division in a marriage can impact prayer to God (1 Pet 3:7). Jesus said in the Sermon on the Mount that if you have a contention with another, go settle it before you offer your gift to God (Matt 5:24).

What are some moments in your life where one relationship, either vertical or horizontal, impacted the other? Were there moments of rebellion vertically that brought you heartache? Were there deep valleys that you experienced with your church family or with your spouse that took a toll on your relationship with God?

CHAPTER 19

TRUE BIBLICAL FAITH

JAMES 2:18–26

Imperative 16: Show Me

INTRODUCTION

Having just made an incredible case for Christian living to be driven by the grace and mercy of God through merging both the heart and mind in service to God, James addresses faith in his 16th imperative. With it, he teaches the true meaning of biblical faith and how, like the kind of relationships we should have with our brethren, it is more than just a mental acknowledgment. True biblical faith is something that can be both seen and shown. It has substance and evidence.

I. EVEN THE DEMONS BELIEVE, SO WHAT EXACTLY IS FAITH? – VS. 18–19

James begins in verses 18–19,

But someone will say, "you have faith and I have works."
Show me *your faith apart from your works, and I will show*
you my faith by my works. You believe that God is one; you do
well. Even the demons believe — and tremble!

James is digging deeper into a thought that he raised in
verse 14 when he said, "Can *that* faith save him?" By
avoiding and mistreating the poor within their congregation, the early church had attempted to create a *type* of faith
that included a mental acknowledgment of God as Lord
while simultaneously ignoring those in need. As we saw in
the previous chapter, God's expectation is that His people be
powerfully connected on a level that is more than just in the
brain. He expects a connection between His children born
out of the heart and mind. This kind of union leads to
sincere actions. He insists upon this because it is what true
faith is all about!

Over the years, faith has been understood by many as
being equal to belief alone. Our 16th imperative tells us
otherwise. The command James gives is the one to "show
me." We can clearly see that there is a connection between
faith and something that can be seen. James suggests that
faith is something people can see with their own eyes and
that can be shown to others, not just something that exists
invisibly in the mind alone. He takes this idea even further
in the following verse. He says, "You believe that God is one;
you do well. Even the demons believe — and shudder!"

Interpretations of James's statement regarding faith and
the demons vary widely. Some are tempted to say that this
verse implies faith *is* something that exists in the mind and
heart alone, and not external. They argue that faith is equal
to belief in God and the demons mentioned did not have

true saving faith because they didn't believe Jesus was the Lord and Christ the Messiah. We know that this explanation isn't accurate though because the demons *did* recognize who Jesus was and verbally expressed it, too. Notice the account in Luke 4:40–41:

> *Now when the sun was setting, all those who had any who were sick with various diseases brought them to him, and he laid his hands on every one of them and healed them. And* ***demons also came out of many, crying, "You are the Son of God!"*** *But he rebuked them and* ***would not allow them to speak, because they knew that he was the Christ.***

Any open and honest student of the Bible has to wrestle with what James 2 and Luke 4 are saying. Both of these passages demonstrate that biblical faith cannot simply mean a mental acceptance, or just believing in one's heart and mind that Jesus is the Son of God and the Christ. As James says, even the demons have arrived at that same conclusion! Yet no one would dare say that they are regenerated and spiritually saved beings. How do we understand James's imperative to "show me your faith," then? If faith cannot be intellectual acceptance and belief alone, what exactly does the Bible mean by faith? This is an extremely powerful and important question and one that can be answered within the great chapter of faith, Hebrews 11.

II. FAITH IS ... A PROCESS COMPLETED IN ACTION — VS. 20–25

Before we break down biblical faith in this chapter, I want to highlight some verses from within it see if you can recognize a pattern.

*By faith, Abel **offered** ...*

*By faith, Enoch was taken up, **having been pleasing** to God ...*

*By faith, Noah **constructed** the ark ...*

*By faith, Abraham **obeyed** when he was called to go out ...*

*By faith, Moses **was hidden** for three months by his parents ...*

*By faith, Moses **refused** to be called the son of Pharaoh's daughter, **choosing** to be mistreated instead ...*

*By faith, **he left** Egypt ...*

*By faith, **the people crossed** the Red Sea ...*

*By faith, Rahab **welcomed** the spies ...*

*By faith, **the walls of Jericho fell after** they had been **encircled for seven days** ...*

Question: Is Hebrews 11 a chapter about **thinking alone** or is it about **doing**, based upon choice and intention?

Again, an open and honest student of the Bible must answer that the great chapter on faith is one of doing, and not thinking alone.

One of the reasons why many misunderstand true biblical faith is because of a mistranslation of Hebrews 11:1. Most modern translations have it worded this way: *"Now faith is the confidence/ assurance of things hoped for, the assurance/conviction of things not seen."* I believe that this has caused many to believe that faith is something that solely exists in the mind. Hebrews 11, however, is not a chapter of thinking, it is a chapter of doing — a chapter of action. At this point, I want to draw your attention to the King James and New King James Versions. Take note as to how they handle this verse. *"Now faith is the **'substance'** of things hoped for, the **'evidence'** of things not seen."* This is more in line with James's intent because evidence and substance are things that can be seen and shown to those around us, unlike mental acknowledgment and belief alone.

It is clear from the differences in translation that the original Greek word behind "substance" must be a tough word to wrap our twenty-first-century minds around. *Hupostasis* is a fascinating little word only used five different times in the New Testament. Three of those instances take place in Hebrews! This term was used to describe the physical effects or substance of something unseen. In those days, before microscopes and advanced technology came along, people could see the evidence and the substance of a reaction or process happening, but they were unable to see the actual event itself.

In Christianity, you could say that *hupostasis* are the actions that people can see us do, actions that tell the world about our invisible connection to the Living God. Said another way, how could someone recognize that we are connected to God? In part, through our words and deeds. When our heart and mind have been merged and shaped by the love of God, that reaction can be evidenced to the world around us by the fruit that we bear. This is why I appreciate the rendering from the King James Version. This translation translates faith as the "substance and evidence" of unseen and hoped for things.

I'll give you another example of *hupostasis* in the book of Hebrews. It appears in the verse used to describe Jesus Himself: *"He is the radiance of the glory of God and the exact imprint of His **nature**"* (1:3). In other words, mankind has never seen God in all His full radiance and glory, but Jesus in bodily form was the physical substance and evidence of God's nature. He was the walking, talking, breathing, speaking, and moving embodiment of God's full personality and being.

Faith is the substance and the evidence of our unseen relationship and connection to the Living God. Rather than think of faith as just belief or an intellectual occurrence, think of faith as a process that begins with God. God has demonstrated His power and ability and He has an established record of faithfulness. These things impact us and how we relate to Him. How we view God and His trustworthiness dictates whether or not we will yield our will to His and follow His guidance, which is the next movement in the process. Indeed, faith is a process that is based upon thinking, considering, and reason, but it is not something that is blind and intangible. True biblical faith involves taking what we know about God and who He is and weighing that out for ourselves in concrete, objective terms, and allowing that to produce actions.

Going back to Hebrews 11, notice what this wonderful chapter says concerning Abraham and Sarah. Although well past childbearing age, Sarah was gifted the ability to conceive and have a son through faith, but notice something interesting about this. It says, *"she **considered** Him faithful who had made the promise."* Just like Sarah, verse 19 says that Abraham, as he was going through the process of offering his son on the altar at God's request, *"**considered** that God was able even to raise him from the dead."* Both Abraham and Sarah, when faced with some extremely difficult decisions, paused to consider (think Jas 1:2!). They thought, they reasoned, and they based their decision to follow instructions on God's pattern of faithfulness. They said, "You know, God has never ever let us down up to this point, nor has He ever given us reason to doubt Him, so based upon the facts, I'm going to do what He says, no matter what the world may say."

Hebrews 11 is essential to understanding true biblical faith. It teaches us that faith happens when we consider His commands in light of His pattern of faithfulness and promises. Then, we follow through on those commands through action, based on a heart of love and trust in God. That's why this chapter of the Bible is really a chapter of action — because true biblical faith is not completed until it has been followed through in *faithful* obedience to God from a heart of love! To the ones that thought that they could make a case for possessing faith because they had mentally acknowledged God and their Savior only, James retorts, "Can *that* hollow faith save you? Because even the demons have that! True biblical faith is evidenced to the world around us by our fruit."

James 2:20–25 drives this incredible point home. It

reads,

> *Do you want to be shown, you foolish person, that faith apart*
> *from works is useless? Was not Abraham our father justified by*
> *works when he offered up his son Isaac on the altar? You see*
> *that faith was active along with his works, and **faith was***
> ***completed by his works**; and the Scripture was fulfilled that*
> *says, 'Abraham believed God, and it was counted to him as*
> *righteousness and he was called a friend of God. A person is*
> *justified by works and not by faith alone. And in the same way*
> *was not also Rahab the prostitute justified by works when she*
> *received the messengers and sent them out by another way?*

Notice that James says that Abraham's "faith was **completed** by his works." Faith is like a circuit. First, you have God, His reputation and His pattern of faithfulness, followed by His instructions and direction for us. Then, just like Abraham and Sarah, there comes our consideration and evaluation, followed by trust and faithful obedience to Him. It is not true biblical faith *until* our belief and trust are followed through in obedience. Faith is not a one-time event allowing us access to God's grace and then stopped. Paul says that faith is also something we are currently standing upon and living in.

> *Therefore, since we have been justified **through faith**, we*
> *have peace with God through our Lord Jesus Christ, through*
> *whom we have gained access **by faith** into this grace **in***
> ***which we stand**; and we exult in the hope of the glory of God*
> *... (Rom 5:1–2).*

So long as the circuit of faith is alive and well, we are

covered by the sacrifice of Jesus and standing in God's grace! A word of caution here ... this is where many misunderstand and fear the Day of Judgment, wondering if they've "done" enough. It is *not* the *action* that saves. It is not the "doing." Those are the *result* of what does save us: belief and trust in God, fueled by love and gratitude for Him. The good deeds are the outcome of the overflow that happens in our heart *because* of salvation. As long as we are walking by faith, we are walking in the light — the place where the forgiveness of Jesus continually cleanses us.

When we live a faith-filled life, one that believes, trusts, and obeys the Lord, we have done exactly what the Lord wishes from His special people. Hebrews 11:6 says,

> *Without faith it is impossible to please Him, for whoever would draw near to God must believe that He exists **(belief)** and that He rewards **(trust)** those who seek Him **(obedience)**.*

Biblical faith comes alive when the three elements of belief, trust, and action are brought together in faithful obedience to God. This is where our relationship with God moves from the mind and into the heart then outward, into the creation, just like He always intended! It is the substance and evidence of our deep connection with the unseen God!

Friendship with God is kind of a strange thought, isn't it? How is it possible to become friends with an all-powerful Being who is infinite in ability? What need would He have of friends? Now that is a question that gets to the heart of why Abraham was called a friend. Jesus expressed a similar sentiment to His disciples in John 15, shortly before His arrest and crucifixion. He said,

No longer do I call you servants for the servant does not know
what the master is doing; but I have called you friends, for all
that I have heard from my Father I have made known to you.
You did not choose me, but I chose you and appointed you that
you should go and bear fruit and that fruit should abide ...
(John 15:15–16).

Friendship is not meant to be interpreted as equality, after all, no one is equal with God. What Jesus was telling His disciples was that their relationship was evolving and growing. No longer did they just do what they were told with no explanation, now they were ready to enter into partnership with God in the fulfillment of His will. Soon, not only were they going to get the full picture of what Jesus's plan was, but they were going to enter into that plan as partners, advancing the Lord's mission to reconcile the world. In this way, Abraham was considered God's friend because not only was Abraham made aware God's intention for the world (*"through you all nations shall be blessed"*), Abraham's faith (belief, trust, and obedience) was going to help advance that intention! Keep this friendship concept in mind, because it will appear again in the book of James.

III. FAITH WITHOUT WORKS IS DEAD – VS. 26

For as the body apart from the spirit is dead, so also faith
apart from works is dead (Jas 2:26).

For the first-century church receiving this letter from James, the lightbulb was out due to a faulty circuit of faith. They were convinced of God's power and they knew God's instructions to treat their fellow man with dignity and respect and service, but they stopped short of completing the circuit when they forgot their gratitude towards God, which led directly to them ignoring the needs of their brethren. Just as the body apart from the spirit is dead, James made sure they understood that their faith apart from works was dead because it was not true faith. Our gratitude and love *for* God and love *from* God is the voltage that keeps the circuit of faith alive; it is what causes us to want to produce fruit. Faith dies when the heart no longer overflows with thankfulness to God for His unmerited gift of salvation.

A lackluster trust and appreciation for Him can be clearly seen in the lack of fruit produced. Spiritual death does not occur when people stop working or trying to do their best. Spiritual death begins much sooner, in the heart. A lack of fruit, or "works" as James calls it, is merely the symptom of what has occurred in the person's connection to God. A person's faith doesn't die because they haven't completed enough good works; the lack of works is a clear sign that a death has occurred earlier in the process itself, in their belief, trust, love, and gratitude toward God.

IV. FAITH IS...HOW WE WALK!

Something that I have heard someone say many times during my time in the ministry is, "I'm losing my faith." Inevitably, when I dig a bit deeper into why they *feel* that way, I usually find that the feeling itself is what they are referring to when they speak of faith. Somewhere along the way, they were led to believe that faith is an emotion. Every human on earth knows that emotions come and go and can change drastically from one moment to the next. Faith is not a feeling that comes and goes. It is the culmination of what God has done and what He has instructed, followed by our rational consideration of these patterns and leading to belief and trust in God. This belief and trust then lead to our faithful obedience to God through visible behavior. There is certainly a feeling of joy that comes from this kind of forward motion and service to God, but faith isn't the emotion being experienced.

Paul has a really interesting way of describing the process of faith in 2 Corinthians 5:7–9,

> For we **walk** by faith, not by sight. Yes, we are of good courage, and we would rather be away from the body and at home with the Lord. So, whether we are at home or away, we make it our aim to please Him.

Notice that for the Christian, "we make it our aim" and "we walk by faith." These are deliberate choices. This is not some fleeting sensation produced by neurotransmitters in the brain; this is the result of decision and intention, based upon a lifetime of trust, love, gratitude, and belief in God!

This entire process of faith is designed to help us transfer trust to our Creator. Our Christian lives executed in faith are exactly that: a life-long transfer of trust from ourselves to our Creator. The more convinced we are of His power and His ability and the greater we increase in gratitude to Him, the mightier our actions that follow will be, with bigger and bigger implications for the world. As James established in verse 18 of his first chapter, God's desire is to have a special people who are like the first fruits of His creation, who bear fruit so that others may taste and see His goodness. These actions are the substance and evidence to the people here on earth that we believe, trust, and love God and are grateful for all that He has done. True biblical faith (belief leads to trust which leads to obedience) is one of the most powerful evangelistic tools that we have! With it, we can win many for the Kingdom!

SPIRITUAL FORMATION SECTION

How do Hebrews 11 and James 2 shape your understanding of what is said in Ephesians 2:8–10: *"Saved by grace through faith ... gift of God (salvation) ... **for** good works"*? How does one inform the other? What is your understanding of their relationship?

CHAPTER 20

CHOOSE SERVANT LEADERSHIP

JAMES 3:1-2

Imperative 17: Let Not Many

INTRODUCTION

I f faith is evidenced by the way we live and the actions that we produce, imagine the importance of our speech! Speech is the primary way that we communicate with the world around us, so it should be the greatest opportunity for us to show the rest of the world the type of God we serve and the belief and trust that we have in Him. The key word here is: should! Our seventeenth imperative focuses on the motives and pitfalls in our speech, starting first with aspiring teachers.

I. IMPERATIVE 17: "LET NOT MANY..." — VS. 1

Since the first chapter of James, we have seen that God's desire for us as His followers and first-fruits people is to evidence our faith to the rest of the world. In doing so, the world can come to know the substance and nature of the God we serve. Our actions are like the divine connection between the spiritual God who made us and this physical world. When lived out, our faith tells a story about God: a story of how He can be believed, surrendered to, and trusted. Sadly, when we produce bad fruit or no fruit at all, we end up telling the wrong story about God. What happens when God's people give God a bad name because they cannot exercise self-control? James chapter 3 is going to address that, starting first with the teachers who should have known better!

> My brethren, **let not many of you become** teachers, knowing that we shall receive a stricter judgment (Jas 3:1).

The imperative is found in the phrase, "let not many of you become." This verse has rightly been interpreted to mean that those who teach in any capacity need to approach that position with humility and diligence, knowing that souls are at stake. When we read James's reference to teachers, our minds quickly gravitate to preachers or Sunday school teachers because we're used to interpreting the Bible through our own twenty-first-century context. But think about the first-century audience. Where would their minds have gone as soon as they heard the word "teachers"? If we pause long enough and really meditate on each word, we can see that behind James's teaching is the voice of Jesus Christ. Let's explore the passage together and see if we can hear both James and Jesus!

Historically, we know that during the lifetimes of James and Jesus, people understood "teacher" to be an official title of honor. For example, in John 20:16, Mary, when she heard

Jesus call her name while at His tomb, said, *Rabboni!* In that verse, John clarifies that *Rabboni* means "teacher." The position of Rabbi or teacher was an extremely well-respected and honored position. The Hebrew word, *rab* which means "great" is even contained within the title of Rabbi. These men were teachers of the Law, great ones who stood out among the people for their wisdom and knowledge. Unfortunately, because of the status that went with the position, there existed a distinct problem with these teachers of the Law that Jesus addressed directly in one of His most hard-hitting denouncements.

Jesus said in Matthew 23:2–12,14:

> The **scribes and the Pharisees** *sit on Moses's seat, so do and observe whatever they tell you, but not the works they do. For they preach, but do not practice. They tie up heavy burdens, hard to bear, and lay them on people's shoulders, but they themselves are not willing to move them with their finger. They do all their deeds to be seen by others. For they make their phylacteries broad and their fringes long, and they love the place of honor at feasts and the best seats in the synagogues and greetings in the marketplaces* **and being called rabbi by others**. *But* **you are not to be called rabbi**, *for you have one teacher, and you are all brothers. And call no man your father on earth, for you have one Father, who is in heaven. Neither be called instructors, for you have one instructor, the Christ. The greatest among you shall be your servant. Whoever exalts himself will be humbled, and whoever humbles himself will be exalted ... "Woe to you, scribes and Pharisees, hypocrites, because you devour widows' houses, and for a pretense you make long prayers; therefore, you will receive* **greater condemnation**.

Can you hear the voice of Jesus echoing in James 3:1? Notice how Jesus connected the Pharisees' love for the title (Teacher), along with a host of other sins, to the **greater condemnation** that they were set to receive. The problem with the Rabbis, or the teachers, was that they loved to be elevated over one another, which (uncoincidentally) was precisely the kind of partiality that was plaguing James's readers. The teachers enjoyed being considered people who had all the answers and could do no wrong, but Jesus pointed out that this was all a show and that it was to have no part in His future kingdom. He explicitly states, *"You are not to be called Rabbi or Teacher among yourselves because you have One Teacher and you are all brothers ... whoever desires to be greatest among you shall be your servant ... ."* Jesus was warning them that if anyone, even those in authority, elevates themselves against their fellow brethren, they would receive "the greater condemnation." Could it be that James is reiterating this warning? Perhaps James is saying, "Do not allow this old system of teacher cults to poison the church, knowing that if any of us become like these teachers, we will receive the greater condemnation, exactly as Jesus warned."

One of the defining characteristics of the church is our equality in Christ. We are all brothers and sisters in Him, just as the Lord intended. We are not permitted to form caste systems or elevate ourselves over one another. Now contrast that with the teachers that we just read about. One of their worst traits was that they loved to be separate and seem higher or "better" than everyone else. They wore clothes that distinguished them in a crowd. They purposely utilized language during their prayers that was lofty and different from those of the average person. And they loved the chief seats in the synagogue, the places of honor. Did we not just read of exactly this behavior and perceived self-superiority in James 2? Yes, we did!

The connections between Jesus's warnings and James 3 don't stop there. Another issue that Jesus had with those who claimed to be teachers or Rabbis was their hypocrisy. He again calls them out regarding this in Matthew 23:25, 27–28:

> *Woe to you, scribes and Pharisees, hypocrites! For you clean the outside of the cup and the plate, but inside they are full of greed and self-indulgence ... Woe to you, scribes and Pharisees, hypocrites! For you are like whitewashed tombs, which outwardly appear beautiful, but within are full of dead people's bones and all uncleanness. So, you also outwardly* **appear righteous** *to others, but within you are full of hypocrisy and lawlessness.*

The Rabbis specialized in making everyone else around them feel unworthy. They caused others to stumble while at the same time appearing to never stumble or struggle themselves. In a show of humility, James disarms anyone who was even thinking of seeking this lofty title by speaking the truth about the responsibility that comes with this position. Where the scribes and Pharisees considered themselves disconnected from the others, in the body of Christ, anyone who teaches will have to answer for what they taught their hearers. In addition to that, and in a wonderfully refreshing show of humility, James pulls back the façade created by the Rabbinical and Pharisaical orders. Teachers do indeed stumble, because they are human just like the rest of us!

II. THE REALITY OF STUMBLING — VS. 2A

To transmit the writings of the New Testament to the widest possible audience, the language that was utilized by the original authors was Greek. Greek was a common denominator language in the ancient world, but it was not the primary language of New Testament writers. James, for example, would have been a native Hebrew/Aramaic speaker, just like Jesus, having grown up in the same home. There are moments in the New Testament where some of the writers' personalities rise to the top if you look through the Greek and seek to hear the conversational language behind the translations. This passage is one such example! The word, "many" in verse 1 and the word "we all" in verse two are actually the same Greek word.

When we take the Greek words for the double use of "many," the word, "teachers," and the word, "stumble" and replace them with what would have been their Hebrew counterparts, what surfaces is a play on words—a common occurrence in the Hebrew language. It goes like this: **"Rab" (many) are trying to become "Rabbis" (teachers), but the "Rab" (we all) are "rabatz" (stumbling)."** In other words, "Rabs" (the many) are trying to be Rabbis or teachers, but the very "rabs" are the ones "rabatzing" (stumbling)! It's a playful exchange meant to simply say, "Be humble! Don't try and follow in the old ways. We all stumble and we're all in need of grace."

That's true wisdom right there! No one has the right to claim perfection, let alone try and bring into the church an outdated system which nurtured division in the past. If anyone could have claimed that title of revered teacher it was James, but notice how James includes himself in the category of the ones who have stumbled. This is rather incredible because we know from history that at this time, James was considered to be a humble and gracious person worthy of extreme honor in Jerusalem. He had gained the respect of both the Jewish religious leaders in Jerusalem as well as the early Church. His wisdom and stature was respected by all, but he includes himself in these humble terms.

III. PERFECTION IS IMPOSSIBLE BUT COMPLETION SHOULD BE OUR AIM — VS. 2B

Simply put, James's words are a condemnation of hypocrisy. These verses were written against anyone who would presume to elevate themselves over others by claiming certain titles (like "teacher"). Just as status and possessions are not reasons for special treatment, neither are titles, educational achievements, or societal roles. Those who engage in that type of thinking are ignoring the reality of their own shortcomings and are indirectly cheapening the sacrifice of Jesus who died for their sins. Obviously, both James and Jesus were passionate about the fair treatment of one another and the acceptance of our need for God's mercy. We are all in need of God's grace and mercy; no human who has ever lived has been perfect (Rom 3:23). If such were the case, there would be no need for Jesus to have come to earth in the first place. As it stands, an inaccurate view of one's failings and imperfections results in hypocritical damage to God's people and church and severely hinders our ability to tell an accurate story about the God that we serve. It also hinders our effectiveness in pushing God's redemption story forward within our circle of influence. It is impossible to glorify God when we're distracted by thoughts of our own grandeur. When we deceive ourselves into thinking that we are more important than our fellow man, it causes us to walk away from them — and the Lord!

James concludes verse 2 by saying, *"If anyone does not stumble in what he says, he is a **perfect** man, able also to bridle his whole body."* The word "perfect" here is the same word that we have seen numerous times throughout James 1 and 2: *teleios*, which means "completion." The idea here is that a person who has mastered the ability to control every part of themselves, both body and spirit, is a person who avoids stumbling. This is a completion process that takes time and patience.

Although, as he says, "we all stumble," the fact remains that we as Christians should still work to bridle, or restrain/control, the body so that we reduce the times that we do stumble. After all, remember James 1:26: *"If anyone thinks he is religious and does not bridle his tongue but deceives his heart, this person's religion is worthless."* Wouldn't it be nice if we all could stumble less with every passing day? To arrive at that level of maturity and control is the standard we should seek to achieve. Each day is a new opportunity to add something to our spiritual discipline so that we become more like God, our Creator. Our lives tell a story about God and one of the worst stories that we can tell is a hypocritical one. To avoid this, God's people should *pursue* holiness with a passion!

SPIRITUAL FORMATION SECTION

We all stumble. For some, that's an easy thing to say. For others, those words could never be spoken out loud. The difference? Pride. The teachers of the Law created a false persona that fed their pride. It made others believe that they were the only ones with issues. Do you struggle with pride? Whose side are you on? Are you yielded and submitted to God? Or are you on our own team?

CHAPTER 21

THE WILL OF THE PILOT

JAMES 3:3–5

Imperatives 18–19: Look and See

INTRODUCTION

J ames 3:3–5 contains two imperatives from James, but they are both essentially the same: the command to "look and see." In our text, James provides tools that can assist in maintaining self-control in our speech so that we become more effective in our spiritual fight to bring goodness and peace into the world. As we saw in the previous chapter, what we're striving for is not sinless perfection (that's impossible) but *teleios*, or completion. We add new spiritual disciplines every day. The 18th and 19th imperatives are going to help us get closer to that goal by focusing our attention on our word power.

I. IMPERATIVES 18 & 19: "LOOK AND SEE!" — VS. 3–5

> *If we put bits into the mouths of horses so that they obey us, we guide their whole bodies as well.* **Look** *at the ships also: though they are so large and are driven by strong winds, they are guided by a very small rudder wherever the will of the pilot directs. So also the tongue is a small member, yet it boasts of great things.* **See**, *how great a forest is set ablaze by such a small fire! (Jas 3: 3–5)*

The imperatives are in James's directions to, *"**Look** at the ships,"* and *"**See** how great a forest is set ablaze."* Again, these commands are meant to draw our attention to the impact that words can have in our lives and in the lives around us. Since the rise of technology and social media, our word power has only grown exponentially. Even words that are not our own, but that are shared, forwarded, and "liked" have our stamp of approval on them and we give them greater reach. Our word-power potential is vast and its effects are permanent!

Christians have it harder than the rest of the world in this area. Our words not only represent us individually, they also contain the added responsibility of exemplifying the Lord since we are co-partners with Him in the re-creation of the world. Because our lives tell a story about God, a stumble in our speech can damage that narrative and give others the wrong impression of the One we serve. James 3:3–5 demonstrates the need for us to exercise control in this vital aspect of daily life. I'd like to spend some time on the ship analogy that James uses to demonstrate the power of the tongue.

This is such a fantastic illustration! It speaks perfectly to the different elements that are involved in day-to-day life and communication. First, you have the ship. This is the great impact and potential influence that our words can have. As he said in verse 5, the *"tongue is a small member but boasts of great things."* Our words can have two outcomes: to bless, or to curse. We can encourage one another, or we can destroy someone's spirit. We can lift up another, or we can plant seeds of doubt and mistrust. As James taught us in the 14th and 15th imperatives, our actions have spiritual ramifications; we can accurately say, then, that words have the capability to alter the course of a person's eternal destiny to some extent. This ship is indeed important, but it cannot do anything on its own. The words themselves are not dangerous; they must be moved and directed.

In addition to the ship, James mentions "strong winds." These are external events that happen on a daily basis and try to force us into a reaction. Our lives are filled to the brim with "strong winds" that test us, winds that push us and pull us. It's easy to identify with the name of Christ in a Church building where there is calmness and a temporary escape from the hurricane outside. What about when we are at work or among friends and acquaintances? What about when someone offends us? What about when something doesn't go the way we want? What about when we receive life-changing test results or are blindsided by betrayal or loss? The winds, like the various trials and tribulations mentioned earlier in James 1:2, will come in varying degrees of strength, but all will demand a response.

A ship also possesses a rudder, which is its mechanical

and steering component. The ship has its potential power and the winds are forceful enough to move it, but the rudder is the part of the ship that harnesses that power by directing it! James equates the tongue with this harnessing agent. Where the rudder goes, the ship turns. In the same way, the tongue produces the movement of our words.

The ship, the winds, and the rudder are all important aspects of the analogy, but none are as important as the "will of the pilot." The decisions of the captain or pilot provide direction to the rudder. The rudder will turn the ship being driven by strong winds and move it in whichever direction chosen by the captain or pilot. James commands us to "look and see," not just at the power words can have, but at the incredible force they can be when harnessed properly. Even in the face of tremendous adversity and struggle, words can be effective opportunities to glorify God.

Whether we bless or curse in our speech ... whether we stumble through the use of our words or use them to glorify God ... it all comes down to our will, the "will of the pilot." The strength of our will determines how motivated and intentional we are concerning our speech. As a minister, I have had the privilege of being invited into the sacred final moments of life for many dear friends in the faith. The giants in the faith who had tremendous strength of will resulting from years of spiritual conditioning and maturity were the ones who entered into this final phase of their lives glorifying God. Even in the face of illness and lack of bodily strength, their speech never departed from giving God glory and thanks for all that He had done for them and continued to do. They used those final, hurricane-level winds to intensify their testimony among all who came to see them and all the medical staff who surrounded them. They were true spiritual giants whose boldness and unwavering zeal for God told a powerful story.

II. THE WILL OF THE PILOT

It's important to strengthen our will, the will of the pilot, if we want our words to match the desires of God's heart. Much of that strength will come from "sets and reps" done in the spiritual gym. The more we allow the trials of life to have their full effect, the stronger we will become. In addition to this conditioning, there are three other principles that can also strengthen our will and help us resolve to use the winds of life for the glory of God.

First, remember our responsibility to be the first fruits of God's creation. This means that we are the city set on the hill, the salt of the earth, and a light shining in the darkness. We are responsible for telling the story of God and of His salvation. We're also responsible for taking the light of Christ and reflecting it for all people to see (Matt 5:16). The light that we shine is meant to illuminate a path for people to find their way out of the world and into the Kingdom of God. Paul says it this way in 2 Corinthians 5:20, *"We are ambassadors for Christ, as though God were making His appeal through us. We implore you on behalf of Christ: Be reconciled to God."* Our speech is one way that God makes His appeal to the world to abandon chaos and choose peace in Christ. It should draw people to him, not push them away. Again, in Philippians 2:14–15, Paul urges,

> *Do everything without complaining or arguing, so that you may be blameless and pure, children of God without fault in a*

*crooked and perverse generation, in which you shine as lights
in the world.*

Remembering always our role as a reflection of God can significantly strengthen our resolve. In my mind's eye, I can still see my mother standing at the door of our humble home. The screen on the door was torn and rolled down, but there was my mom behind it, every morning. Without fail, she would yell out to us, "Remember who you are and remember where you are going!" This was her way of inviting us to take the name of Jesus with us. We had very little, but we had all we needed. I left home and traveled to places that I never dreamed of. But no matter how far I go, I can still hear those words. They strengthened the will of this pilot to persist through winds that cannot be described in words. To God be all the glory!

Second, show gratitude to the Lord for His gifts. Thankfulness has a way of helping us to live a more optimistic and hope-filled life. Gratitude also breaks the downward spiral that happens when trials begin to pile upon each other and increase in weight. Often when this happens, we can only see the negative in life, but that is just tunnel vision. The reality is that God's children are blessed beyond measure and are constantly surrounded by blessings. As James has taught us, even the trials themselves are blessings. In moments of turbulent winds, we have to be intentional about focusing on these blessings, and the best way we can accomplish that is through gratitude.

In ancient times, under the Law of Moses, the children of Israel celebrated a very special offering. It took place a few days after the Passover in the spring, at the beginning of the grain harvest. They were commanded to bring the first fruits of the harvest to the Lord, but this wasn't about just offerings. Deuteronomy 26:1–3 says,

> When you come into the land that the LORD your God is giving you for an inheritance and have taken possession of it and live in it, you shall take some of the first of all the fruit of the ground, which you harvest from your land that the LORD your God is giving you, and you shall put it in a basket, and you shall go to the place that the LORD your God will choose, to make his name to dwell there. And you shall go to the priest who is in office at that time and say to him, "I declare today to the LORD your God that I have come into the land that the LORD swore to our fathers to give us ..."

In other words, this act was meant to be a way of saying, "I believe, I know, and I recognize that God kept His word and this basket was only made possible because of God's faithfulness." Deuteronomy 26 continues in verses 5–11,

> And you shall make response before the LORD your God, "A wandering Aramean was my father. And he went down into Egypt and sojourned there, few in number, and there he became a nation, great, mighty, and populous. And the Egyptians treated us harshly and humiliated us and laid on us hard labor. Then we cried to the LORD, the God of our fathers, and the LORD heard our voice and saw our affliction, our toil, and our oppression. And the LORD brought us out of Egypt with a mighty hand and an outstretched arm, with great deeds of terror, with signs and wonders. And he brought us into this place and gave us this land, a land flowing with milk and honey. And behold, **now I bring** the first of the fruit of the ground, which you, O LORD, have given me." And you shall

set it down before the LORD your God and worship before the
LORD your God. And you shall rejoice in all the good that the
LORD your God has given to you and to your house, you, and
the Levite, and the sojourner who is among you.

You and I are the first fruits now. Just like the children of
Israel were instructed to acknowledge with a heart of gratitude how they were blessed through the actions of previous
generations (Deut 26:10), we too should also take the time
to nurture that spirit within us. We should give thanks to
Jesus for making it possible for us to be called an heir with
Him. We should also give thanks for the unbroken spiritual
genealogy that brought us the gospel. Fostering a heart of
gratitude to the Lord and a spirit of thankfulness for all the
blessings that we have will strengthen our resolve to drive
the ship down a God-glorifying path.

Lastly, utilize long-term, spiritually-based thinking. The
world is notorious for being a transitional place, existing
day to day, hour by hour. The world acts and reacts and lives
like tomorrow doesn't exist and isn't important. It is
certainly true that we don't know whether there will be a
tomorrow here on earth, but even if the world was to be
destroyed today, there would still be an eternal tomorrow.
As Christians, we of all people should be focused on the
long-term, just like God is. Since we are spiritually eternal
beings, we need to bring eternity into our daily interactions.
Regarding this, Paul says in 1 Corinthians 9:24–25,

Do you not know that in a race all the runners run, but only
one receives the prize? So run that you may obtain it. Every
athlete exercises self-control in all things. They do it to receive
a perishable wreath, but we, an imperishable.

Paul's point is that we are currently running a long-distance, spiritual "race." The prize of that race will not be given here on earth; it will be given in the days of eternity after this life is over, in that great tomorrow. Keeping eternity in mind will motivate you to exercise self-control in your day-to-day life and strengthen your resolve when the winds come unexpectedly.

SPIRITUAL FORMATION SECTION

Does your ship need maintenance? Has the rudder turned in a direction that ended up bringing pain? Many like to blame their tongue ("I just couldn't hold my tongue!") as though it was the tongue that decided on the treacherous course. As we saw, it is not the tongue that makes the choice, but the will of the pilot. Inner spiritual strength is critical to withstanding the temptation to allow the winds to drive us toward a place of sin with our speech. Think about a time when your words brought you the most heartache that you can ever remember. Evaluate the following:

1. Your Ship — When did you say it?
2. Your Rudder — What was said? How did you say it?
3. Your Winds — What were the circumstances?
4. You, the Pilot — What triggered the response? Did you speak from a place of emotion and instability or were you intentional about what was said? What was your motive? What was your intended desire?
5. The Will of the Pilot — What could you have done differently? If you had remembered your

status as a representative of the Lord, would that
have changed your words? If you had weighed
what you wanted to say against the sacrifice of
Jesus to see if those words were worthy of what
Jesus did for you, would you still have moved
forward? Did your words have long-lasting
consequences? In that moment, were you
thinking of the long-term and even eternal
consequences? Would thinking of the eternal
have changed how you responded?

CHAPTER 22

THE DEADLY POISON OF THE TONGUE

JAMES 3:6–8

INTRODUCTION

One of the most poisonous animals on the planet is the Komodo Dragon. This monitor lizard has venom that is injected into its prey when it bites. Unlike other animals that have speed and agility to aid them in their hunt, the Komodo Dragon only needs to bite its prey and the poison will do the rest. After an incubation period of several days, the bitten animal falls dead and the Komodo Dragon follows its scented trail to the feast. Although there are no imperatives within James 3:6–12, we're going to see James elaborate on the destructive capability of the tongue. Like the Komodo Dragon, our words can have long-lasting and deadly effects. Fire and poison destroy and reintroduce chaos into the creation. If we're not careful and intentional about our speech, our words can erase the progress that we and others in the Kingdom of God have made.

I. THE POISON-PRODUCING TONGUE

> ... *How great a forest is set ablaze by such a small fire! And the tongue is a fire of worldly unrighteousness. The tongue is designated among our members as what stains the whole body and sets on fire life's cycle having been ignited by the fire of hell. For every kind of beast and bird, of reptile and sea creature, can be tamed and has been tamed by mankind, but no human being can tame the tongue. It is a* **restless** *evil,* **full of deadly poison** *(Jas 3:5b–8).*

If it feels like this passage sounds similar to the self-control teaching from James 1, that's because it is and there's a reason for it! The word "restless" in James 3:8 is the same as the one translated "unstable" in James 1:8. The idea is that the tongue may be subdued every now and then, but over the course of one's life, things will happen and we will go through moments of weakness. Some of these moments will be so strong that if we're not intentionally thinking about how we're to respond, and if left unchecked, we may lose control over the tongue, causing it to be unstable and unruly.

The tongue has tremendous influence and potential, but remember that if we stumble in its use, it's not the tongue's fault, it's ours. The tongue is the medium by which we communicate, but as Jesus said, *"Out of the abundance of the heart, the mouth speaks"* (Luke 6:45). The real instability is within our hearts and minds. Although our words were never intended to be deadly poison and fire, they can be used for this purpose. The choice is ours.

The Bible is filled with cautions regarding our speech

and the various types of deadly poisons that can come from our tongues. I want to spend some time looking at some of these poisons, followed by ways we can neutralize the venom.

Ephesians 4 speaks about an incredibly potent venom called corrupting talk:

> Let no **corrupting talk** come out of your mouths, but only such as is good for **building up**, as fits the occasion, that it may give grace to those who hear.

Corrupting talk, like the deadly poison of the Komodo Dragon, breaks down, disintegrates, and destroys. This is why Paul says that the only kind of speech a Christian should use is the speech that builds up. Corrupting talk can take the form of slander, which is when we destroy a person's reputation and credibility. It may also take the form of gossip, quarreling, arrogance, and disorder, all of which are condemned by Paul in 2 Corinthians 12:20 because they break down unity among God's people. And worst of all, they disintegrate the strength of our unified light.

Another deadly poison of the tongue is found in the works of the flesh outlined by Galatians 5:20: "*outbursts of wrath and rage.*" This particular poison targets a community of believers by breaking down harmony and trust and even fracturing the spirit of the receiver. This poison is produced by a person who has lost all control over their flesh and has turned over their will to anger and rage. This has no place within the Kingdom of God. As Christians, we ought to be the very model of self-control, not people out of control. Sadly, those who give in to rage and anger tend to be short-sighted, not thinking of the consequences that their behavior can have, and certainly not considering its eternal implications. I've heard people say from time to time that their outbursts were only a result of "speaking their mind." They say this as though it was a badge of honor. Christians should feel free to speak their mind because their mind *is* the mind of Christ (1 Cor 2:16) but that would never involve anger or loss of control over their speech.

Lastly, some of the deadliest poison that we can produce comes not in the form of corrupting talk or outbursts of rage, but in what the Bible calls, "sowing discord." In the list of the six things that the Lord hates and the seven that are abominations to Him from Proverbs 6:16–19, the final one listed is *"one who sows discord among brothers."* This particular sin is especially highlighted because it personally insults the Lord Himself. The injury done when brethren form groups and inflict damage against one other doesn't just impact them personally, it sends a message to the world that the Lord is divided and lacks the ability to lead His people in a unified way.

The Corinthian church's discord had become so well known that Paul had even heard about it from a sister in Christ named Chloe and her fellow Christians in Corinth. He writes to them,

> *I appeal to you, brothers, by the name of our Lord Jesus Christ, that all of you agree, and that there be no divisions among you, but that you be united in the same mind and the same judgment. For it has been reported to me by Chloe's people that there is quarreling among you, my brothers. What I mean is that each one of you says, "I follow Paul," or "I follow Apollos," or "I follow Cephas," or "I follow Christ."* **Is Christ divided?**

Being someone who has insulted the Lord by sowing discord and division within His first-fruits people is a scary place to be! Jesus began the church to usher in an unprecedented era of life, a time not seen since Adam and Eve (1 Cor 15:23). Sowing dissension and disagreement within this new special place is like pushing in the opposite direction! That's why Paul went on to tell Titus,

> *As for a person who stirs up division, after warning him once and then twice, have nothing more to do with him, knowing that such a person is warped and sinful;* **he is self-condemned** *(3:10–11).*

God's special first fruit community of people needs to be pushing in the same direction. Not their own individual directions, but the one that furthers God's will!

II. TOOLS TO NEUTRALIZE THE DEADLY POISON OF THE TONGUE

With all the poison that can flow from our tongues, it is crucial to find ways to neutralize it. I want to offer some preventative measures from the Scriptures to do just that.

First, give others the benefit of the doubt and be slow to react. James said as much back in his first chapter:

> *Know this, my beloved brothers: let every person be quick to hear, slow to speak, slow to anger; for the anger of man does not produce the righteousness of God (19–20).*

Pausing before responding gives us enough time to gather all the information before we say something that could end up eroding unity instead of building it up. There is a story that I heard a preacher share and it has stayed with me through the years. I want to share it with you because it demonstrates this need for us to pause long enough to obtain all the facts before reacting.

One night, a preacher was seen with his arm around one of his church members, stumbling out of a bar. The two were observed by another church member as she was driving by on her way home from work. When she arrived home, she was shaken by what she saw, but rather than call the preacher and ask about it, she called another member and told her what she had seen. That member, completely upset by what was told to her, called one of the deacons, who called his fellow deacon, and so on. The fire grew and began to spread. Days went by and little did the preacher know that word was going around the community that he was a drunk! By the time he found out, the damage was done and he had lost credibility in the community and within the congregation.

The preacher was fired from his position and after he collected his possessions and relocated his family, he returned one day to the member who had first seen him that night. He brought a sheet of paper and asked her to tear it into tiny pieces. Once torn, he took the pieces and scattered them into the wind. Then he said, "Help me find them all." They collected as many as they could but inevitably, some were lost. They set the pieces on the table and tried to put them all together again. The sheet could not be made whole.

The preacher said, "What you didn't know is that the person that I was seen holding was a brother in Christ that called me. I was helping him with his sobriety. He had long suffered with alcoholism and he had relapsed. Crying, he called me to drive him home. I walked in and helped get him home safely. The wrinkled and incomplete paper represents my reputation. I could try and talk to every single person who was told that I stumbled out of the bar, but not only would that break the brother's spirit who relapsed, I could never know of all who heard the mischaracterization."

The lesson is clear: pause long enough to avoid answering from a place of emotion, check your motives and your motivation for speaking, and always pause long enough to gather the facts. Otherwise, you can do irreparable harm.

Second, remember The Golden Rule's Cousin. Treat others as God has treated you. Watch what Paul says in Ephesians 4:31–32,

> *Let all bitterness and wrath and anger and clamor and slander be put away from you, along with all malice.* **Be kind to one another***, tenderhearted, forgiving one another,* **as God in Christ forgave you.**

We've been shown extraordinary kindness, grace, and mercy in Christ Jesus. The blessings that come with salvation ought to be extra incentives to disarm that deadly poison of the tongue. This passage teaches us that bitterness, wrath, anger, clamor, slander, and malice should not be found in the heart of one who has been forgiven by the Lord. Our hearts should be filled with love and compassion for our fellow man, just like love and compassion have been shown to us.

Lastly, remember the heavy price paid for the church and its unity. When we get upset with brethren in the church (which does happen from time to time!), our next steps should be carefully thought out and then taken prayerfully because our unity was made possible by the precious blood of Jesus. Knowing how valuable God considers it — so valuable that He gave His son for it — we cannot help but take special care to not dishonor it. Paul tells the Ephesian church,

> *With all humility and gentleness, with patience, bearing with one another in love, eager to maintain the unity of the Spirit in the bond of peace. There is one body and one Spirit—just as you were called to the one hope that belongs to your call (4:2–4).*

Such a heavy price was paid for that one body! Being mindful of that will help us to avoid the fire and poison that our tongues can potentially spew and replace them with love and hope.

SPIRITUAL FORMATION SECTION

Once bitten, the Komodo Dragon's prey is as good as dead, even though it will appear fine for a while. Some of us carry poison from bites we received in the past, poison that still affects us today. The worst kind of poison is the poison that remains from a person who has passed away and cannot be confronted. In these circumstances, it may seem as if there is no resolution possible since we cannot discuss things with them and settle the matter.

Have you been bitten in this way? Do not feel like you have no options. Do not suffer in silence. Something you may find helpful is to speak directly to the person as though they were alive. When you are ready, choose a quiet and solitary time and imagine that they are sitting in a chair opposite from you. Speak what is on your heart, but do so as though the Lord was present at this meeting as well. The reason why it is important to visualize the Lord standing in your midst is because the Lord Himself says, *"Do not take revenge, my dear friends, but leave room for God's wrath, for it is written: 'It is mine to avenge; I will repay, says the Lord"* (Rom 12:19).

God says, "I will repay." Don't read those words to mean just punishment toward the offender; read these words as a repayment to you! You've lost so much time on this sadness and pain. What was owed to you by the offender will never be paid by them, but the Lord says, "Send it to Me and I will repay you." Turn that debt over to the Lord and do not carry it any longer. Let the joy of the Lord replace your heartache and sadness.

Likewise, if you poisoned someone along the way, please make it right. That may make all the eternal difference in the world.

CHAPTER 23

SHOW OTHERS A BETTER WAY
THROUGH OUR WORDS

JAMES 3:9–12

INTRODUCTION

Over the course of this book, we've seen that there is so much more at stake than just our relationships when we stumble in our speech! It involves nothing less than our personal acceptance of our role to rebuild the creation, being yielded to God's authority as our Creator. It involves shaping our heart and mind in the image of God, honoring what He honors, and loving what He loves. Although our passage from James 3:9–12 contains no imperatives, James is going to continue to build upon what was previously stated regarding the power of the tongue. He's going to strengthen his case for us to step up to our first fruits responsibility by taking us back to the theme of creation. In this section, James draws heavily from the creation language to turn our attention to God's original design for the world. There are three distinct references to the Genesis creation here. In those references, we will find tools to help us rise as co-partners in the New Creation.

I. "THESE THINGS OUGHT NOT TO BE SO ..." VS. 9–10

> *With it we bless our Lord and Father, and with it we curse*
> *people who are made in the likeness of God. From the same*
> *mouth come blessing and cursing. My brothers, these things*
> *ought not to be so (Jas 3:9–10).*

This passage begins by informing us that not only does the tongue have the capability to bring both life and death, its poison is also covert and stealthy. The tongue is able to bless God and make that blessing known using beautiful and eloquently spoken words, but at the moment of our choosing, it can also release hurtful poison and curses. This is because the tongue is a tool wielded by the heart and mind. If the tongue is unstable and used for dual purposes, it's because it is being employed by a double-minded and chaotic person.

That's the first connection to the days of the creation: the paths of order and chaos. Genesis 1:1–2, says,

> *In the beginning, God created the heavens and the earth. The*
> *earth was without form and void, and darkness was over the*
> *face of the deep. And the Spirit of God was hovering over the*
> *face of the waters.*

The word "formless" means "chaos" and "without order or purpose." Then, as the creation process began, God proceeded to establish levels of order and stability out of it. I also connect Genesis 1 with our passage here because we are called to be creators, just like our Creator.

The second reference to the first creation in our James passage is also found in verse 9 when he says, "we curse people who are made in **the likeness of God**."

On the sixth day of creation, God said,

> *"Let us make man in our image, after our likeness. And let them have **dominion** over the fish of the sea and over the birds of the heavens and over the livestock and over all the earth and over every creeping thing that creeps on the earth ..." And God blessed them. And God said to them, "Be fruitful and multiply and fill the earth and subdue it ..." (1:26–28).*

In other words, God instructed Adam and Eve to "continue the work I started and partner with Me in the creation process. Continue to bring order and peace out of disorder and instability."

This is really at the heart of what it means to be created in the "image of God:" the fact that we are partners with God, passionately and creatively pursuing order and having a leadership role within His creation. In the beginning, the Lord removed the chaos that existed in the world and replaced it with peace, and in like manner, He charged His new image-bearers with continuing this wonderful work. Image-bearers do this by acting as peacemakers, patterning their work after God, who is peace.

He did this because He intended for us to be able to mirror His character, creativity, leadership, and love in the world He created. Of all people, Christians should understand the importance of stability and self-control, knowing that we represent the Lord. Our task on earth is to reflect this order in the creation, honoring God's original intention for us as image-bearers. If we, as Christians, are both blessing and cursing, adding to the instability and chaos into world, like James says, "this ought not to be so."

When we honor our own desires and passions to the exclusion of God's will, we are essentially choosing to worship self over God! This is why Paul calls covetousness "idolatry" in Colossians 3:5 and why he calls on us to avoid what is "earthly" about ourselves.

The third reference to the Genesis creation is in James 3:11,

Does a spring pour forth from the same opening both fresh and salt water? Can a fig tree, my brothers, bear olives, or a grapevine produce figs? Neither can a salt pond yield fresh water.

In Genesis 1:11, when God was removing chaos and replacing it with order, one of the statements He made was,

Let the earth sprout vegetation, plants yielding seed, and fruit trees bearing fruit in which is their seed, each according to its kind, on the earth.

And it was so. From that point forward, even after the ground was cursed because of man's sin, the creation continued exactly as God commanded, *"according to its own kind."* Ever since the beginning, creation has honored God's intention and design for it. A seed grows the same kind of plant from which it came; a sunflower seed does not grow a pumpkin. An animal gives birth to the same kind of creature as itself; a sheep does not give birth to a dog. There are clear rules and processes that creation must follow because that was God's divine design.

Humans, on the other hand, are the only part of the creation that can and have dishonored the purpose intended for them by the Lord. The Genesis 1:11 reference to replication is incredibly powerful when we tie that concept to what James said back in his first-fruits verse: *"Of his own will he birthed us by the word of truth, that we should be a kind of first-fruits of his creatures."* Jesus said that Christians grow from the seed of the Word (Luke 8:11), and as the first fruits of the New Creation, our responsibility is to replicate ourselves after the seed, not reintroduce darkness into our lives and the corrupted world.

II. TOOLS TO HELP MAINTAIN STABILITY IN AN UNSTABLE WORLD

The world is a chaotic place on its own. Mankind has always attempted to live according to what they believed was right. With no unified standard, each person does what is right in their own eyes. Even the standards that mankind has created over the course of human history have proven to be flawed and most have changed remarkably from decade to decade.

What the Lord offers, however, is an alternative to all of this turmoil caused by sin. He has instructed His newly-created children to go and create peace in the world based upon His standard of righteousness. If we're going to do that, we're going to have to remain as stable as possible in this unstable world. Here are a few tools that can help us stay grounded.

Be committed. The tongue is notoriously unbalanced

because of similarly erratic hearts. As we saw in James 1, instability of heart and mind comes from an unwillingness to commit to God. To avoid this, we need to make the words of the Psalmist our aim: *"**I am resolved** to obey your statutes to the very end. I despise those whose loyalty is divided, but I love your law"* (119:112–113). Regarding the lukewarm commitment of the church at Laodicea, Jesus said, *"I know your works: you are neither cold or hot! So, because you are lukewarm, and neither hot nor cold, I will spit you out of my mouth!"* (Rev 3:15–16).

Jesus's expectation for His church is full commitment, firmly on His side.

Use godly vision in order to maintain stability. We know we are not to curse our fellow man because they too were created in the image of God, but that kind of perspective requires spiritual training. So much has already been said about being spiritually discerning, so I will simply reiterate that our eyes need to see others as Jesus did: as people of value. But even more than this, we need to see the entire world as God sees it, not just the people in it. For example, do we see our marriage as a spiritual institution that God joined together and not just a certificate on paper (Matt 19:4–6)? Do we see children as spiritual blessings from God, not just added responsibilities or potential burdens (Ps 127:3)? Do you see God's mind and His creativity in nature around you (Ps 19:1–2)? Do you also see the life in the animals of nature and have regard for their spirit (Prov 12:10)? Being more spiritually aware of God in every facet our daily lives is a compelling way to focus on what endures in an ever-changing world.

Be true to your purpose! Romans 7:4 tells us,

*Likewise, my brothers, you also have died to the law through the body of Christ, so that you may belong to another, to Him who has been raised from the dead, **in order that we may bear fruit for God**.*

Being true to our purpose in Christ and bearing new spiritual fruit is another way of honoring God's status as the Creator and His authority over us. One statement that I have heard many times in my ministry is, "I don't know where God is leading me." Often, this is not really a question of God's direction; it's instead a statement of frustration with how God fits within the direction that they want to go. A Christian's purpose in life is to nest our talents, gifts, and resources into God's will for the total re-creation of the creation. We live new spiritual lives, molded and shaped by His goodness, so that collectively we might push forward in removing the chaos that has ravaged this world and teach those around us a better way of life.

If we remain committed, see ourselves and the world around us as God does, and stay true to our purpose in Christ Jesus, we will be doing exactly what God wants us to do! James used these three references to the Genesis creation to get us to explore a much bigger story. He turns our attention to the choice that faces us each and every day, the same choice that plagued Adam and Eve — the choice of whether we will worship ourselves, or God!

SPIRITUAL FORMATION SECTION

New spiritual growth comes from planting the seeds of the fruit of the Spirit: love, joy, peace, patience, kindness, goodness, faithfulness, gentleness, and self-control. The Word of

God is also described as a seed. We have so many options to choose from in order to bring new spiritual growth. Which seeds have you sown the most of? Which are you still lacking? Of the seeds that have already been sown, spend time in prayer, asking God to give the increase (1 Cor 3:6).

CHAPTER 24

SHOW OTHERS A BETTER WAY THROUGH OUR DEEDS

JAMES 3:13

Imperative 20: Show

INTRODUCTION

With the 20th imperative from the book of James, we're going to continue the big-picture concepts from the previous chapters concerning God's desire for the creation, but we're going to move past just words and into deeds. In the last chapter, we saw three distinct references James made to the Genesis creation and God's visions and intentions. Now, James adds another layer to his discussion by pointing to our responsibility to evidence what we know and show the world a better way to live.

I. IMPERATIVE 20: "SHOW!" — VS. 13

James asks, *"Who is **wise and understanding** among you? By his good conduct **let him show** his works in the meekness of wisdom"* (3:13). The imperative is found in the words, "let him show." First and foremost, this verse challenges modern thinking on faith and religion. As we've seen previously, there is a popular thinking within Christian circles that our religion and our beliefs are supposed to be privately held, hidden from the world, and retained only in the mind, between ourselves and God.

James's command here is quite the opposite. James says to "show" God's wisdom and understanding to the world through good works. Public testimony and service aside, James has a deeper message implied through his curious use of the phrase, "wisdom and understanding." It's like he is pulling from a known biblical expression to reinforce the responsibility of God's people to go and "show" the world a better way of life that reflects the goodness found in being in a covenant with God. Let's explore that a bit further.

In Deuteronomy 4:5–7, before God's people went into their new and promised land, the Lord said,

> **See**, I have taught you statutes and rules, as the LORD my God commanded me, that you should do them in the land that you are entering to take possession of it. Keep them and do them, for that will be your **wisdom and your understanding in the sight of the peoples**, who, when they hear all these statutes, will say, "Surely this great nation is a **wise and understanding** people." For what great nation is there that has a god so near to it as the LORD our God is to us, whenever we call upon him?

The Lord wished for His people to go into the land He had given them and be a beacon of light and influence to those around them. You probably already noticed that connection to our passage from James, but did you notice "wisdom and understanding"? In this way, James linked the Christian mission with the original one given to Israel to influence the nations around them.

Our mission, however, is one based on the fullness of the redemption plan in Jesus. It is a spiritual mission, and instead of the promised land, the Lord expanded our focus to the entire world (Matt 28:19). The Lord told the children of Israel that when they went into the land, their conduct — guided by the Law of Moses — would cause the people around them to be amazed at how wise and understanding the people were. By borrowing from the same language, I believe that James is saying to us: be careful how you speak and act because it is our turn now, on a worldwide level to realize the Lord's intention to influence others!

Our faith is not private and it was never intended to be private. Our faith is the substance and evidence to the rest of the world that there is something bigger and more meaningful available to them than just empty life pursuits. Peter said it this way in 1 Peter 2:11–12,

> Beloved, I urge you as sojourners and exiles to abstain from the passions of the flesh, which wage war against your soul. Keep your conduct among the Gentiles honorable, so that when they speak against you as evildoers, they may see your good deeds and glorify God on the day of visitation.

Our speech and our conduct should cause others to associate us with God and should "show" the world the way to find Him.

II. CHALLENGES FACING THE WORLD TODAY AND OPPORTUNITIES TO "SHOW" THE WORLD A WAY FORWARD

Through advances in technology, we are the most connected people in the history of the world and yet, we struggle with loneliness and isolation. We're struggling to connect with others on a deeper level than just social media comments and messages. So much more could be said about the challenges that humanity faces, but amidst it all, there is hope. As we learned in James 1, for Christians, trials and tribulations come paired with opportunities to shine a bright light and show the world a better way of life.

The church must be a place of sanctuary and encouragement within a suffering world. Unfortunately, churches can fall into the trap of being too inwardly focused, but that is not what will accomplish our mission. Instead, we are instructed to be a place where people love one another sincerely and wholeheartedly! Generations befriending generations; cultures, languages, races, and ethnicities, all coming together to love one another as God has loved us! There is power in that kind of connection. The church was designed by God to be a place of connection and support, a place where we bear one another's burdens. That genuine love, friendship, and support must then radiate outward to those drowning in the sea of chaos.

People are desperately searching for something genuine — a deep connection with others and a community to invest in. The church can and should be the answer to that longing, but that is only possible when we align with God's will and character and be true to our mission within this new "let there be light" era.

We can also "show" the world a better way of life by being "in the world but not of the world." Jesus prayed for His followers,

> *I do not ask that you take them out of the world, but that you keep them from the evil one. They are not of the world, just as I am not of the world.* **Sanctify** *them in the truth; your word is truth. As you sent me into the world, so I have sent them into the world. And for their sake I* **consecrate** *myself, that they also may be sanctified in truth (John 17:15–19).*

The word "sanctified," has its origins in the Law of Moses and means to be set apart. It is a term very closely related to "consecration," which is also found in John 17:19. We were designed by God to be the answer to the world's upset, a choice for those seeking peace from the seas of chaos. With more and more hopelessness in the world, we have an amazing opportunity to demonstrate what hopefulness in Christ looks like. Hope is powerfully connected to giving meaning and purpose to suffering. Hope helps us to endure and persevere, knowing that better days are ahead. Hope connects God's people and keeps them moving in the same direction.

Finally, God's people have a prime opportunity today to "show" others a life of real meaning and fulfillment to a lost generation. After Solomon had enjoyed every conceivable pleasure in this life, watching his empire grow and then seeing the destruction that came from his sins, at the end of his life, he determined, *"Now all has been heard; here is the conclusion of the matter: Fear God and keep his commandments, for this is the duty of all mankind"* (Eccl 12:13). There are so many in the world who are unhappy and filled with despair.

They're desperately searching for something to fill the hole in their spirits, but they don't know what it is they're searching for or where to turn.

It is not uncommon to hear people today say, "I don't know what I'm supposed to be doing," or, "I feel like I don't have a purpose." Man was created by a Creator to passionately and fervently pursue Him. When we honor God and live according to the way of life that He has shown us through His Word, we will have an abundant life of joy, contentment, and peace. What an opportunity we have in this day and age. May the overflow of our hearts move us to change the world, one blessed interaction at a time!

SPIRITUAL FORMATION SECTION

Ecclesiastes 3:11 says,

> He has made everything beautiful in its time. Also, he has put eternity into man's heart, yet so that he cannot find out what God has done from the beginning to the end.

Mankind instinctually recognizes that there is something greater than itself "out there." It has an understanding of infinity and eternity, but that understanding is limited and has been placed in hearts to push them to search for the answer: God. You can be the light that guides them the rest of the way! Do you know anyone who is searching?

CHAPTER 25

WHOSE SIDE ARE YOU ON?

JAMES 3:14–18

Imperatives 21 & 22: Do Not Boast & Do Not Lie

I ntroduction
       So far, James chapter 3 has been all about choices!
Which side will we choose? Will we choose God and His
intention for our lives or will we choose self? James isn't the
only one who outlined a choice of two options. Moses
described a critical choice between *"life and death ... blessings
and curses"* (Deut 30:19). Joshua insisted on a decision
between the LORD and the false gods *"beyond the Euphrates
River and in Egypt"* (Josh 24:14–15). Paul described a choice
between "the flesh" and "the spirit" (Gal 5:16–18). Jesus
taught of a choice between two paths, the "narrow gate"
and the "broad gate" (Matt 7:13–14).

       Our 21st and 22nd imperatives are once again going to
present a decision with two options, but this time it will be
presented as a choice between the "earthly" way and "the
way from above." James uses these two imperatives to draw
a very important line of distinction between Christians who

are fully yielded to the Lord, and Christians who attempt to mix some of the world in with the truth, creating their own personal flavor of Christianity. One will further God's will and intention for the world and the second will result in wavering and chaos. One will make faith come alive and cause a believer to be fruitful in the Lord; the other leads to a dead faith.

I. IMPERATIVES 21 & 22 — VS. 14-15

Before we get into our verses, let's establish some context. The heart of what James has been saying since the start of his book is the same ultimate truth that was established in the early days of the creation. God alone has authority as the Creator over His creation and His expectation is that we would honor Him through the creation, not enjoy it apart from Him. That has always been our problem, though, because accepting that truth means that we must also yield our lives to Him in humble surrender. God has never been our enemy, and He has only ever wanted the very best for us. In the Garden of Eden, there was only one path to walk, the path where mankind would yield to God and acknowledge His authority as the Creator. This path was supposed to be a path of life and ultimate peace, walked daily in the presence of God!

As we know, acknowledging God's full authority by obediently following His instructions proved to be too diffi-cult for Adam and Eve. Instead, mankind attempted to create another, blended path of authority: a path that would supposedly give them freedom *from* God and the right to dictate *for themselves* what was good. This evil and alterna-tive path began with Satan when he told Adam and Eve in

Genesis 3:6, *"God knows that in the day you eat of it, your eyes will be opened and you will be like God, knowing good and evil."* Satan planted seeds of doubt and pushed cracks into the relationship between God and His creation and he did so by succeeding in convincing Adam and Eve that they had it within themselves to be equals with God. An alternative path was opened that day, and it's the path that ultimately resulted in Jesus's sacrifice on the cross. This is the root and the guiding principle behind the earthly way of life that James is going to describe. It is a way that is unstable, unspiritual, and demon-like because it's based on the old Satanic lie mankind has been buying into for centuries. The lie that the creation does not need the Creator and that what is good can be established by our own passions, apart from our Creator.

As we approach James 3:14–15, it is important to know that James is not speaking to non-Christians here. He's speaking to the church! From that truth alone we can infer that there were Christians choosing a path of sin, even after pledging their allegiance to Jesus through obedience to the gospel. Once, they had been on the right path. But now they were attempting to incorporate earthly and unspiritual behavior into the body of Christ — seeking to somehow combine the two paths into one. It's the very issue James also addressed in James 1:8 when he wrote about the double-minded! He writes,

> *If you have bitter jealousy and selfish ambition in your heart,* **do not boast** *and* **do not lie** *against the truth. This is not the wisdom that comes down from above, but is earthly, unspiritual, demon-like (Jas 3:14–15).*

"Do not boast" and "Do not lie." These two commands direct attention to what is really taking place when Christians try to live with one foot in the world and one in the Body of Christ. Not only are they continuing the legacy of sin that was started in the Garden of Eden, they are also fighting "against" the truth by re-introducing darkness. The creation and all that flows from it are precious gifts meant to be informed by our relationship with God, not used apart from Him. The boasting and lying that James is referring to is the boast and lie that says that God is not enough and cannot be trusted or followed. Whether it is acknowledged on our part or not, when we choose a path that is not under God's direction, this becomes our boast and lie as well. Any attempt by Christians to create a form of spirituality that decreases God's sovereignty and authority over our entire existence is not only contrary to God, but is a lifestyle that is absolutely against all goodness and truth!

The Word of Truth tells us that we *can* have an abundant life; in fact, Jesus said that this was part of the reason why He came (John 10:10). However, the Word has been clear from the very start that if you want to experience that abundance, your life has to be informed by what the Creator calls good. When our resources, time, family, recreation, work, and relationships are all aligned with God's love and wisdom from above, we *can* experience abundance. Peace within cannot exist when we are re-introducing chaos and darkness into the world.

One of Satan's lies says that God wants to strip people of their rights, privileges, and any enjoyment in life. The misconception that many have concerning Christianity is that it is a restrictive and constrictive way of life, but it could not be further from reality. What the Lord wants, and what

He has always sought, are followers who honor and love Him with all their heart, mind, soul, and strength. With this as our foundation, we are then able to *use* the creation in a way that blesses God and enriches our lives. Just as a parent's greater experience and knowledge help us to foresee trouble and warn our children so that they can avoid heartache, our Father gave the Word of Truth to protect (not suffocate!) us.

The beauty of the wisdom of God is that it came directly from the mind that created us, a mind capable of seeing every life that has and will ever live. The Lord, infinite in His power to see every decision that mankind has ever made and their outcomes, produced a set of principles by which to live by so that we would have the most abundant life possible on this difficult earth. God's wisdom, when fully received and yielded to, is not just able to help us navigate through all the highs and lows of life, it is also able to teach us how to grow from our hardships.

The Christians in James's letter must have had a difficult time surrendering to God's manner of living because their actions were incongruent with God's character. As Jesus famously said at the Sermon on the Mount, *"You shall know them by their fruits"* (Matt 7:16).

II. HALLMARKS OF THOSE STANDING ON THE SIDE OF TRUTH — VS. 16–17

How can we know if we, as Christians, are truly standing on the right side of truth and yielding to the wisdom from above? As if he anticipated that logical question, James gives his readers his own take on Jesus's "know them by their fruits" teaching by saying,

For where jealousy and selfish ambition exist, there will be
disorder and every vile practice. But the wisdom from above is
first pure, then peaceable, gentle, open to reason, full of mercy
and good fruits, impartial and sincere (Jas 3:16–17).

There is so much to learn here! First, let's take a look at
what the life that refuses to submit looked like. James says
that you will know those who are living for themselves,
according to the passions of their flesh, because their lives
will contain "disorder" and "vile practices." God is not a God
of disorder. In fact, as we saw earlier in James chapter 3, God
established order out of chaos. God is not the author of
confusion, but the God of peace (1 Cor 14:33). Since we, the
Church, reflect God's goodness and character, we too are not
a people of confusion and disorder. Anyone who brings
about turmoil and instability has obviously chosen what
side they are on— and it is not Christ's! The first-fruits
people are consistent, full of God's character, and determined to do the right thing. Their kindness and compassion
should be unshakeable. Christians do not cause misunder-
standings and conflict by picking and choosing certain parts
of the Scripture to obey because we believe and accept the
entirety of God's Word.

It's just as easy to see the ones who are fully committed
to God because these Christians choose to live lives that are
"pure, then peaceable, gentle, open to reason, full of mercy and
good fruits, impartial and sincere." They are pure because
they're fully aware of who they represent and the price that
was paid for their sins. They do not abuse the gift of God's
grace and mercy. They are peaceable and gentle because
they know the church family is the body of Christ and they
endeavor to keep the unity of the Spirit in the bond of peace

(Eph 4:3). They know that damage inflicted on their Church family is also against Christ because the church is His body (1 Cor 1:10–13; Col 1:18). They remain open to reason because their hearts are humble and pliable, not arrogant, proud or hardened. If they are at fault, they glorify God by repenting of their sin and making the proper restitution. If a brother or sister in Christ is sinning, they gently show them their error in a spirit of love and compassion. They are full to the brim with mercy and good deeds because they know that Jesus expects them to show the same kindness and care to others as He first showed them. They also know that if they cannot be merciful, no mercy will be shown to them (Jas 2:13).

Lastly, Christians who are firmly committed to God and to His authority are "impartial and sincere." Their sense of value and self-worth doesn't come from their own hands or any external factors, but from the name of Christ Himself worn upon their hearts. They feel no need to deceive others by pretending that they are something that they are not, nor do they shame others for their backgrounds or lack of possessions or status. They are grateful for all that they have and are deeply humbled for all the blessings that the Lord has entrusted to them!

III. CREATORS OF RIGHTEOUSNESS

James chapter 3 closes this wonderful section on choice by inviting us yet again to become participants in the will and story of God! As we know, we have free will and whoever we choose to follow in our hearts and minds will be evident to all because it will outpour into action. This is the very root of Jesus's Sermon on the Mount! James ties all of these themes together in one incredibly deep verse:

The wisdom from above is first pure, then peaceable, gentle, open to reason, full of mercy and good fruits, impartial and sincere. But the fruit of righteousness is sown in peace by peacemakers (Jas 3:17–18).

Notice, again, the similarities between these special verses and the Sermon on the Mount. Jesus said, *"Blessed are the pure in heart, for they shall see God"* (Matt 5:8). James writes that the wisdom from above is "pure." Jesus said, *"Blessed are the peacemakers, for they shall be called the sons of God."* (Matt 5:9) James writes that wisdom from above is "peaceable" and sown by "peacemakers." Jesus said, *"Blessed are the merciful, for they shall receive mercy"* (Matt 5:7). James writes that the wisdom from above is "full of mercy." Jesus specified that *"every healthy tree bears good fruit"* (Matt 7:17). James writes the wisdom from above bears "good fruits." And where Jesus says, *"Love your enemies and pray for those who persecute you ... be perfect (teleios -complete) like my Father is perfect,"* James writes that the wisdom from above is "impartial" (balanced, well-rounded, and complete).

It makes perfect sense why the Sermon on the Mount would have such strong connections to these words from James because the sermon was more than just instructions, it was about giving the people a glimpse into what to expect from the Kingdom of God! Jesus was painting a picture for His listeners — picture of what the new Kingdom of God was going to look and act like. He was giving a message of anticipation!

In like manner, James gives his readers something to aspire to and a sense as to what humanity can accomplish when connected to God. Instead of decay, God's first fruits citizens of the Kingdom of God could go on to cause new spiritual growth. Through the spiritual power of God and through spiritual transformation, it is possible for us to be creators – just like God.

What are we creating? According to James, we are creating the very righteousness, character, and holiness of God ... but we're doing it visibly, in this physical world! We're bringing something unseen and spiritual from God and translating it into something visible that can change people's hearts! That is why faith is the substance and evidence of the unseen connection to God!

To the Corinthian church, Paul said it this way,

> *I planted, Apollos watered, but God gave the growth. So neither he who plants nor he who waters is anything, but only God who gives the growth. He who plants and he who waters are one, and each will receive his wages according to his labor. For we are God's fellow workers. You are God's field, God's building (1 Cor 3:6–9).*

We often limit Paul's reference here of "planting" to teaching the gospel. While that is certainly part of it, this actually speaks to so much more. The reference to sowing, watering, and growing is a metaphor for the collective witness of the church: revealing a more abundant, joyful way of life to others, then planting the seed of hope in their hearts and minds whenever they become receptive to it. Afterward, "watering" this seed with the continuous demonstration of what it means to be a citizen of the Kingdom of God will bring about the blossoming of new life through faith in Him. What a miracle!

In the beginning, God created the world to be a place of peace. Unfortunately, sin came in and destroyed that peace, but now, both Jesus and James are urging, "Church, it is *your* time to be makers of peace!" Each small seed is sown with this hope in mind. Peace is our intention and our disposition. It is our assignment from God, our mission to the world, and the reward of our relationship with the Savior. It's the one thing the world desperately craves and we are called to provide it to them, not because they deserve it or because they showed it to us first, but because God has redeemed us and told us to share it with others!

Every day is a new opportunity to exercise the privilege of choosing to serve God. Even if every innate pillar of our lives was to be removed, we would still be left with the ability to choose God. That choice lives within our hearts and minds and should drive every decision we make in this life.

Above all else, guard your heart, for everything you do flows from it (Prov 4:23).

Your heart and mind are the sources of a stream of emotion, thought, and deed. Purify that stream with the holiness of God's wisdom from above. Do not let your heart and mind fall for Satan's ancient lie. Trust that God knows what is best for you and that He wants us to have an abundant life. Choose to become a participant in the wonderful redemptive work of Jesus. Choose to plant spiritual seeds wherever you go and water those seeds through your unwavering devotion to God.

SPIRITUAL FORMATION SECTION

The seeds that come from the fruit of the Spirit are so important to the path of wisdom. These actions all but ensure that we stay on that path and accurately reflect the goodness of God to others. I want to issue a challenge. See the fruit of the Spirit (love, joy, peace, patience, kindness, goodness, faithfulness, gentleness, and self-control) as the only responses that you are allowed to have toward others. When faced with a situation, no matter what it is, turn to the fruit of the Spirit and use them to guide your responses.

CHAPTER 26

WHEN CHRISTIANS WAVER

JAMES 4:1–4

INTRODUCTION

We've seen how there is a choice to make between two paths, one leading to life and the other to struggle. One yields to God; the other lives for self. In this chapter of James, we see the issues that arise when the wrong path is chosen. By the end of our discussion, it will be clear that the best place for us is sitting as close as we can to Him, under the shadow of His wing. There are no imperatives in this text, but James is going to take us even deeper into our understanding of what takes place — both inside and out — when we struggle with sin. He will also give us tools to help fight the good fight of the faith.

I. WAVERING EXPOSED — VS. 1–3

James 4:1 begins, *"What causes quarrels and what causes fights among you? Is it not this, that your **passions are at war within*** *you?"* This is such an interesting statement from James because it gives us a diagnostic look at what happens when individuals enter into conflict, both within the church and in relationships. Essentially, James is saying that the outward quality of our lives reveals the spiritual health of our inner being. The condition of our heart and its connection to God is directly related to the types of lives that we lead, which is why a lack of God-honoring works is an indicator that something is terribly wrong within the heart of a believer.

Have you heard the analogy of the spilled cup and how it relates to our actions? What is spilled, when bumped, is only what is in the cup. If there was coffee, when bumped and spilled, only coffee is going to fall out. If water or tea, then only water or tea is going to spill out. In the same way, when life "bumps" us, what is in our heart and *only* what is in the heart will always spill out into the open. As Jesus says in Luke 6:45,

> *The good person out of the good treasure of his heart produces good, and the evil person out of his evil treasure produces evil, for out of **the abundance (overflow) of the heart** his mouth speaks.*

When there's contention between individuals, the real question ask is: What's taking place within the person that is causing the overflow from their heart to be blame, criticism, and judgment? What battle is taking place within their heart that is causing their words to erupt in anger and rage?

Paul mirrors this teaching in Romans 15:5–7,

*May the God of endurance and encouragement grant you to live in such **harmony with one another, in accord with Christ Jesus**, that together you may with one voice glorify the God and Father of our Lord Jesus Christ. Therefore **welcome one another as Christ has welcomed you**, for the glory of God.*

Harmony with each other begins with being in accord (i.e., complete agreement) with God. If we're not in agreement or in sync with God, it's going to affect our relationships with others. In like manner, if we're not in accord with one another within the body of Christ, it's going to affect our relationship with God. The two go hand in hand. It may not be possible to fully live in peace with those in the world, but to this, Paul exhorts in Romans 12:18, *"If possible, so far as it depends on you, live peaceably with all."*

I truly do appreciate James's acknowledgment of our inner and outer battles. As we all know, none of us are sinless and we all stumble. Every one of us is on a lifelong journey of sanctification — the pursuit of holiness — and we are all seeking to rid ourselves of sin, one day at a time. There will be struggles between the flesh and the spirit that will spill over into our relationships with others. James calls this struggle a "war" for a reason. It is spiritual warfare to put away the flesh and strengthen the spirit to be more like God! Look at how Paul describes it to the church at Galatia:

*The desires of the flesh are against the Spirit, and the desires of the Spirit are against the flesh, for **these are opposed to each other**, to keep you from doing the things you want to do (Gal 5:17).*

To the Church at Rome, in Romans 7:14–15, 19–23, Paul described this tension in this way:

> *For we know that the law is spiritual, but I am flesh, sold under sin. For I do not understand my own actions. For I do not do what I want, but I do the very thing I hate ... For I delight in the law of God, in my **inner being**, but I see in **my members** another law <u>**waging war**</u> against the law of my mind and making me captive to the law of sin that dwells in **my members**.*

Just knowing how intense the battle is helps us to better understand what takes place within a Christian when they struggle with sin and why some choose a path that leads away from God. Additionally, knowing this struggle can also help us to be more compassionate with others because we never fully know the struggles of others.

James continues,

> *You **desire** and do not have, so you murder. You **covet** and cannot obtain, so you fight and quarrel. You do not have, because you do not ask. You ask and do not receive, because you ask wrongly, to spend it upon **your passions** (4:2–3).*

Look at the root from which these evil actions are stemming: desire and covetousness. Desire and covetousness are products of the choices we make and what we decide to value. Desire is *epithymos*, which literally means to "*set* your passion upon something." Using today's common language, we would say something like, "I have my heart *set* on that." The word "covet" is *zelos*, which means figuratively to "boil." Setting your heart on something and then boiling over in desire for it doesn't sound like a passive situation does it? No, it doesn't — it sounds like an active, chosen focus.

Utilizing James's words for desire and covetousness and these insights into the tension between the flesh and spirit, I want to tell a story to describe what happens when Christians waver. Imagine that you have two paths. One path is "set on" the earthly lusts of the flesh and the other on the wisdom from above. Now imagine a Christian, passionate for God, beginning their journey on the right path. Then one day, the Christian sees something that they desire on the other side, on the path of the flesh. The desired object could be anything and is different for every person. Maybe they see a world where they are lifted up above all others. A world where they are given the best seats while many are forced to move out of the way or sit on the ground (we saw that in James chapter 2). It could be a world where they get to decide how they're going to approach God, a world where their relationship with God is on their terms and not His (we saw that in James chapter 3). Whatever the temptation is, it calls to them to switch paths but that switch doesn't happen immediately. They see a life that feeds their earthly passions and they begin to give in to it. They begin to set their heart on what they see before them. Little by little, they are drawn toward that temptation and their growing and burning desire for it makes each step easier and easier, until, as James says, they "boil over." Then (as we saw in Jas 1:14–15) when opportunity for sin and the desires of the flesh join together, sin is conceived and the Christian has wavered.

Even so, that person is still a Christian! They are still a child of God, so at this point, there is an all-out war raging within them. Their passion for God and the passion for this lust of the flesh are fighting against one another. Only one can claim the victory.

Every decision that we make will feed one side or the other. Every decision that we make will cause one side to pull harder than the other. Every decision we make will tell the world around us who won that particular battle. Each time we give in and yield to sin, the more that sin will grow stronger in our lives and the less of a struggle there will be moving forward. And then finally, once that sin has become full grown, James 1:15 says that it will bring forth spiritual death.

Paul elaborates on this spiritual death in Galatians. It appears that some within the Galatian church were dealing with their own pride-related sin. They were attempting to blend Jesus's teachings with their own practices from the old Law of Moses and present the combination as another gospel (Gal 1:6–7). This resulted in Paul reiterating to them the consequences of giving in to temptation and compromise. Paul says,

> *You are severed from Christ, you who would be justified by the law; you have fallen away from grace. For through the Spirit, by faith, we ourselves eagerly wait for the hope of righteousness. For in Christ Jesus neither circumcision nor uncircumcision counts for anything, but only faith working through love (Gal 5:4–6).*

There is a full-on war within us daily, and the side that will win is the side that we choose to feed. We are all tempted by different things. For some, it is pride, wealth, and prestige. For others, like the Galatian church, it was the love of control over others using a twisted theological framework. For James's early readers, it was a combination of all of those areas. Whatever it is, the temptation will eventually cause us to voluntarily leave the shadow of God's wing. It will lead us towards death by causing us to be "severed from Christ" and spiritually "fallen away." Make no mistake about it, this does not happen overnight. It is a decline that will be evident to all, first taking place in the heart, then being made evident in action or lack thereof.

II. SPIRITUAL ADULTERY — V. 4

Adulterers! Do you not know that friendship with the world is opposition to God? Therefore, if one is willed to be a friend to the world, they stand as God's adversary (Jas 4:4).

Spiritual death isn't the only consequence of giving into sin; spiritual adultery is another. All throughout the Old Testament, the Lord described any type of mixing with the world and idolatry as spiritual adultery. He is and has always been clear that He expects His people to be sanctified, or set apart and different than the world around them. He expects faithfulness from those who are in a covenant relationship with Him. It is interesting that he calls spiritual adultery as a "friendship with the world." This reinforces the idea that people are not just led away from God immediately, a passion and desire are cultivated first leading to a friendship. Ultimately this friendship leads to an affair with the world.

This is the second time that friendship has been mentioned in the book of James. The first was in James 2:23, in reference to Abraham. Abraham was called a "friend of God" because he believed in God, trusted in God's power and direction, and followed through in faithful obedience to God out of the overflow of that belief and trust. Abraham was also a friend of God because he knew what the Lord was intending to do with the world and he participated in advancing that intention through obedience to God's direction. Sadly, those who were pursuing an affair with the world were adversaries to God because they chose to advance the world's desires over God's.

Whichever side that we choose to advance and partner with is the side that we have chosen as friends. This is critical to understand because I wonder if we see our actions in that way. Do we see our sin as essentially us pushing in the opposite direction as God? To this point, Jesus powerfully stated, *"Whoever is not with me is against me, and whoever does not gather with me scatters."* (Matt 12:30).

A Christian's heart cannot move forward when it is divided in affection between God and the world. Having said that, James is not saying that we have to treat non-Christians as enemies. Rather, he means that anything we willingly do that approves of, or supports the world's efforts to dethrone God, in turn, makes us God's adversary. This is not because He hates us, but rather because we have made ourselves to stand in opposition to Him. Friendship involves partnership, so partnership with the world comes at cost for the Christian. Even then, God's love for us does not go away (Matt 5:44–45). The Lord is a "consuming fire, a jealous God" (Deut 4:24) — and for good reason! He is an impassioned God who wants our affections and our very selves because He created us and has given us so much. He is our Father and we are His children and He loves us with His special gifted love. When God's own people, the people who wear His Son's precious name and who were bought and forgiven by the precious blood of His Son's sacrifice, have their passions shift from Him to the world, that grieves the Lord.

We choose how much of the world we are going to set our heart upon and become passionate about. We decide the moment when God stops being enough for us, and we choose to walk away from Him. We tip the scales in either direction by the little concessions that we make each and every day. Don't be fooled, though — our God is passionate about having a relationship with us! He does not let us go easily. Every citizen of the Kingdom of God is special in His sight. He has given the Holy Spirit to dwell within each one and help to keep us near. I love how Paul encouraged Timothy to stay on the right track. He said,

> Hold on to the pattern of sound teaching you have heard from me, with the faith and love that are in Christ Jesus. Guard the good treasure entrusted to you, with the help of the Holy Spirit who dwells in us (2 Tim 1:13–14).

The Holy Spirit is a powerful force of accountability for us. Sin "grieves" the Holy Spirit, which in turn pricks our consciences.

III. TOOLS FOR SPIRITUAL BATTLE

We don't want to be God's adversary by pushing in the opposite direction. We don't want to grieve the Spirit. We don't want to be lured away from the path of righteousness. So, what can we do? How can we protect ourselves against the desires of the flesh, which are contrary to God?

Remember what brought you from death to life. Paul writes,

> Do not present your members to sin as instruments for unrighteousness, but present yourselves to God as those who have been brought from death to life, and your members to God as instruments for righteousness (Rom 6:13).

In moments of weakness, when we feel temptation and our desire to abandon God starts to grow, remember that we "have been brought from death to life." Remember the price that was paid to pay your sin — debt in full. Remember that it was the blood of Christ that paid it! There is power in focusing on the sacrifice of Jesus and the grace God showed toward us. Titus 2:11–12 confirms,

> The grace of God has appeared, bringing salvation to all people, training us to renounce ungodliness and worldly passions, and to live self-controlled, upright, and godly lives in the present age.

Make it a practice to renounce and avoid the path of the flesh by remembering God's grace and asking if the desired action is worthy of that sacrifice; this exercise is one way to train ourselves in Him.

Walk by the Spirit! The Holy Spirit is a key ally by our side in the spiritual battle within us:

But I say, **walk <u>by</u> the Spirit,** *and you will not gratify the desires of the flesh ... And those who belong to Christ Jesus have crucified the flesh with its passions and desires. If we live by the Spirit, let us also* **keep in step <u>with</u> the Spirit.**

The fruit of the Spirit are: love, joy, peace, patience, kindness, goodness, faithfulness, gentleness, and self-control. Make these nine traits your only possible responses to the world and the difficulties of life. When insulted, choose patience and self-control. If provoked to anger, choose peace. When disrespected, choose kindness. If there is pressure on you to put aside what you believe to accommodate others, choose faithfulness instead. When experiencing trials and deep valleys, search for the blessings and choose joy. If you find yourself weighted down by guilt and shame, choose love. Love yourself the way God loves you, and love the Lord with all your heart, mind, soul, and strength! When the traits of the Spirit are your only responses, every word and action advances the Kingdom of God and brings new spiritual growth into the world!

Pay attention to the Holy Spirit. In this spiritual struggle, we must constantly remind ourselves that the Spirit of God abides in us as the seal of our salvation (Eph 1:13). The Lord is not going to force us to be faithful to Him because He gave us a free will, but just knowing that the Spirit is within us, aware of every thought, intention, and action can help keep us accountable. The seal of salvation is meant to serve as a reminder that we are a people of purpose and belonging. Stay focused on who you are and where you are going!

Use knowledge to stay strong. We have been given insight into how a person is tempted and lured away. We have also been given examples of those who have withstood and finished the race. We have instructions from Scripture on what choices are wise and which are not. Use all of this knowledge to your advantage! David wrote in Psalms,

> With all my heart I have sought You; do not let me stray from Your commandments. I have hidden Your word in my heart that I might not sin against You (119:10–11).

John echoes this teaching saying, *"My little children, I am writing these things to you so that you may not sin ..."* (1 John 2:1). We are not ignorant of Satan's schemes and devices (2 Cor 2:11). It may seem like he has the advantage because of how long he has been studying mankind, but the Lord has given us everything we need to defeat him and make the right choices! We have been made alive in Christ; we are fellow heirs with Jesus (Rom 8:16–17). The Lord is not going to allow us to be tempted beyond our ability (1 Cor 10:13). If you're experiencing a trial, choice, or decision that is pulling you away from the path of righteousness, remember: you are going through this because you have at your disposal all that you need to choose victory in Christ. The way of escape is there, but you must be willing to take it!

SPIRITUAL FORMATION SECTION

This passage pulls back the curtain on why people choose a lifestyle that dishonors God. Quarreling, fights, division, and wandering from God, all highlight the inner battle that is taking place inside of the waverer. Honestly ... we've all been there! Think back to the last conflict that you had with someone. What deeper battle was taking place? Think of those actions as just the tip of the iceberg above the water, the rest of it buried in darkness. What was going on that others could not see? How does James's insight help us to be patient with others?

CHAPTER 27

STAY IN STEP WITH THE SPIRIT

JAMES 4:5

INTRODUCTION

When Christians waver, they do so because they have chosen to pursue some need of the flesh (the lust of the flesh, the lust of the eyes, or the pride of life). There is a tension that exists within us between our heart, mind, and spirit, which longs to be like God, and our flesh, which longs to live for self. James 4:5, again, has no imperatives, but in this verse, James is going to dig even deeper into understanding the consequences and implications of sin. This is going to set the stage for what will be the most imperative-filled verses in the entire book! In our text here, James is going to appeal to the presence of the Holy Spirit as additional motivation for God's people to live for Him. Let's follow James into the richness of God's word and understand why the Spirit is crucial to our spiritual maturity.

I. UNDER THE SHADOW OF HIS WING

Verse 5 says: *"Are you thinking that the Scripture speaks with emptiness? The Spirit, which He made to dwell in us, yearns jealously."* This statement immediately follows James's rebuke of wavering Christians who were attempting to be both friendly with the world and in a relationship with God. Now he is reinforcing what he just said by asking them, "Do you think that all of what was written in the Scriptures concerning God and what He's done for mankind to rebuild this broken relationship was written for no reason, in vain, and with emptiness?"

Ouch! That's a really convicting question because it calls friendliness with the world and wavering in faith as exactly what they are: attempts to live out a form of Christianity that is not found in the Scriptures. Every time that mankind has attempted to blend the Lord with their own thinking on how to live, it has always ended up in catastrophe and heartache. James's opening comment is essentially asking them, "Don't you think that hasn't already been tried before? The pages of the Scriptures are filled to the brim with people who attempted that blended lifestyle and it always ended badly."

Over and over again, the Scriptures demonstrate that the best possible place for God's children is close to Him instead of attempting to have a relationship with our Creator on our terms. Being close to God isn't just about following His rules or putting His wisdom into practice, it's also about enjoying the peace that can only exist when we are that close. I love the Psalmist's way of describing this special place:

*He who dwells in the shelter of the Most High will abide in the shadow of the Almighty. I will say to the LORD, 'My refuge and my fortress, my God, in whom I trust.' For he will deliver you from the snare of the fowler and from the deadly pestilence. He will cover you with his pinions, and **under his wings** you will find refuge (Ps 91:1–4).*

The God we serve seeks us and desires us to be close to Him, *under His wings*, where He is responsible for our good and protection. One of the ways that the Lord has proven to us that He desires to be close to us is through the Holy Spirit. As James says here, *"The Spirit, which He made to dwell in us, yearns jealously."* The Holy Spirit dwelling within us is God's New Covenant form of presence. I believe that if God's people were to fully comprehend the movement of God's presence over the course of human history, it would fundamentally change the way we see what is at stake in the Christian life! A full appreciation for what it took for the presence of God to finally abide within us would instantly convict any who would seek to live in a way that is incongruent with all that the Lord did to bless us with this gift. I believe that is why James chose to go this route here, at this particular junction in his argument.

As we've done several times before, I'd like to understand James's reference to God's presence by taking the long way around. I assure you; it will be so worth it! As we're going to see, God's Holy Spirit is synonymous with His presence and is one of the most powerful expressions of His desire to be close to us, His special creation.

II. THE BLESSING OF GOD'S PRESENCE

God's presence is one of the most powerful blessings of being in a relationship with Him. Throughout the ages, through the various covenants and dispensations of God's plan, that presence has taken on different forms, but nevertheless, it has always been constant. We see this, even in the very beginning of the creation.

Although God is Spirit, the very first glimpse that we are given of Him takes place in our physical universe. Genesis says that He *"hovered over the surface of the waters"* (vs. 2). In that opening scene, the Spirit becomes a sort of divine connection between God and this new physical world that is about to be arranged. The Spirit of God, in this moment, represented intention and possibility, but most of all, the Spirit represented God's desire to be present with His creation. As the Psalmist says in Psalms 139:7, *"Where can I go away from your Spirit or where can I flee from your presence?"*

But shortly after the fall of Adam and Eve, because of the rampant wickedness of man, Genesis tells us that the Lord said, *"My Spirit shall not always strive* (contend*) with man forever, for he is flesh* (fleshly): *his days shall be 120 years"* (6:3). There's the tension again that we saw in James 4:1, Galatians 5:17, and Romans 7. The Spirit and the earthly (fleshly) way of life were and *are* opposed to each other. Therefore, God made the decision to remove His Spirit from mankind following a 120-year period of mercy. During this time, Noah preached in hopes that mankind would repent. But none obeyed, so the earth was destroyed. The presence of God was removed from the world. Yet, this wasn't the end of the story; it was only the beginning. God was determined to rebuild that broken relationship and restore His presence among His people once more.

God's presence soon returned to mankind, but this time, on a limited scale, starting first with Abraham. First, God called Abraham (Gen 12), then He spoke to him again (Gen 13 and 14), before establishing a covenant with him in chapters 15 and 17. Finally, the Lord returned to talk to Abraham in person and reiterate to him the promises that He had made with him, giving him a glimpse into what He had planned (Gen 18). Little by little, the Lord was preparing the world, for His divine return, but it would not be until Exodus that the Lord would take the next big step.

In Exodus 6:3, when the Lord was ready, He told Moses,

> *I appeared to Abraham, to Isaac, and to Jacob as El-Shaddai*
> *— "God Almighty" — but by my name the LORD (Jehovah) I*
> *did not make myself known to them.*

The Lord didn't just want His people to know that it was He, the God of their forefathers, that was going to rescue them. The Lord was showing His people that there was more to His power than even Abraham, Isaac, and Jacob understood. They would come to know that the God they were following out of Egypt was nothing less than the Creator of the universe. The presence that formed the universe was prepared to mobilize His creative power once more and soon they would come to know the power within His name.

When He decided to reveal Himself as Jehovah to His people, it was an indication that He was ready to initiate a new era of His presence and with this newly restored relationship would come the blessing of His presence. Finally, through the Tabernacle and the Ark of the Covenant, the presence of God would arrive once more. The Bible tells us,

Now the Presence of the LORD appeared in the sight of the Israelites as a consuming fire on the top of the mountain ... Let them make me a sanctuary, that I may **dwell** *in their midst ... (Exod 24:17; 25:8).*

Unfortunately, at the very moment when the Lord was speaking to Moses and revealing His plan to bring His presence back to the earth, the children of Israel were making a golden calf-god to represent God and claim His presence on their own terms. Sadly, even Moses's own brother, Aaron, built an altar before the calf and declared that a feast should take place in honor of Jehovah (Exod 32:4). I believe that Aaron and the people believed that Jehovah led them out of Egypt, but where they went wrong was declaring the image of the calf to represent the presence of God. The people were so starved for the presence of God that they were willing to create an image (idol) of God instead of wait on the true presence of God to be revealed when the Lord was ready. They resorted to mixing the world of Egypt into the holiness of Jehovah to create their own blend of closeness to God.

In response to this, the Lord told Moses,

Go now, lead the people where I told you. See, My angel shall go before you ... But I will not go in your midst, since you are a stiff-necked people, lest I destroy you on the way ... [And] When the people heard this harsh word, they went into mourning, and none put on his finery (Exod 32:34; 33:3–4).

The people were crushed. The presence of God set them

apart from the nations and accomplished signs and wonders beyond their comprehension. Without this presence, the people knew that they were truly lost. Even Moses, in one of the most heartfelt sections of Exodus, begged the Lord saying,

> *Unless You go in the lead, do not make us leave this place. For how shall it be known that Your people have gained Your favor unless You go with us, so that we may be distinguished, Your people and I, from every people on the face of the earth? (33:15)*

In other words, **"Without your presence, how are we any different from the rest of the world?"** Is James's reason for referencing the Spirit and presence of God for God-honoring behavior toward others becoming clearer? Let's keep going!

The Lord relented and granted Moses this request but He carefully laid out the terms of the covenant, terms that included their faithfulness to Him and Him alone. They were to tear down the altars to the image and were even commanded to maintain holiness and purity within their camps since God's presence would be there with them:

> *Because the LORD your God walks in the midst of your camp, to deliver you and to give up your enemies before you, therefore your camp must be holy, so that he may not see anything indecent among you and turn away from you (Deut 23:14).*

In other words, if they did not maintain their faithfulness and holiness, God would remove His presence from them. There, in the tabernacle and the Ark of the Covenant, the Lord traveled with His people. During the days of the first kings in Israel, the Lord replaced the temporary structure of the camp with the permanently fixed temple. At the dedication of the temple, King Solomon declared,

> *The LORD has said that he would dwell in thick darkness. I have indeed built you an exalted house, **a place for you to dwell** in forever ... But will God indeed dwell on the earth? Behold, heaven and the highest heaven cannot contain you; how much less this house that I have built! Yet have regard to the prayer of your servant and to his plea (1 Kgs 8:12–13, 27–28).*

For the first time since the creation of the world in Genesis, the presence of God was going to be permanently fixed on earth, albeit on a much smaller scale and only for a brief moment. Still, this was cause for celebration! The world was about to receive a part of what it had lost so long ago!

Unfortunately, the nation of Israel again abandoned God and forsook His presence, so the Lord allowed them to be taken into captivity. Notice the way 2 Kings recounts what happened:

> *The LORD was very angry with Israel and **removed them from his presence**. Only the tribe of Judah was left and even Judah did not keep the commandments of the LORD their God, but lived according to the customs Israel had introduced (17:18–19).*

During those days of captivity, Isaiah also spoke these painful words:

*They rebelled and **grieved his Holy Spirit**; therefore he turned to be their enemy, and himself fought against them. Then he remembered the days of old, of Moses and his people. Where is he who brought them up out of the sea with the shepherds of his flock? **Where is he who put in the midst of them his Holy Spirit** ... Like livestock that go down into the valley, the Spirit of the LORD gave them rest (63:10–11, 14).*

The Spirit of God has always been the link between God, who is Spirit, and the closeness that He desired with His people. The divine presence that resided with the people of Israel at various points in their history was proof of this. But after the destruction of their nation, even though the Lord permitted them to rebuild, the glory they had once had would never be the same. It was clear they were in need of a Savior. If the presence of God was going to come down on a worldwide scale, it would have to be done by someone more powerful than humanity. This realization that mankind was unable to usher in this new era on their own was very much a part of God's ultimate plan.

The outlook may have seemed grim, but God was not through with His plan! Our God does not abandon His creation, no matter what happens. His love is fierce and He is unwilling that anyone should perish. When it seemed like the glory and presence of the Lord had gone for good, the prophets began to speak a message of hope! The presence of the Lord was coming again, but in a form that would catch the world by surprise! Listen to Ezekiel's words:

*And I will make a covenant of peace with them; it will be an everlasting covenant. I will establish and multiply them, and **I will set My sanctuary** among them forever. **My dwelling***

place will be with them; I will be their God, and they will be
My people (Ezek 37:27).

The dwelling place of the Lord's presence would be
different than before, though. God's plan to bring His presence to the world was not going to involve a Tabernacle or a
Temple. Little did the world know that God's presence was
headed directly into the heart of His people! Ezekiel
continued,

> I will give you a new heart and **put a new spirit within you;**
> I will remove your heart of stone and give you a heart of flesh.
> And I will **put My Spirit within you** and cause you to walk
> in My statutes and to carefully observe My ordinances (Ezek
> 36:26–27).

The closeness that the Lord longed for since the beginning would soon arrive! Finally, at the right moment in
time, Jesus came, and with Him came the new era of God's
presence. Describing Jesus's work after His death, burial,
and resurrection, Peter said,

> What God foretold by the mouth of all the prophets, that his
> Christ would suffer, he thus fulfilled. Repent therefore, and
> turn back, that your sins may be blotted out, that **times of
> refreshing may come from the presence of the Lord,** and
> that he may send the Christ appointed for you, Jesus (Acts
> 3:18–20).

Jesus ushered in an unprecedented "time of refreshing"
in "the presence of the Lord" by bringing peace between
man and God through His sacrifice, and through faith (Rom

5:1–2). The gospel message of grace granted humanity an opportunity for our sins to be remitted and for us to be reconciled to Him (Rom 5:9–11). This is what God has wanted since the very beginning! During these last days, His presence would dwell on earth once again, but this time in His people and the church! Paul explained it all in his second letter to the Corinthian church.

> What agreement can exist between the temple of God and idols? For **we are the temple** of the living God. As God has said: "**I will live with them** and walk among them, and I will be their God, and they will be My people." "Therefore, come out from among them and be separate, says the Lord. Touch no unclean thing, and I will receive you" (6:16–17).

Now, the Lord would dwell within His children. No longer would they need to travel to a fixed location to worship Him. He would be in their midst! This is why Paul exhorted,

> Do you not know that your body is **the temple of the Holy Spirit** who is in you, whom you have received from God? (1 Cor 6:19)

Peter quoted the Prophet Joel in Acts 2:16–17 when he explained, "This is that which was spoken through the prophet Joel: "In the Last days it shall be, God declares, that **I will pour out my Spirit on all flesh.**" Joel had prophesied about a time when God's presence would no longer be limited to just one person, one family, one nation, or one Temple, but would be available to all people. In response to Peter, the people had cried out, "Men and brethren, what shall we do?"

What does a person need to do in order to receive such an amazing gift?

The answer was, *"Repent and be baptized every one of you in the name of Jesus Christ for the forgiveness of your sins, and you will receive the **gift of the Holy Spirit**"* (Acts 2:38).

III. THE PRESENCE OF GOD AND THE HOLY SPIRIT

This is why James says, "If you think friendliness with the world is acceptable and that mixing the divine with the corruption of the world is permissible, then you must certainly believe that the Scriptures were written in vain and are empty because they tell a different story. The Scriptures teach us that the Lord worked through an incalculable number of people, places, spans of time, and events to bring mankind to the point to where we were ready to receive the blessed presence of God through the gift of His Spirit who abides in us. Live in a manner that honors God's gift, not in a way that brings dishonor."

The Scriptures teach that Lord has been working toward rebuilding His divine presence and relationship with His people since the very moment it broke down. The presence of God, now represented by the Holy Spirit of God, is a blessing that is unique to the New Covenant of Jesus Christ. Paul tells us that the Holy Spirit is the same Spirit that was "promised," and is the guarantee of our inheritance as Christians (Eph 1:13–14). The Spirit did not come under the Law of Moses but through Jesus's redemptive work on the cross.

Having been sent to us personally, the wonderful gift of the Holy Spirit comes with the expectation that we should live lives that reflect the level of blessing involved with it. For Christians, who now have the Holy Spirit dwelling within them, showing any friendliness to sin both minimizes God's sacrifices and hurts the Spirit within us, who longs for us to be close to God. Ephesians 4:29–31 reads,

> *Let no corrupting talk come out of your mouths, but only such as is good for building up, as fits the occasion, that it may give grace to those who hear. And **do not grieve the Holy Spirit of God**, by whom you were **sealed** for the day of redemption. Let all bitterness and wrath and anger and clamor and slander be put away from you, along with all malice. Be kind to one another, tenderhearted, forgiving one another, as God in Christ forgave you.*

Moses once asked God, "Without your presence, how are we any different from the rest of the nations?" Moses understood that God's presence sets His people apart and sanctifies them for a special divine work, renewing within them the desire to mirror God's goodness. Now James asks us to honestly assess where we are in our own spiritual life. Are we living in a way that ignores the presence of God? Or are we living in a way that honors the journey that the presence of God traveled to arrive in our hearts?

SPIRITUAL FORMATION SECTION

When Christians waver and choose the wrong path, we're not just choosing a route that lives for self, we're creating distance between ourselves and God. When the children of Israel crossed into the Promised Land, they set up twelve stones in a place called Gilgal to commemorate that special day, the day that God fulfilled His covenant with them. Sadly, the people abandoned God's will for the land and in the final moments of Joshua's life, the Lord sent a messenger to them. Judges 2:1–5 says that the Angel of the Lord traveled from Gilgal to Bochim, the place where the people were gathered. An angel does not need to travel, but the Angel traversed the distance to show the people how far they had departed from the Lord. On arriving, He asked them, "What is this that you have done?" Distance between ourselves and God is dangerous, but it is usually not realized until everything is falling apart. Meditate on this thought and reflect on how close you are to the shadow of God's wing.

CHAPTER 28

CLOSING THE GAP WITH GOD

JAMES 4:6–10

Imperatives 23–32 Submit to God. Resist the Devil. Draw near to God. Cleanse your hands. Purify your hearts. Be wretched and mourn. Weep. Let your laughter be turned to mourning. Humble yourselves.

INTRODUCTION

In James 4:5, we looked at the connection that James makes to the Holy Spirit, the presence of God, and what the Scriptures recorded regarding these truths. We traced the presence of God through the beginnings of creation, from Abraham, and then to Moses. We saw the presence of God referenced at Mount Sinai, in the tabernacle, the temple, and then concluded with the prophesied indwelling Holy Spirit through the work of Jesus. Based on all this history spoken to us in the Scriptures, James asked his wavering brethren, *"Do you think all that was written in vain?"* (4:5) No! On the contrary, we know why God's actions were preserved in the written record. It was to illustrate how zealous God is when it comes to having his special creation close to Him. He doesn't want to live apart from us. The Lord wants to abide in us through His Spirit (1 John 3:24), until the day that we will see Him face to face forever! James 4:6–10 is going to contain an explosion of imperatives from James! This is the moment that James has been leading up to! These ten imperatives will demonstrate that since God desires to be close to His creation, anything that stands between us and God has to go! Let's begin in verse 6.

I. CLOSE THE GAP — VS. 6

He gives more grace. Therefore it says, "God opposes the proud but gives grace to the humble" (Jas 4:6).

James is quoting Proverbs 3:34 here. When you compare that section of Proverbs in your English Bible with James 4, the wording isn't an exact match because of the movement between languages. However, the wisdom in the Proverb is clear: *"At scoffers, He scoffs, but to the lowly He shows grace."* Scoffer is not a term that we used often in daily life, but we all know the characteristics of these individuals. They are masters at taking what you held dear and poking holes in it to cause you to question your beliefs. They are proud, arrogant, haughty, and argumentative. Scoffers also seem to portray their lifestyle as just a bit better than everyone else's.

Sadly, because of these traits, there is a great distance between a scoffer and the Lord God. The Psalmist adds, *"Though the LORD is on high, He attends to the lowly; but the proud He knows from afar" (Ps 138:6).* There are great blessings in the Lord and He desires to shower those blessings to His creation, but the scoffer does not enjoy the fullness of the Lord's gifts because they are unwilling to see value in what the Lord has to offer. The space between the two is created when the scoffer becomes repulsed by the idea that they are accountable to someone else and they are not the true masters of their lives.

Scoffers firmly believe that God is not worthy to sit in the chief seat of their heart. What a presumptuous (and sad!) thought, especially knowing that the very air we breathe belongs to Him. The life we have within us comes from Him. And the earth that we enjoy? He made it! The Proverb James quotes from goes on to say, *"Be not wise in your own eyes; fear the LORD, and turn away from evil"* (3:7). In other words, close the gap between you and the Lord. Those who exercise pride, scoffing, arrogance, vanity, and mockery, invite the Evil One into their lives, whether knowingly or not. These traits directly contribute to the promotion of Satan's lie that man and God are co-equal with each other and that man can live apart from God.

II. IMPERATIVES 23–32: DRAW NEAR TO GOD! — VS. 7–10

In response to these proud scoffers, James lands TEN imperatives!

> **Submit** *yourselves therefore to God.* **Resist** *the devil, and he will flee from you.* **Draw near** *to God, and he will draw near to you.* **Cleanse** *your hands, you sinners, and* **purify** *your hearts, you double-minded.* **Be wretched** *and* **mourn** *and* **weep. Let your laughter be turned to mourning** *and your*

joy to gloom. **Humble yourselves** *before the Lord, and he will exalt you (Jas 4:7–10).*

The imperatives in these verses are:

- Submit to God.
- Resist the Devil.
- Draw near to God.
- Cleanse your hands.
- Purify your hearts.
- Be wretched.
- Mourn.
- Weep.
- Let your laughter be turned to mourning.
- Humble yourselves.

Ten separate imperatives are contained within four verses! From this bold showing, we get the impression that the early church was in the fight of their lives and to avoid sinking back into chaos, changes needed to be made.

The fruit of a scoffer's heart is disorder and chaos. I cannot help but wonder if the issues that James is addressing tried to be resolved within the church family first, at the lowest levels. Perhaps there were attempts, but pride stood in the way of reaching peace. Pride creates distance between people because it first creates distance between us and God.

Combining James's imperatives, he's saying that, "Our souls long for the presence of God, but in order for us to draw near to Him, we must humble ourselves by submitting to God's authority as the Creator. We have to resist Satan's Genesis 3 tactics and draw near to God, under the shadow of

His wing. If we've been involved in spiritual adultery and uncleanliness, it is time to wash our hands and purify our hearts once and for all and be rid of what has stained our relationship with God. We must grieve our mistakes in repentance and humble ourselves once again!"

Although James was addressing the issues of that day, the same truth applies to us. If changes must be made to bring us closer to God and under the shadow of His wing, then we must make those changes today! If we're drowning in the sea of chaos, then we need to mourn our rebellion to God and turn back to shore. Today is the day to expose whatever darkness abides within us to the light that shines in the face of Jesus Christ! If necessary, apply some or all of the ten imperatives to do it. Do not remove yourself from the fight by falling asleep. Feel these ten imperatives from James as his way of reaching through the book and shaking us until we awaken! What is at stake is nothing less than the presence and closeness of God. As Moses lamented before God, if His presence is not with us, then how will we be distinct among the nations of the world?

From my perspective, the references to celebration turning to mourning and the purification of the heart and hands carry an additional meaning that I believe would have resonated with his readers given their similarity to other well-known passages of Scripture that speak to this very concept. For example, in Exodus 33, the chapter we read previously regarding God's presence, the children of Israel were laughing and celebrating their new false god, but when they heard that the presence of God was going to be withdrawn from them, *"they mourned and no one put on his ornaments"* (Exod 33:4).

David also comes to mind as one who failed God and mourned his sin. He says in Psalm 51:10–11,14,17,

Create in me a clean heart, O God, and renew a right spirit within me. Cast me not away from your presence; take not Your Holy Spirit from me ... Deliver me from bloodguiltiness, O God, O God of my salvation, and my tongue will sing aloud of your righteousness ... The sacrifices of God are a broken spirit; a broken and contrite heart, O God, you will not despise.

David's spiritual discernment was far beyond his time, but this sensitivity to the divine made him painfully aware that there was no remedy for the sins that he had committed before God. David was perhaps the first of that covenant dispensation to realize the full weight of God's grace because without God's mercy, there was nowhere he could have turned to within the Law of Moses to cover adultery and murder. The shocking realization that God's presence could be removed due to their actions caused them to humbly return to God with a *broken spirit and a contrite heart.*

Notice James's next reference to the "hands and the heart" and their similarity to Psalm 24:1–4:

The earth is the LORD's and the fullness thereof, the world and those who dwell therein, for He has founded it upon the seas and established it upon the rivers. Who shall ascend the hill of the LORD? And who shall stand in His holy place? He who has clean hands and a pure heart, who does not lift up his soul to what is false and does not swear deceitfully.

Again, I see no coincidence to James's wording and the Psalm because the messages are the same: His glory, His authority, His dwelling place, and His presence are what we should yearn for each and every day. Again, it is amazing how spiritually discerning David was for his time. Here, he speaks from his own perspective on how to draw closer to God's presence, but he's doing so during the days of the tabernacle, which housed the Ark of the Covenant. Even during these early days, when the presence of God was represented by these physical objects, David understood that humility of the soul, purity of the heart, and clean hands made one closer to God! The truth of his statement can be seen reflected in Hebrews 10:22 and 12:22:

> Let us **draw near with a true heart** in full assurance of faith, with **our hearts sprinkled clean** from an evil conscience and **our bodies washed with pure water** ... you have **drawn near** to Mount Zion and to the city of the living God, the heavenly Jerusalem ...

Sadly, mankind has always been in a struggle between growing closer to Him by yielding our will versus satisfying our own short-sighted desires. When Christians choose the latter, they waver and eventually grow apathetic. James 4:6–10 is meant to shake these believers into realizing how far they have drifted away from the Lord. His words are not just written to convict; after all, conviction without repentance and change of direction gains us nothing. These verses give us clear guidance on how to close the gap between ourselves and the Lord. He wants us to abide in Him and He in us!

Every Christian should long for the Lord and desire to sit as close as possible to Him! But if that's not the case, then something has gone very wrong, and James calls that to our attention. The only way to draw near to God is to do it in a fully surrendered manner and on His terms. You cannot embrace two opposing forces, just as you cannot make opposites exist simultaneously. Trying to live with one foot in the Kingdom of God and one in the world is dangerous and will only result in chaos. John gives this same wisdom in 1 John 3:4–6, saying,

> *Everyone who makes a practice of sinning also practices lawlessness; sin is lawlessness. You know that he appeared in order to take away sins, and in him there is no sin. No one who abides in him keeps on sinning; no one who keeps on sinning has either seen him or known him.*

To see God is to know Him experientially. More will be said about this soon, but for now, know that John and James are both imploring us to push in the same direction as the Lord. Draw close to Him by aligning your priorities with His. Seek to remove chaos from the world, not add more to it through lawlessness.

III. DRAW NEAR TO GOD

In the early days of the gospels, we read that the people were ready for healing and they were ready to enjoy the blessings that flowed from God, blessings that they heard from the reading of the Word in the synagogues. But in the first century, even the sacred temple, the very symbol of God's presence, was tied to a Roman-aligned leader and overtaken by corrupt financial practices. Where could they go to be connected to God?!

It was during those desperate days that the gospel message began to be sent out. Part of that message inspiring hope was the personal connection to the presence of the Lord. Peter taught them that they did not need to be in the temple to be close to God anymore. Instead, if they repented of their sin and accepted Christ's sacrifice for the salvation of their souls, a "time of refreshing" would come from the presence of the Lord (Acts 3:20–21). What a time to have been alive! It must have been exciting to know that the hand of God was about to rescue His people and set the captives free (Luke 4:18)!

Since that time, the gospel message has traveled all over the face of the earth, from generation to generation, being revealed from faith to faith (Rom 1:17). It is a message of hope and closeness with God. To solve the issues pressing against the unit of church, James implored them to be convicted and head back to the blessed shadow of God's wing.

What about you? Do you need the reminder as well? Where are you in your journey? How long has it been since you felt the peace that comes with surrendering to God? Is there anger, sadness, deeply rooted pain, bitterness, or shame that has prevented you from drawing near to the refreshing presence of God? Is there something standing in the way of that?

The Lord's presence is not in a tabernacle; it's not in a temple. And it's not far away — it's near (Phil 4:4)! God has chosen to have His Holy Spirit dwell within us (1 Cor 3:16). He has given His Word to us as well. He has blessed us with prayer so that we can send our anxieties, our frustrations, and our thanksgivings, at any time of the day or night to His throne. He has given us the body of Christ, the church. In every corner of the planet there are like-minded believers who meet regularly and who work together to live out their heart's expression to God.

James is imploring his readers, if there is anything standing in the way of drawing near to God, settle it and remove it! Have someone help you work through it, if needed, but whatever you do, do it in a spirit of repentance and humility. Don't rob yourself of the peace of God that flows from being close to Him.

Philippians 4:6–7 says,

Do not be anxious about anything, but in everything by prayer and supplication with thanksgiving let your requests be made known to God. And the peace of God, which surpasses all understanding, will guard your hearts and your minds in Christ Jesus.

For James's audience, they needed ten imperatives to get the message across to them. Some of us have hard heads and hearts too, and it may take a while to come to the realization that God does indeed know best and He can be trusted. Take action today and know that you are not alone in this journey! Just as Satan was active in the garden, he is still on the prowl, *"like a roaring lion, seeking someone to devour"* (1 Pet 5:8). In your reading today, you saw James stand boldly in front of us all and said in the most forceful way that he could, "Resist Satan and his lies!" Resist him and draw near to God. May we choose for ourselves, every single day, to sit as close as we can to the Lord our God!

SPIRITUAL FORMATION SECTION

If the children of Israel were considered "toddlers" in the eyes of the Lord when they came out of Egypt (Hos 11:1–4), then the wilderness-wandering years where they needed to be provided food and clothing but still wanted their own way could be considered the teenage years. That would make the dark days of the books of Judges through Samuel their collegiate time. The reign of Solomon took place at the peak of their wealth, so it would not be unreasonable to think of those years as their prime adulthood phase. The division, financial ruin, and servitude years came during their "retirement." Each stage of their life was marked by tension with God. In each one, they insisted on their own way and their faithfulness to God came and went in waves. It's amazing how their story resembles the tension that exists in our own lives between our will and God's will.

What has your life been like? Visualize each stage by drawing a line down the middle of a sheet of paper. Label that line, "Closeness to God." At the top of the line, write the number zero, and at the bottom of the line write your current age. Draw a second line to represent the course of your life. Start at zero and draw how close you have been to the Lord. Once the line is drawn, think of the days that were most difficult and then the ones that were most joyful. Is there any correlation between these to the closeness to God that you can identify?

CHAPTER 29

YOU'RE IN MY SEAT, SAYS THE LORD

JAMES 4:11–12

Imperative 33: Do Not Speak Evil

INTRODUCTION

Affter the children of Israel sinned at Mount Sinai by creating a false god out of gold, the Lord told them that His presence would not travel with them anymore. Moses went down from the mountain and was furious with the people. He challenged all who were on the Lord's side to join him. Afterward, 3,000 people were put to death in their rebellion. Moses then implores God to allow His presence to accompany Israel again. The Lord responded saying, *"This very thing that you have spoken I will do, for you have found favor in my sight, and I know you by name"* (Exod 33:17).

Moses didn't stop there; in a wonderful scene in the book of Exodus, Moses asked for proof of God's presence, to see the glory of God Himself so that he would know for certain that God was ready to be there with them once again (Exod 33:18). In the midst of the sea of chaos that the people had created, the Lord allowed Moses one brief glimpse of His glory as He passed by. The divine always has a way of calming the sea.

At that exact moment, as if to reveal what His presence really meant and what its spiritual significance was going to be, the Lord invoked His name (Exod 34:5), and said the following words,

> *The LORD, the LORD, a God merciful and gracious, slow to anger, and abounding in steadfast love and faithfulness, keeping steadfast love for thousands, forgiving iniquity and transgression and sin, but who will by no means clear the guilty, visiting the iniquity of the fathers on the children and the children's children, to the third and the fourth generation (Exod 34:6–7).*

The Lord's people had a decision to make and their choice would have eternal consequences. Imperatively speaking, James has also presented all of his readers the same two paths. To the one who will submit to the Lord and yield themselves to Him, He is *"merciful and gracious, slow to anger, and abounding in steadfast love and faithfulness [and] forgiving iniquity, transgressions and sin."* But to the one who declines God's merciful plea, seeking to be their own law-giver, they will stand on their own and be judged according to all that they have done. A lesson was learned that day on the mountain. After this scene, Moses bowed his head down to the ground and worshiped. He said, *"If now I have found favor in your sight, O Lord, please let the Lord go in the midst of us, for it is a stiff-necked people, and pardon our iniquity and our sin, and take us for your inheritance"* (Exod 34:9). The people chose, on that day, to yield to the Lord and allow Him to take His rightful place of honor.

Many years later, Isaiah would summarize God's sacred position in this way: *"The LORD is our Judge; the LORD is our Lawgiver; the LORD is our King; He will save us"* (33:22). The seat of Lawgiver, Judge, and Savior belongs to one and one alone, the LORD! What happens when we try to sit in that seat? James addresses that in our next imperative.

I. IMPERATIVE 33: "DO NOT SPEAK EVIL ..." — VS. 11–12

> *Do not speak evil against one another, brothers. The one who speaks against a brother or judges his brother, speaks evil against the law and judges the law. But if you judge the law, you are not a doer of the law but a judge. There is only one Lawgiver and Judge, the One who is able to save and destroy. But who are you to judge your neighbor? (Jas 4:11–12).*

Our imperative is found in verse 11 with the command against evil speaking. When taking into account what was previously written regarding the prideful scoffers, it appears as though they were creating discord within the church. James specifically refers to their behaviors as "evil-speaking." Now, we know that Christians are told to make determinations every single day as to whether something is right or wrong, but this behavior had apparently crossed the line into forbidden territory. To see that line, we have to understand judgment itself.

The theme of judgment is strong in the Bible, but unfortunately, it is one of the most misunderstood. I'm sure we have all heard someone say, "You can't judge me because Jesus says not to judge." When used as a defense, usually this implies that the individual does not want their actions or decisions to be critiqued. Sometimes people use this as a blanket policy to live their lives how they see fit and avoid answering questions about the chaos that ensues.

Biblically speaking, judgment can mean to make a determination or it can also describe the act of pronouncing a sentence. In a sense, we make judgments or determinations every single day! There's no escaping that reality, especially when it comes to distinguishing between right and wrong. To interpret Jesus's directive, *"Judge not lest you be judged,"* (Matt 7:1) as, "We should stop deciding whether something right or wrong," is not only flawed, but dangerous. Jesus was not teaching us to purposefully avoid deciding whether something is right or wrong; He was forbidding us from condemning (sentencing) others to death based on our own flawed sense of what is right. This is clearly seen in the very next verse, which asserts, *"For with the judgment you pronounce you will be judged, and with the **measure you use** it will be measured to you."* Without using God's standard of righteousness, we are left to use our own best sense of what is right and the end of that dark path is death (Prov 14:12; 16:25). Additionally, to interpret Matthew 7:1 in this way would cause a contradiction within John 7:24, which says, *"Do not judge by appearances, but judge with righteous judgment."*

God's judgment is righteous judgment. It is righteous judgment because He will not say declare something evil as good, and He certainly will not be partial in the way He carries out judgment. It is a righteousness based on His very character. In this Christian age, His judgment is infused with grace and mercy because His divine demand for justice was satisfied by the blood of Jesus for those who accept this gracious gift. This is something that only He can do and only He can offer. Through Jesus, the penalty for our sin is covered and we do not receive the death sentence owed to us for sin. On the other hand, if we choose to replace God and His judgment with our own standard, choosing to sit in His seat as judge, then the subsequent works-based, grace-absent criteria that we use will be applied to us too, when it is our turn to stand before God. Grace and forgiveness are unique traits to God's standard of righteousness that are given by God to those who are willing to receive it in the manner that He has determined. All other standards of righteousness, outside of God's standard, are weighed on their own merit and ability. What a scary thought when we consider how imperfect and fragile, we are as humans. Works-based systems of holiness, result in measuring one another and divisions. Pride can also cause believers to misuse knowledge and abilities to hurt fellow believers (1 Cor 8:1–3).

In James's culture, the teachers of the Law — the Scribes and the Pharisees — were masters at creating complex standards of holiness that they used to measure one another. Over time, these extra standards called the traditions of the elders became deified. Jesus often preached against them and their traditions because they manipulated the people into thinking that they represented God when they spoke, even though the measurement that they were using was a mixture of what God had given Moses and their own interpretations.

The extra-biblical traditions ultimately ended up

corrupting God's original intent for the Law of Moses. The Law wasn't meant for His people to cut one another down; it was meant to be used to teach His people about His holiness and the need for a Savior. The precious laws of human dignity and the fair treatment of others were meant to show the ancient world that there was a sanctity to life. Life was precious and that truth can and should be lived out. Sadly, by the time Jesus arrived, the Law and the religious traditions had been transformed into weapons to hurt one another. They even tried to use them against Jesus Himself (Matt 15:2).

Jesus memorably confronted them about this in Matthew 23. He told the people listening, *"They* [the Scribes and Pharisees] *tie up heavy, burdensome loads and lay them on men's shoulders, but they themselves are not willing to lift a finger to move them"* (vs. 4).

It is easy to recognize God's law over all others because God's teachings are meant to save, not destroy. John 3:17 says that even God, when He sent His Son to usher in the New Covenant, *"did not send His Son into the world to condemn the world, but in order that the world might be saved through Him."* If God — the only One truly qualified to condemn anyone — did not do so, then neither should we. That seat is reserved for God and God alone. There is a day that is reserved for that kind of sentencing, where people will receive life or death, but that day has not yet arrived (Heb 9:27).

In our first-fruits, Kingdom of God era, we are to be a people of peace and healing, not chaos and condemnation. Within the Kingdom of God, we are co-equal with each other as members and fellow servants of God (Gal 3:28). We all have different functions within the church, but we are all under the authority of God. In the equal body of Christ, we support and encourage one another. Sometimes we have to provide correction and admonishment (1 Thess 5:14) in order to warn those who are slipping (2 Thess 3:15). We sometimes have to rebuke and exhort brethren with complete patience (2 Tim 4:2), but we do so as their brethren in a spirit of gentleness (Gal 6:1), without haughtiness or superiority. All of these actions require us to exercise judgment, but it is based upon God's righteous standard, nothing else. Unfortunately, James's audience was yet again seeking to bring in the old traditions and fallen ways of doing things into their first-fruits assembly. They were guilty of evil speaking by sentencing their brothers and sisters in Christ, but this is not all that they were guilty of doing.

Notice, James says they *"speak evil against the law and judge the law."* This reinforces the point that when we use the guidance that God gives His people to hurt one another in condemnation, not only are we exercising a function that does not belong to us, we are also injuring the very law of God itself. We're evil-speaking against the law when we misrepresent and mischaracterize its intention. The fruit that we produce when we interact with the world around us and with our fellow first-fruits believers gives significant insight into what seat we are attempting to sit in!

II. "RIGHTEOUS JUDGMENT" VERSUS "EVIL SPEAK"

It's interesting that James says one can be guilty of evil-speaking both individuals and the very law of God itself. I want to explore this evil-speak principle a bit further, not just because James commands us to avoid such a path, but because it is also critical to maintaining a healthy view of self in the Kingdom of God. In the context of our text from James, evil speaking occurs when an individual member of the body of Christ seeks to rise above their fellow brethren and to give their own opinion, preferences, or the traditions of men, the same weight as God's Law. In doing so, they end up sitting in a seat that does not belong to them. What follows is a mentality where an individual breathes condemnation toward others instead of helping to heal. Rather than invest their time, effort, and resources into others, they instead create an *us versus them* climate within their social circle.

It's no surprise that James wasn't the only one to address this issue. Paul also had some words about this in Romans 14:4, *"Who are you to judge someone else's servant? To their own master, servants stand or fall. And they will stand, for the Lord is able to make them stand."* The implication is that we're all servants! What right has one servant of God to rise up, sit in the seat of Jesus, and pronounce condemnation based on their own flawed standard? In verse 12 of our text, James words it this way, "Who are you to judge your neighbor?" Again, the judgment that was taking place here is not determining whether something was right or wrong, it was the inappropriate use of God's law to condemn and self-elevate.

It seems that the old religious system was slowly seeping into the first-fruits people of God. Since the natural order is for the Lord our Creator to be the Law-giver to us as His creation, when Christians rise up and bind their own opinions or beliefs upon their fellows, the end result will always be quarreling and chaos. If you want to see if the brethren are following the pure wisdom of the Lord as He intended, you need only look at the fruit that is being produced. Conflict between Christians happens when God's natural order is violated. Any time an individual's views or preferences runs contrary to God's wisdom, disorder will ensue, as it always has. Righteous judgment uses the instructions of God and His methods of discernment to resolve conflict and nurture peace among our neighbors. "Evil-speak" opens the door to all kinds of dishonorable actions.

Additionally, righteous judgment also means that we recognize that when someone does something different, it does not mean it is sin. In a very famous section of his letter to the Corinthian church, Paul addressed an issue within their congregation where individuals were condemning one another due to meat. One group freely ate of meat that had been given by others as a sacrifice to the local gods, and the other group could not fathom why Christians would even touch such tainted meat. In addressing the issue, Paul said,

> But take care that this right of yours does not somehow become a stumbling block to the weak. For if anyone sees you who have knowledge eating in an idol's temple, will he not be encouraged, if his conscience is weak, to eat food offered to idols? And so by your knowledge this weak person is destroyed, the brother for whom Christ died. Thus, sinning against your brothers and wounding their conscience when it is weak, you sin against Christ. Therefore, if food makes my brother stumble, I will never eat meat, lest I make my brother stumble (1 Cor 8:9–11).

There was already a stream within the early church that

struggled with even touching and tasting something they deemed to be unclean (Col 2:21). It's not hard to imagine why. After all, the laws and traditions they followed were deeply engrained within their daily lives. But rather than take one side or another, Paul brilliantly states that his position is for the strong in conscience to meet the weaker conscience brethren where they were at in their spiritual development. To do otherwise would be sin for the strong because it would place an opinion in a position of greater importance over their soul, for which Christ died. Paul also adds something James has referenced before, "to wound the weak is to sin against God Himself."

James commands us to stay within our proper and healthy position before the Lord. Do not fall into the trap of believing that God and His gifts can be used to hurt others. To do such a thing is to commit the sin of evil speaking. If our thoughts and hearts are molded by gratitude to God, we will naturally overflow in compassion toward others, even those that are as lost as sheep with no shepherd (Matt 9:36).

III. BRINGING CORRECTION

Within the body of Christ, there will be moments when we have to provide correction and be open with someone about their sin. This is part of discerning between what is right and what is wrong. I want to walk through that process so that we can avoid crossing into "evil-speak" and sitting in a seat that belongs to the Lord. Let's start at the top!

Imagine that you have discovered something that you feel is sin and you feel it needs to be addressed. The first step, before we do anything else, is to ask: "Is this really sin or is this preference and opinion?" The reason why that is important is, again, if we step outside of God's revealed Word and attempt to bind our own opinions on others, then we're guilty of replacing God as the Law-giver! Proverbs 18:13 tells us, *"If one gives an answer before he hears, it is his folly and shame."* There is too much at stake for us to neglect our own due diligence before we act. Be sure that you are using the right standard of measurement and not being clouded by your own fleshly desires to exert your will on others! Be self-aware so that you do not become guilty of becoming the stumbling block that Paul warned against.

Let's suppose that we have prayerfully and scripturally considered the issue and what we determined is that the issue was sin. Before we come even remotely close to talking to the person about it, we must enter into the process of self-examination. Jesus said,

> *Why do you see the speck that is in your brother's eye, but do not notice the log that is in your own eye? Or how can you say to your brother, "Let me take the speck out of your eye," when there is the log in your own eye? You hypocrite, first take the log out of your own eye, and then you will see clearly to take the speck out of your brother's eye (Matt 7:3–5).*

Examining ourselves is critical because it helps us to approach our brethren from a position of equality and humility, and not one of loftiness. After all, as Paul said, we are co-equal servants of God. These verses in Matthew chapter 7 have always amazed me because they give perfect insight into what God sees when imperfect people correct each other. Notice that Jesus never said that the person didn't actually have a speck in his eye, or that there was no fault and no right to approach him in correction. What He said was that even if we feel our cause is just, we need to make sure that we're actually seeing clearly. What are our motives for addressing this with our brother? Proverbs 21:2 says that *"Every way of a man is right in his own eyes, but the LORD weighs the heart."* In other words, we may speak and act like our cause is just, but ultimately the Lord knows our true intent. We are flawed and fractured human beings and we are notorious for having patterns of behaviors that others notice, but that escape our awareness. Jesus asks for this self-examination in order to help us pause long enough to identify any areas that are skewing our rationale so that we do not end up destroying each other.

At this point, even if our cause is inarguably just and the offense is without a doubt a sin, we still need to evaluate our own triggers. Galatians 6:1 clarifies, *"Brethren, if anyone is caught in a transgression, you who are spiritual should restore him in a spirit of gentleness. Keep watch on yourself, lest you too be tempted."* The brother or sister in Christ may be struggling with an issue that we are still healing from. Even with the truth and a right spirit, self-examination may reveal that it is not wise for us to proceed because doing so would put us in danger as well. Knowing our weaknesses and limitations and really examining ourselves is critical so that we don't end up hurting ourselves in the process. This does not mean that we turn away. What this means is that we will have to prepare our hearts and be prepared to be open about our own struggle with sin.

Finally, once all this personal work is done, we are to prayerfully and humbly show the brother or sister their fault. Leviticus 19:17 gives some amazing insight into this process. I love the way the verse is rendered in The New Living Translation because it does the best at explaining what is being said here in Hebrew concerning the heart during this confrontation: *"Do not nurse hatred in your heart for any of your relatives ... Reason frankly with your neighbor, lest you incur sin because of him."* Be open and honest about what has happened and why you feel the way you do about their actions. If you do not, bitterness will spread and cause you to stumble when you take matters into your own hands.

Vengeance, just like pronouncing condemnation, is not a function that belongs to us, it belongs only to God (Deut 32:35; Rom 12:19). Only God has the purest motives, the ability to see into the very depths of a soul and its intentions, and is absolutely impartial. That is why these incredibly serious responsibilities fall on Him. We cannot fathom the weight that comes from wielding judgment that leads to spiritual death and vengeance, so we should leave them to God and seek as much peace as possible, within our power (Rom 12:18).

Ultimately, the result of righteous judgment on our part is restoration and healing, not condemnation that leads to spiritual death. The motivation for righteous judgment should be spiritual life for the accused, not injury because of our own selfish ambition or insecurities. If the brother or sister comes back to the truth and returns from their wandering, your love for them will have covered a multitude of sins (1 Pet 4:8). This is what pleases God! Bringing new spiritual growth at the heart of being the first-fruits children of God.

On Mount Sinai, God covered Moses with His hand to symbolize the atonement (covering) that His presence would provide at that time. But as God moved past Moses, I envision His hand lifting up and revealing His glory as it passed by. At that moment, the Lord began speaking of forgiveness of sin, iniquity, and transgression (the three types of errors that mankind commits). The Hebrew word here for forgiveness is *nasah,* which means "to lift up." This word is not atonement, which was all that the children of Israel had for their sins, transgressions, and iniquities. This was something different altogether. I read the lifting of the covering that was shielding Moses and its subsequent revealing of glory to correspond with what the Lord was saying. One day, the Lord would lift the sins of all who would come to Him and remember them no more.

On that day, glory will be revealed unlike anything the world had ever known. This would be an act born out of steadfast love. This was the forgiveness through remission of sins that Peter spoke about when the crowd asked, *"What shall we do?" Peter said, "Repent, and let every one of you be baptized in the name of Jesus Christ for the remission of sins; and you shall receive the gift of the Holy Spirit."* (Acts 2:38)

As recipients of that special forgiveness in Jesus, we should be a people committed to peace and the preservation of it. We should be committed to showing others how to receive that special gift for themselves, and a people committed to honoring God as the sole Judge, Law-giver, and Savior! Each and every day provides us two paths to choose from. One path elevates our pride over God. The other path draws us closer to God through humility and the God-honoring treatment of others. The world desperately needs the latter. May the Lord strengthen our resolve to be His hands and heart in the world!

SPIRITUAL FORMATION SECTION

What kinds of conflicts have you seen within the Church? Now that we have discussed what is "evil-speak" and what is righteous judgment, which side would you say the conflict was on? Did the conflict appear valid, but was later determined to be a result of trying to impose someone's will over another? How can churches *"endeavor to keep the unity of the Spirit in the bond of peace"* (Eph 4:3)?

CHAPTER 30

COME ON, NOW...

JAMES 4:13–17

Imperative 34: Come Now

INTRODUCTION

There has been much in the book of James that has addressed how our choices and relationship with God are intertwined and directly impact the way we treat one another. As we have seen, the choices that we make on a daily basis either push our first-fruits, God-assigned mission forward, or they don't. They either co-partner with God or stand as God's adversary. So far, James has focused intently on the fair treatment of others within the church family. What we are about so see is that our first-fruits way of life is not just specific to the Church, it actually encompasses every aspect of our identity.

Everything in the Christian life should be connected to God, but in this imperative, we are going to see a frustrated James address Christians who were attempting to create distance between themselves and God in yet another area:

business. His reason for this will be fully given in chapter 5, but for now, he sets the stage for that dialogue in these verses.

I. IMPERATIVE 34: "COME NOW!" — VS. 13–17

> **Come now,** *you who say, "Today or tomorrow we will go into such and such a town and spend a year there and trade and make a profit" — yet you do not know what tomorrow will bring. What is your life? For you are a mist that appears for a little time and then vanishes. Instead you ought to say, "If the Lord wills, we will live and do this or that." As it is, you boast in your arrogance. All such boasting is evil. So whoever knows the right thing to do and fails to do it, for him it is sin (Jas 4:13–17).*

"Come now" is our imperative in this text. Today, we might say, "Come on, now!" It's an expression of frustration, usually occurring when something that should have been very obvious isn't being understood by someone else. We might also say, "Come on, now! Surely you can see ...!" Given the intensity of James's wording, one might wonder as to why he was frustrated. The answer to that question is found in the contrast that he makes between the two types of Christian business owners. On the one hand, James highlights the fact that there were some who had mentally and even spiritually created a sub-section of their lives where they put their business plans. These Christians were, in essence, creating space between their professions and God. We know this because of what James offers as an alternative.

James says that instead of creating separate plans, one should say, "If the Lord wills." Saying *if the Lord wills* is yet another way to acknowledge God's role as the Creator. We may have our plans, but since the Lord rules our entire heart, we might instead say, "This is what I want to do, but in the end, I want it only to come to pass if it furthers God's desire for me as His first-fruits creation and our work in the Kingdom of God." Invoking God's will is one significant way that we can make sure that we are indeed pushing in the same direction as the Lord!

Within our ability to think and reason, we often make the biggest plans possible, letting our dreams and ambitions run wild. Plans are absolutely fine, but again, when we make them, we have to make sure that the Lord is included. In fact, true first-fruits decision-making also involves incorporating our knowledge of what God wants us to accomplish into our plans. In that regard, we ask, "If I go to such and such town and spend a year there in order to make a profit, is God and His will for His first-fruits people motivating me? Since my life is but a vapor, is that precious year-long droplet of life God has extended to me going to be used there to advance His will or mine?" To the one who forgets to evaluate their business proposals in this light, James says, "Come on, now!"

In Genesis 1 and 2, Adam and Eve were supposed to have recognized their place within the creation, honoring God *through* it and *through* their work in it, but as we know, that did not end up being the case. Our temptation, like that of the first human beings and James's early readers, is to attempt to separate all that we do. For some believers, there is real temptation to compartmentalize our work, play, education, family, faith, and friendships. We tend to try to keep them separate from one another because we want to dictate how those streams are to flow. We may be fine with relinquishing control of one or more of those streams, but certainly not all.

What God designed in the beginning wasn't compartmentalization. It was one single identity, comprised of unique components, but all informed by God's character and will. We can hunt; we can fish; we can grow things and we can produce items of value. We buy, sell, trade, and build. We employ, we have friendships and families, and so much more. These blessings are absolutely wonderful, but notice how they all flow from the special image of our Creator. We mirror creativity, creation, and closeness with others because this is what is divine within us. What we love and what we do should be enjoyed, but within the context and guidance of the Lord, not apart from Him. Our identity should be informed *through God* and not apart from Him. An identity that infuses the divine, girds each strand with meaning and purpose. Crisis, in one or more areas of our identity, is unavoidable, and having divine meaning and purpose wrapping each component of who we are will help us to persevere. Crisis, without God's meaning and purpose, inevitably leads to a personal identity crisis.

II. GODLINESS WITH CONTENTMENT

If there is one who knows that they are on a path outside of the shadow of God's wing, traveling down a road that elevates their own personal interests over God's intention for them, James's point is plain: *"for him, it is sin."* Sadly, we will see in James chapter 5 what the unmitigated love for wealth over God leads to. Every time we step out from under the shadow of God's wing and attempt to cross over to another, self-focused path, it comes at a cost. That cost will eventually be paid by the ones we love, as well as ourselves.

The life that we have is a precious gift from God. It is a strand, pulled from our Creator and extended to us to empower us to express our unique character. James reminds us that as precious as this gift is, our time in this physical world is *a mist that appears for a little time and then vanishes.* Life certainly does not always feel that brief, especially during the days of our youth. We have a constant feeling of unlimited possibility, but the follow-along frustration of wanting more or wishing time would just move quickly so that we can realize our goals. Unfortunately, in the constant going and coming, or as James says, in the *"such and such,"* we can lose sight of the ultimate will of God to drive out the darkness from the world.

In his late life, John relayed this truth by saying,

*Whoever keeps his word, in him truly the love of God is **perfected**. By this we may know that we are in him: whoever says he abides in him ought to walk in the same way in which he walked. Beloved, I am writing you no new commandment, but an old commandment that you had **from the beginning**. The old commandment is the word that you have heard. At the same time, it is a new commandment that I am writing to you, which is true in him and in you, because **the darkness is passing away and the true light is already shining** (1 John 2:5–8).*

The "perfecting" is again, this idea of completion. Aligning our love with the Lord is a process. This completion process is lifelong because as the years go by, we become attached to different values and experience different ambitions. Each phase of our lives has its own goals and attractions, but ultimately our soul should long for what is beyond this physical world. Aligning with God helps tamper the chaotic unrest that follows these pursuits. I love the way John invokes the old truth that is new again to his readers because it has taken on a new context and a new expression in the lives of new believers in Jesus. Children of God must know that in this new *let there be light* era, darkness is being pushed away from the creation and soon, this work will be done. Every day serves as an opportunity to partner with God and drive out the darkness within ourselves first, then use our unique gifts and abilities to shine that light into the world (Matt 5:16). *"The night is nearly over; the day is almost here. So let us put aside the deeds of darkness and put on the armor of light"* (Rom 13:12).

One truth that is emphasized in Scripture that can assist us in staying focused on God's will and expressing our unique character in a way that is God-aligned is Godliness through contentment. Paul reminded Timothy of this truth in 1 Timothy 6:6–10,

> ***Godliness with contentment is great gain, for we brought nothing into the world, and we cannot take anything out of the world.*** *But if we have food and clothing, with these we will be content. But those who desire to be rich fall into temptation, into a snare, into many senseless and harmful desires that plunge people into ruin and destruction. For the love of money is a root of all kinds of evils. It is through this craving that some have wandered away from the faith and pierced themselves with many pangs.*

In this passage, there is a contrast between two approaches to life. First, there is the approach that honors God for the blessings that have been given and understands that this life must be viewed through the lens of the eternal. Paul says that this mentality leads to great gain! On the other hand, there's the other approach that is restless and desires to extend that boundary, just like the individuals James was addressing. Obviously, only one lives under the shadow of God's wing and is nested in His will. This is truly tragic because our time in this physical world is just a vapor and it makes no sense to live for self here when what we have gained cannot go with us. Jesus said it best when He said, *"What good is it for someone to gain the whole world, yet forfeit their soul?"* (Mark 8:36)

The Lord designed our identity to be realized in our role as His children, not from anything sourced in the physical world. Paul writes, *"I have been crucified with Christ. It is no longer I who live, but Christ who lives in me. And the life I now live in the flesh I live by faith in the Son of God, who loved me and gave himself for me"* (Gal 2:20). There is nothing wrong with enjoying God's creation, or pursuing our earthly talents through business, but we must do so through the Lord and not apart from Him. As Paul says, it should be Christ who lives in us and through us.

The soul that finds its fullness and identity in God and not finances is the soul that will arrive at the point of contentment, and godly contentment ensures that this soul will thrive no matter what season it may find itself in.

His delight is in the Law of the LORD, and on His law he meditates day and night. He is like a tree planted by streams of water, yielding its fruit in season, whose leaf does not wither, and who prospers in all he does (Ps 1:2–3).

James is both warning his readers to always be cognizant of God's will and asking that they evaluate whether their goals or ambitions are pushing that will forward. We need to sit as close as we can to the Lord. The *such and such* that James speaks of is something familiar to us all! The busyness of the day has a way of leading us away and causing us to think that there is always more time later. Stay grounded, stay aligned with God, and infuse the Lord's will into everything that you do! When you do, you will find rich meaning and purpose, even in the difficult seasons. A life that is expressed in this way is a life that is pushing the darkness out of world and patiently waiting for the time when there will be no more night (Rev 22:5)!

SPIRITUAL FORMATION SECTION

1 Peter 4:10–11 says,

As good stewards of the manifold grace of God, each of you should use whatever gift he has received to serve one another. If anyone speaks, he should speak as one conveying the words of God. If anyone serves, he should serve with the strength God provides, so that in all things God may be glorified through Jesus Christ, to whom be the glory and the power forever and ever. Amen.

The manifold, or varied, ways that the grace of God appears in the lives of His children is through the diversity in methods used by His children to employ their talents for

Him! What are your talents? Have you used your talents and blessings through God, or apart from Him? What are ways that you can use your talents for His glory? The possibilities are endless!

CHAPTER 31

TAKE HEART, GOD SEES ALL

JAMES 5:1-6

Imperatives 35–37: Come Now & Behold

INTRODUCTION

The closer our heart and soul are to God, the more our identity and pursuits will be aligned with the will of God. The more aligned we are, the more effective we will be in our first-fruits, Kingdom of God mission. Every aspect of who we are, every blessing we enjoy, and the decisions that we make, all must fall under the Lord's guidance and must serve His divine intent. Space, however, creates opportunities for sin and comes with consequences.

In our next three imperatives, James is going to reveal why he commanded his readers to bring urgent changes to the aspects of their lives that they were hiding in darkness. At first it may have seemed like James's commands regarding the fair treatment of others and business practices were two separate issues, but in the most severe language yet, James 5:1–6 is going to reveal that they were indeed related. This passage should serve as a warning of what people are capable of when they allow parts of their identity to fester in the darkness, away from the accountability and oversight of God.

I. IMPERATIVES 35–37 — VS. 1–6

> **Come now**, you rich, **weep** and howl for the miseries that are coming upon you. Your riches have rotted and your garments are moth-eaten. Your gold and silver have corroded, and their corrosion will be evidence against you and will eat your flesh like fire. You have laid up treasure in the last days. **Behold**, the wages of the laborers who mowed your fields, which you kept back by fraud, are crying out against you, and the cries of the harvesters have reached the ears of the Lord of Hosts. You have lived on the earth in luxury and in self-indulgence. You have fattened your hearts in a day of slaughter. You are accustomed to condemn and have murdered the righteous person. He does not resist you. (Jas 5:1–6).

The imperatives here are, "Come now!" "Weep" and, "Behold!" They are contained within a passage that is quite shocking. It is easy to see why James just unleashed ten imperatives aimed at becoming more aligned with God before addressing these specific behaviors. There is no way around the appalling nature of what was occurring within this early church. Some may interpret the rich as a generic category of antagonists. While I don't find that interpretation necessarily wrong, my view is that James was targeting a specific group of people who were well-known by the local church. I believe that these rich individuals were the same as the ones who were being given the best seats in the congregation, by individuals who were potentially attempting to rise in status and authority (Jas 2:1–4).

I interpret the rich as not just known, my view is that they were fellow believers for two reasons. First, because of how James organizes the conversation here, i.e., how he raised the fair treatment of others, starting first with the stain of sin (Jas 1:21; 2:2), then how he commanded that business must align with the will of God (Jas 4:13–16). We've seen James's mastery of this method of rebuke numerous times throughout the book, and I believe that he is employing it once more with this passage. There is a pattern to how James gives correction to believers, and I see its culmination in this passage.

Second, I believe that the fact that James has been speaking to the rich with authoritative correction and clear guidance on how to repent, indicates that these were specific individuals who had a connection to the Kingdom of God. As we know, all of God's Word is authoritative, but if this was a faceless and generic reference to the rich of the world, would James have use precious space in this powerful letter to go as detailed in his admonitions as he did? I believe that these sections contain the commands that they do because the group being addressed saw James as an authoritative source and would have taken his words to heart.

If the rich were indeed the same individuals as those in James chapter 2 who were being welcomed into the assembly and being given the best seats at the expense of the lowly, that would mean that their fraudulent behavior was either unknown to the church or it was known, but not questioned, because of their position of privilege. Their status and influence possibly acted as a cloak to hide their evil deeds and shielded them from anyone looking too closely at their lives.

What appears to have happened is that the riches and status that the wealthiest among them enjoyed, caused them to believe that they could abuse their laborers with no repercussions. They withheld desperately needed wages and had caused the abused to send their cries up to the Lord (verse 4). As we saw in James 1:25–27, the Lord is the voice for the voiceless and He is the defender of the defenseless and He is the ear that hears their distinct cry. The wealthy and connected thought that they could hurt others and somehow still enter into the assembly as though they were favored by God. How wrong they were! Wealth and possessions are not evil in and of themselves, but what *is* condemned as evil is the use of God's creation to injure our fellow man. The possessions that we have are only on loan to us. We brought nothing into the world and we will take nothing out when we leave. Paul says,

> *He (Jesus) is the image of the invisible God, the firstborn of all creation. For by him all things were created, in heaven and on earth, visible and invisible, whether thrones or dominions or rulers or authorities — all things were created through him and **for him**. And he is before all things, and in him all things hold together ... So that in all things **He may have preeminence**. (Col 1:15–18).*

The Hebrews writer drives the point home even further: "*He is the radiance of the glory of God and the exact imprint of his nature, and he upholds the universe by the word of his power"* (3:1).

The belief that we (and not God) own our possessions is self-deception. The proof of this is in the fact that when that breath of life is taken out of our bodies and we are called by God to leave this world, we leave absolutely everything behind where it is. Unless our belongings are moved by someone still living, they will gather dust and return to the earth through decay. The only parts of our being that we will take with us when we die are our heart, mind, and soul. They are God's gift to us. As living beings, created in His image, we have the free will to choose how we spend our brief time on earth and what we will do with the temporal and eternal gifts that we have been given.

Sadly, the abuse of possessions that we are reading in James 5 was not an isolated incident in the first-century Church. The pursuit of riches had caused numerous brethren to elevate themselves and become calloused to the pain inflicted on others. Paul told Timothy,

> *But those who desire to be rich fall into temptation, into a snare, into many senseless and harmful desires that plunge people into ruin and destruction. For **the love of money** is a root of all kinds of evils. It is through this craving that some have wandered away from the faith and pierced themselves with many pangs ... As for the rich in this present age, charge them not to be haughty, nor to set their hopes on the uncertainty of riches, but on God, **who richly provides us with everything to enjoy**. They are to **do good**, to be **rich in good works**, to **be generous** and **ready to share**, thus storing up treasure for themselves as a good foundation for the future, so*

that they may take hold of that which is truly life (1 Tim 6:9–
10, 17–19).

Instead of blessing others and glorifying God with their material wealth, the rich that James is correcting defrauded their workers and used their power and influence to hurt those who could not resist them. The workers relied upon their wages to support themselves and their families, but even the just wages due to them were being withheld as though real human beings were not counting on them to survive. In a show of great power and force against this travesty, James invoked an ancient title: Lord of Hosts (Jas 5:4)!

The title "Lord of Hosts" comes from the Hebrew Scriptures and means "God of Armies." It is a title that the Lord wears when it is time for Him to make war! The Lord does not stand by while the stranger, the widow, the orphan, and the defenseless are hurt. The Lord of Hosts is their Defender, and His power is invoked by the cries of the maligned. James's words give the guilty the sense that their evil was now exposed and the Lord was preparing for war against their fragile empires. Should they take no action, the Lord would take matters into His own hands.

Not only was the fair treatment of all people a priority for God, since the beginning, even the very wages owed were sacred and were not permitted to be withheld longer than necessary. Leviticus 19:13 reads, *"You shall not oppress your neighbor or rob him. **The wages of a hired worker** shall not remain with you all night until the morning."* Perhaps this was the reason why James pulled from Leviticus 19 as much as he did.

Again, Deuteronomy 24:14–15 reads,

You shall not oppress a hired worker who is poor and needy,
whether he is one of your brothers or one of the sojourners who
are in your land within your towns. You are to pay his wages
each day before sunset, because he is poor and depends on
them. **Otherwise he may cry out to the LORD against**
you, and you will be guilty of sin.

The rich were committing grave offenses and had hardened their hearts toward those they injured. Again, the evidence is clear, the further that we move from God, the colder and harder our hearts become toward Him. The more distance created, the more misaligned our hearts become with His values and character. This should serve as an example to us regarding what can happen when we attempt to keep a part of our identity separate from God. But, rest assured, God sees all!

Whether we have an abundance of this world's goods or not, our Christian aim should be the same: to be as close to God as possible and to honor God's will for us as His first-fruits people. This heartbreaking passage reminds us that we as human beings are capable of some terrible things when we choose to live for self and not for God. Even Christians can be lured from God by their own desires. The only way to truly prevent these kinds of Christian failures and wrongdoings from taking place in our own lives is to stay close to God. The closer we are to God, the more we will grow to be like Him.

II. "SOME TRUST IN CHARIOTS"

This passage has shown us the importance of yielding our identity to God and refrain from trying to keep pieces of our life separate from God. There is nothing wrong with comforts, making a good living, and enjoying the fruit of our labor. The pain comes from buying into the lie that these streams make us better than others or that parts of these blessings can remain separate from God's oversight. These thoughts are products of man-made constructs and have no place in a Christians heart and mind. As Paul said earlier, wealth and the preservation or increase of wealth, has led brethren away from the shadow of the Lord.

To avoid falling into that pitfall and to avoid creating separation between you and the Lord, I want to offer all of the words of Psalm 20. This is a beloved Psalm that reads like a call to war. This Psalm is like the prayer of a warrior who is about to step into battle. I offer this Psalm for reflection because there is wisdom contained here that speaks directly to trusting in man-made constructs. The Psalmist says,

> *May the LORD answer you in the day of trouble! May the name of the God of Jacob protect you! May he send you help from the sanctuary and give you support from Zion! May he remember all your offerings and regard with favor your burnt sacrifices! May he grant you your heart's desire and fulfill all your plans! May we shout for joy over your salvation, and in the name of our God set up our banners! May the LORD fulfill all your petitions! Now I know that the LORD saves his anointed; he will answer him from his holy heaven with the saving might of his right hand. **Some trust in chariots** and some in horses, but we trust in the name of the LORD our God. They collapse and fall, but we rise and stand upright. O LORD, save the king! May he answer us when we call.*

Whether it be chariots, horses, or any other physical possession, nothing can replace the peace that comes from surrendering to God's oversight and authority. When our hearts are aligned with God, He will grant us our heart's desire and fulfill our plans because our success furthers His will. This Psalm is all about finding favor through divine alignment and surrender. There is a somewhat hidden connection between the remembrance referenced in verse 3, when the Psalmist says, *"May he remember all your offerings"* and verse 7. The connection is not easily seen because verse 7 is rendered, *"Some trust in chariots and some in horses, but we trust in the name of the LORD our God."* In Hebrew, the verse can be read, *"In these chariots and others in horses, but we, in the name of the LORD our God, we will make remembrance."* The Psalm is opened and closed in remembrance. God remembers His people and His people remember Him. In the "day of trouble," what we remember and seek to take hold of first is that which we truly trust and have built our identity upon. For some, when moments of crisis arise, they place their trust in their chariots and horses, but God's people remember the Lord and they take comfort in the fact that they know the Lord remembers them.

If you are struggling with surrendering your trust in your chariots and horses, worried that when your "day of trouble" comes that you will be left alone, cast those thoughts aside. The Lord knows who you are and you are loved. The Hebrews writer said it in the most absolutely perfect way: *"Keep your life free from love of money, and be content with what you have, for he has said, 'I will never leave you nor forsake you"* (Heb 13:5). If parts of your life are as hidden from God as Adam and Eve who hid their shame, I implore you to hide no more. You are not a child of darkness, recycling more darkness into the world. You are a child of God who is called to live in the light and expose what is hidden to the glorious light of Christ. Paul says,

> *Therefore do not become partners with them; for at one time you were darkness, but not you are light in the Lord. Walk as children of light (for the fruit of light is found in all that is good and right and true), and try to discern what is pleasing to the Lord. Take no part in the unfruitful works of darkness, but instead expose them. For it is shameful even to speak of the things that they do in secret. But when anything is exposed by the light, it becomes visible (Eph 5:7–13).*

Although James was addressing the wrongs of a time long past, our struggles are still very much the same. The good news is that the same Lord who had such a deep and intense love for those that were being wronged, continues to reign today and knows your every worry and fear. Sit as close as you can to the Lord *"and the peace that surpasses all understanding, will guard your hearts and your minds in Christ Jesus"* (Phil 4:7).

SPIRITUAL FORMATION SECTION

Sitting as closely as we can means finding ways to stay grounded and anchored in our faith. John describes spiritual anchoring and grounding as "abiding in Him" and the way that he says that we abide in Him is to *"walk as Jesus walked"* (1 John 2:6). Jesus gave thanks, He glorified God, and He made sure that He left every person He met better off than they were before they approached Him. Determine in your heart to walk as Jesus walked. Spend the day glorifying God, giving Him thanks for every blessing, including the small ones, and do what it is your power to brighten the day of every person you meet.

CHAPTER 32

STAND FIRM BY SENDING UP

JAMES 5:7–9

Imperatives 38–43:
Be Patient. See. Be Patient. Establish.
Do not grumble. Behold

INTRODUCTION

S ome of the worst pain that we can feel in this life comes from moments where we feel absolutely power-less and voiceless. What do we do when we've entered into the deep valley of pain and suffering? How should the Chris-tian respond? What do we do when we feel like we have suffered an injustice? Who is our defender? In our 38th through 43rd imperatives, James reveals three responses to suffering that will answer those questions. Although James's wisdom regarding suffering and pain was originally addressed to the desperate situation of the brethren described in our previous chapter, it is still as useful and pertinent today as it was to them. Our settings may have changed, but our responses to suffering have not.

I. IMPERATIVES 38–43 — VS. 7–9

> **Be patient**, therefore, brothers, until the coming of the Lord.
> **See** how the farmer waits for the precious fruit of the earth,
> being patient about it, until it receives the early and the late
> rains. You also, **be patient**. **Establish** your hearts, for the
> coming of the Lord is at hand. **Do not grumble** against one
> another, brothers, so that you may not be judged; **behold,** the
> Judge is standing at the door (Jas 5:7–9).

This section of Scripture begins with the word, "therefore." "Therefore" is the bridge connecting the injustices in the previous verses to James's response here. Before we go any further, I want to highlight the fact that there are three times as many imperatives addressed to the defrauded brethren as there were to the ones who committed the crimes! They are: "Be patient," "See/behold how the farmer waits," "You also be patient," "Establish your hearts," "Do not grumble," and "Behold, the Judge is standing at the door."

James is pushing the brethren to endure their trials patiently and refrain from taking matters into their own hands. Just imagine what life must have been life for them! At this point in history, the Christian way of life was not seen as honorable. In fact, Paul's teachings alone cause people to believe that he was advocating practices that were illegal under Roman law (Acts 16:21) and against Caesar (Acts 17:7). If first-century Christians had a dispute, suffered an injustice, or experienced persecution, where could they safely go for help?

As modern-day Christians, thousands of years removed

from the pains of the early church, it's tough for us to envision this type of environment. While our own pain, suffering, and trials may not be the same, what James offers is powerful, even in the present day. Let's explore James's guidance on suffering a bit deeper.

II. WISDOM FOR THE SUFFERING

First, he says,

> *Be patient and establish your hearts ... Be patient like the farmer who waits for the precious fruit of the earth, being patient about it, until it receives the early and late rains ... You also be patient and establish your hearts.*

This is absolutely amazing! Let's stop to think about this illustration and how it would have been received at that time. Imagine that you were one of the workers who had just completed a harvest for your employer. Now that the harvest was over, you expected that this farmer/landowner would have given you your wages, but instead you were cheated. Now, you hear James telling you, "Be patient like the farmer who waited for his harvest." How would you have reacted? This would have been like rubbing salt in an open wound because the one being offered as exemplary in the illustration was the very one who had withheld the wages. It's easy to see how this would have been hard for the defrauded brethren since they were right in the middle of that conflict. I can imagine them thinking, "I *was* patient! I did my part. I mowed and I harvested, but I was the one who has been wronged."

It's not easy to be patient during moments of pain and

suffering, regardless of the reason. But it's especially difficult when specific people are the cause of our distress and
heartache because there's a face associated with our pain.
These Christians were injured and they knew who to blame.
Because of that, James tells them to "establish" or
strengthen their hearts and fight the urge to retaliate. In his
reference to the early and late rains, I read a subtle homage
to Jesus's teachings in Matthew 5:43–45:

> You have heard that it was said, "You shall love your neighbor
> and **hate** your enemy." But I say to you, "Love your enemies
> and pray for those who persecute you, so that you may be sons
> of your Father who is in heaven. For he makes his **sun rise on**
> **the evil and on the good**, and sends **rain on the just and**
> **on the unjust.**"

The harvesters knew firsthand that there were two parts
necessary for producing the "precious fruit of the earth."
First, their own part. The labor involved in working the land
as mowers and harvesters were vital to the first-fruits. This
is the part they controlled. Then, there was the sunshine
and rain, both of which came from God and could not be
influenced by the farmer or harvester. I have no doubt that
these workers prayed diligently for sunshine and rain so
that they could continue their work and provide for their
families. So, in this subtle manner, James is reminding them
that the very rain that made the harvest possible for their
unjust employers had actually been provided because God
willed it to be so. The decision to send the rain and sunshine
was God's alone.

I read James's reference to this specific teaching of Jesus
because the point of that teaching was about doing good to

all, even those who persecute you. Christ pointed out very early on that there would be people who were going to revile them. There would be those who were going to slap them in the face, sue them for the very clothes on their back, and force them to go places against their will (Matt 5:38–42). Despite all of that, Jesus's teaching was crystal clear: love completely like God and do not take vengeance into your own hands.

The responsibility of God's children is not to execute justice on God's behalf. It is to respond in such a way that surprises the world. This is possible because our kind response is not based on the individual, it is based on our trust and confidence in the Lord's absolute control and ability to defend. The same Lord who sends the rain can also cause a drought or hail storm. He acts according to His own will and punishes wrongdoers when He deems the time to be right (Rom 12:19).

The second word of guidance that James gives to those suffering is found in verse 9: *"Do not **grumble** against **one another**, brothers, so that you may not be judged ... the Judge is standing at the door."* This a reference to a principle described in Leviticus 19, which we looked at in James 4:11–12. As I mentioned previously, the New Living Translation perfectly captures the Hebrew imagery in its translation, *"Do not **nurse** hatred in your heart for any of your relatives. Confront people directly so you will not be held guilty for their sin."* "Nursing" a grudge means to feed into ill will and bitterness. It's tempting and easy to do, and it's our choice; but if we feed that poison, it will cause us to react to our trial in a way that dishonors God. James reminds his brethren that he does not desire this additional hurt for them because they have been through enough. He urges them to let God, who is standing at the door, act on their behalf! Knowing that the Judge is at the door inspires confidence because it gives the sense that the Lord is just on the other side and can hear everything taking place. It eases our minds to know that God is not fooled by anyone.

But it should also invoke responsibility within our own hearts as well. The Judge's posture at the door is not just one of action, it's one of accountability. Think of the places where our most secret conversations and our whispered gossiping against each other tend to take place — in our homes, in our cars, at our offices. Think of where our most poison-filled venting sessions happen. Now, imagine how different those exchanges would be if we knew that Jesus was standing just on the other side of the door or wall, listening to every word.

The reality is that we don't have to pretend as though He is on the other side of the door. We already know that he absolutely hears every word we say and that we will have to *"give account for every careless word"* (Matt 12:36). So regardless of what has happened to us, two wrongs do not equate to a right. Do not nurse feelings of animosity, hate, or ill will. They will cause you to sin right along with the ones who originally injured you.

Remember, too, that the Holy Spirit of God lives within you and is also keeping us accountable when we remember that our conduct can grieve *"the Holy Spirit of God, by whom you were sealed for the day of redemption"* (Eph 4:30). Paul continues, by saying that when we keep the Lord close to our hearts, that will allow us to *"get rid of all bitterness, rage and anger,"* and *"be kind and tenderhearted to one another, forgiving each other just as in Christ God forgave"* (Eph 4:31–32). The same Spirit also *"intercedes for the saints"* when there are no words to pray (Rom 8:26–27). As God's children, we are never alone and we are never without help!

Finally, James gives one last critical word of wisdom that is especially powerful for those of us enduring pain caused by others. James commands the suffering Christians twice to "Behold!" or "See!" Suffering can cause distortion in the way that we view ourselves and those around us. For example, with physical pain, it's hard to enjoy events like family get-togethers when symptoms prevent us from fully engaging or participating. We may feel guilty about this, or question our value in the eyes of our loved ones. As our bodies begin to be able to do less and less, individuals can feel lost since their very lives have been disrupted. The body that we once relied upon and never questioned can suddenly betray us in the worst imaginable way. When we go through deep valleys like this, it can significantly impact our mental and spiritual health. We may even begin to feel like God is distant and far away, but James is saying, "Behold!" or, "See, the Lord is at hand." In this difficult life filled with sighs and groans, the Lord wants us to know that although we may feel like He is distant, He is present and near us in a posture of action.

By sending twice as many imperatives to those who had been defrauded, James is forcefully advocating for trust and surrender to the Lord. As Christians, it is so important to trust God with all of our pain and suffering. Yes, we would like an answer immediately. Yes, we would like to see our wrongs avenged in the way that we would like, at the moment of our choosing. Yes, it is unfair that sometimes the actions of others cost us dearly. Yes, we share in the same pain and suffering as the rest of the world and sometimes we hurt more than the world because we love and trust people. Ultimately, no matter what happens in this life, the end of the road that God's first-fruits people are traveling on, will lead to beauty beyond compare (Rom 8:28). It is okay to let out sighs and tears, but wrap those tears with a groan as well. A special kind of groan that takes place inwardly, in the spirit. The inward grown that longs for redemption and restoration of all things in Jesus (Rom 8:23). Take heart knowing that as God's special first-fruits people, despite all of the ups and downs, you are pushing forward on bringing that day closer. When the Father decides that the world is ready, our labor will be done and we will be made whole again! May that day quickly come!

SPIRITUAL FORMATION SECTION

There are some lessons that only deep suffering can teach. Trials are one thing, but the harmful and hurtful actions of others toward us have their own unique poisons. I am reminded of Job who, after having gone through all that he did, said this, *"I had heard of you by the hearing of the ear, **but now my eye sees you**"* (42:5). What lessons have pain and suffering taught you through the years? Meditate on these.

CHAPTER 33

GOD'S PATTERN OF FAITHFULNESS

JAMES 5:10–11

Imperatives 44 & 45: Take Hold & Behold

INTRODUCTION

To aid the suffering Christians in their struggle to make sense of why they were experiencing these injustices and to help them navigate that deep valley, James provides two more lessons in how to respond that are equally applicable today. James is going pull strength directly from the cloud of witnesses that surround us all and use one example of strength in the midst of violent storms. We are not alone in our suffering; in fact, we are in good company with others who endured disaster, trials, and challenges in our spiritual ancestry. His 44th and 45th imperatives command us to take hold of the examples set before us as if they were treasures that could be held close to the heart. James is going to also call us to "behold" or see and analyze how they came to understand the Lord's purpose in the pain. No conversation of God-honoring actions in times of pain and suffering is complete without a conversation about Job. As we are going to see, it is Job that James calls forward from the cloud to bring relief. In like manner, invite you to enter verses 10 and 11 with a heart that is ready to listen to Job's testimony. May his life be a blessing to you as it was for James's early readers.

I. IMPERATIVES 44 & 45 — VS. 10–11

> Brothers, **take hold** of the example of the prophets' suffering and patience, prophets who spoke in the name of the Lord. **Behold**, we consider those blessed who remained steadfast. You have <u>heard</u> of the steadfastness of Job, and you have <u>seen</u> the purpose of the Lord, how the Lord is compassionate and merciful (Jas 5:10-11).

James's imperative to "take hold" of the examples of the prophets is a command to acknowledge that others have suffered in the past. Hardship all too often leads to isolation because we fall out of alignment with those around us. Where others are celebrating, we are secretly burdened and anxious. It goes without saying that taking hold of the examples that we have of suffering and patience means learning from them and modeling our responses after theirs. "Taking hold" means to grasp onto something and really make it your own, like a prized possession you look at often to remember something important. It also means to allow ourselves to be influenced by past events and be open to receiving any wisdom in them. This is why James gives the second imperative to "behold" or "see" that if we follow their example, we too will be blessed. Just because we consider the prophets of the past to be pillars in the faith, doesn't mean that their ability was beyond our own. They were human, just like us, and if we "take hold" of their example, we will overcome just like they did!

In verse 11, James turns our attention to Job, perhaps the most famous of all biblical examples of staying true to God despite losing everything. What James does in this text is absolutely masterful! Using his own unique way of using key words to give us hints at where to look, James is not just pointing to Job as a general example of someone who made it through tremendous suffering, he's also hinting at a specific place within Job's life to find what his early readers needed to hear to endure and persevere. Although Job's suffering was the result of Satan's desire to humiliate God, Job unlocked a critical truth from that suffering that gave meaning and purpose to his tragedy. It is that specific moment that James is pointing to using two deeply insightful words in this section. Notice the words "heard" and "seen" in verse (v.11).

These two words were uttered by Job himself at a moment of revelation and personal realization when he was finally able to speak to God directly. Up until that point, he had endured but he struggled to understand his deep pain and trials, but when he uttered these two words, it was at the moment that God's purpose for it all had become clear to him. On the other side of his suffering, after his conversation with God, Job said, *"My ears had **heard** of You, but now my eyes **have seen** You"* (Job 42:5). Let's take a closer look at Job's story and see if we can piece together the purpose and meaning that Job arrived at on the other side of his suffering. My hope is that you may *take hold* of this truth that Job realized and that you will hold it close during your trials.

II. JOB: THE "EXAMPLE" OF SUFFERING

There was a man in the land of Uz whose name was Job, and that man was blameless and upright, one who feared God and turned away from evil. There were born to him seven sons and three daughters. He possessed 7,000 sheep, 3,000 camels, 500 yoke of oxen, and 500 female donkeys, and very many servants, so that this man was the greatest of all the people of the east. His sons used to go and hold a feast in the house of each one on his day, and they would send and invite their three sisters to eat and drink with them. And when the days of the feast had run their course, Job would send and consecrate them, and he would rise early in the morning and offer burnt offerings according to the number of them all. For Job said, "It may be that my children have sinned, and cursed God in their hearts." Thus, Job did continually (Job 1:1–5).

The beginning of Job tells us exactly what we're dealing with here. These verses are like a little window into understanding the "Aha!" moment that Job has later. So, who is Job? What kind of man was he? What did Job's identity consist of?

Our identity is made up of the things that motivate us to get out of bed every morning and move forward. It's how we see and describe ourselves as a person. We know from this opening passage that Job was a follower of God. He was extremely wealthy. He was also a family man, married with ten children. He was a man of prominence and his reputation was honored even in the lands known for their wisdom ("the greatest of all the people in the east"). He was a businessman with a vast number of servants who answered to him. During those days, boundaries of territory were enforced by the sword, so he would have had to have been both a protector and an excellent statesman. He was no doubt intelligent, healthy, and capable. If we envision personal identity as a circle, we could say that Job's identity was a balance of: faith, family, possessions, wealth, status, business, health, and earthly wisdom.

Then, in the first chapter of the book, Job's life begins to be dismantled. In verses 13–19, Job's sheep, oxen, donkeys, camels, and land have been stolen and his servants are all killed by invading armies. But the worst is yet to come in verses 18 and 19. While the messengers were telling Job what had happened to his wealth, *a great wind came across the wilderness and struck the house and it fell on Job's children and they all died."*

In the opening of this tragedy, Job didn't just lose his family, possessions, wealth, status, and business, he lost most of his identity as a person. Our identity is who we are and what we hold on to that gives our lives meaning. Without his children, his status, his possessions, or his business, Job is left fallen on the ground, practically lifeless.

Little did Job know that his suffering was just getting started! In chapter 2, we read,

> So Satan went out from the presence of the LORD and struck Job with loathsome sores from the sole of his foot to the crown of his head. And he took a piece of broken pottery with which to scrape himself while he sat in the ashes. Then his wife said to him, "Do you still hold fast your integrity? Curse God and die" (2:7-9).

Job's identity had been mostly destroyed already,

leaving only his health and his marriage, but now those had collapsed. What reason did he have to go on living? When a person's identity is fractured it is difficult to move forward because identity is attached to actions and even routines. Despair sets in when identity-fractured individuals are left feeling as if there is no reason for them to even exist.

Disasters strike on a daily basis and we have all either experienced it for ourselves or have known someone who has gone through identity-crushing circumstances. We've all known of individuals who were once parents, but then lost a child. Were once married, but the marriage fell apart. Were once business owners, but the business collapsed and the doors were permanently closed and all the workers had to be laid off. We know individuals who were once physically strong and could get up and go here and there, but because of a change in health, had to rely on others for all aspects of life. Instead of being afflicted with one of these tragedies, Job was struck by them all. Every single pillar of his life collapsed into dust. His entire sense of self was destroyed in the space of a few days. For Job, despair was settling in and overtaking the light which once shined bright.

III. A "PURPOSE" FOR SUFFERING

It is not long after the destruction that we begin to see some flaws within Job and within his faith. Job 3:11 reads, *"Why did I not die at birth, come out from the womb and expire?"* Put another way, Job is asking, "If I do not have my children, my marriage, my business, my health, and my status, what is the point of living? If all of this was going to happen, what was the point of bringing me into the world?"

Job chapter 3 contains quite a few verses involving themes of light and darkness, themes indicating a major shift in thinking on the horizon.

"Let the daylight be darkened."

"Let gloom and darkness come."

"Let thick darkness claim the day."

"Let the stars darken and let them not hope for light again."

"Let me be like a child who never saw light."

"Why is light even given to those in misery?"

"Why is light given to a man who is hidden from God?"

These mark the beginning of Job's understanding. He's been dismantled, he's destroyed, he's been reduced to absolutely nothing, and it is here that he questions the very point of life itself, using light and darkness to illustrate his desperation. Job was now ready to receive with meekness the implanted word of God.

When the Lord finally responds to Job (36 chapters later!) He does so first by invoking the same references to the darkness that Job invoked, but He does so by calling out Job's posture: *"Then the LORD answered Job out of the whirlwind and said: "Who is this that darkens counsel by words without knowledge?"* (38:1–2) In other words, "The only darkening that is happening here is the darkening and obscuring of real wisdom by a person who is lacking in it!" The Lord asks Job a series of pointed questions, beginning first with the creation and how it was assembled. He asks Job to explain (if he can) the origins of creation, to explain why they were assembled the way they were, and its purpose. He asks him about the stars and the reason for their constellations. He asks Job about the animals which fill nature — what their purpose was, what was the reason behind their characters and construction.

Then the Lord turns to the creation itself. He says, *"You couldn't even compete with the Behemoth or the Leviathan and yet you wish to contend with the One who created them? ... Whatever is under the whole heaven is mine"* (Job 41:11). This entire opening statement of the Lord was meant to do one thing only: demonstrate to Job that he is utterly out of his element.

Once God finished illustrating to Job how infinitely little Job understood or controlled, Job yielded to Him. Job's title of the "greatest of all the people in the east," and all the wealth and status he and his family enjoyed, had doubtless given Job the illusion that he was a man in control. I wonder if his faith was also informed by the pillars of his identity. Either way, it was clear from this conversation that the Lord felt Job's faith was not yet complete.

God was not insulting Job, but rather enlightening him to the truth that although Job was never actually in control, the One who was could be trusted. By describing the deep complexities of creation, the Lord demonstrated the infinite nature of His power and all that He was responsible for. He was teaching Job that even though his suffering assured him that he had no clue what his tomorrows would bring, neither did he know how any of the rest of the creation functioned, but it did so perfectly nonetheless! The same God who held creation and dictated its unfolding could indeed be trusted with Job's life, too. He learned that there were elements of his own world that could not be grasped, even if he lived a thousand lifetimes, but imagine the relief of knowing that if God could cause all things to work together for good in that arena, then He certainly could do the same for him. Job learned a powerful lesson of trust in the midst of suffering. Perhaps he had once understood this concept, but now he lived it experientially. This is the heart of wisdom when compared to knowledge alone.

Watch how Job responded in the first six verses of chapter 42:

> *Then Job answered the LORD and said: "I know that you can do all things, and that your purpose cannot be thwarted ... I have uttered what I did not understand, things too wonderful for me, which I did not know ... I had **heard** of you by the hearing of the ear, but now my eye **sees** you; therefore I despise myself, and repent in dust and ashes."*

Job shows us that a finite and fragile human being can be taught the most fundamental truth in all the Scriptures: "God is enough and even if every aspect of someone's identity was destroyed, a person could still CHOOSE to love and trust God." It took Satan stripping Job of everything he had for him to understand that powerful truth, but he learned the lesson well. In this moment of clarity, Job said, "I understand now that Your purpose cannot be thwarted." Not only is God infinitely powerful, but there is a purpose and a reason behind not just His creation, but behind all of His actions. Job was a part of that greater plan. He may not have understood it fully, but God was enough for him and he was determined to honor Him with the only thing that couldn't be taken from him: his free will to choose! Once Job came to this realization, his faith grew from just hearing to seeing: "I had heard of you ... but now my eye sees you."

The prophets and Job were blessed in their perseverance because although they experienced hardship, they had full confidence in God. They could not truly comprehend God's plan, but they knew that He was enough and chose to remain close to Him. They knew that no matter what, they would be alright as long as they were with Him. God is working His sovereign plan and there will be pain along the way, but we must trust that we are contributing toward something much greater, and — best of all — that we are in good hands!

James's words and his use of Job's life as proof are humble reminders that there is so much more at work in God's divine providence and plan that we will never be able to fully comprehend. I have every confidence that as James's early readers sat with these words, their countenance was lifted and their souls refreshed. If you're going through difficult times, please believe with all your heart that God is enough for you and that He can be trusted. Just like Job, you may not know what your tomorrow will look like, but you know that your tomorrow rests in the hands of One who loves you and desires to bring you closer to Him. No matter what happens in this life, God is enough! Choose God!

SPIRITUAL FORMATION SECTION

The mission of easing the suffering of others has, in part, been entrusted to us as the church. We have the opportunity and privilege to be God's hands and heart in this broken and painful world. Who are the ones in need? How can you provide them encouragement and strong support? Seek them out and tell them God sent you!

CHAPTER 34

DO NOT DISTORT THE TRUTH

JAMES 5:12

Imperatives 46-47: Do Not Swear &
Let Your Yes Be Yes/No Be No

INTRODUCTION

James chapter 5 is a chapter of warning against those who desire to live compartmented lives, away from the complete oversight of God. It is also a chapter of encouragement to the defrauded because James directly addresses the abuses of power that were taking place and offers words of encouragement to endure. This is why it may seem, at face value, that verse 12 does not fit with the rest of the chapter. This verse contains excellent wisdom — no doubt about that — but it can be tough to see how his guidance on oaths fits within a context that first dealt with suffering and will end with prayer. Our 46th and 47th imperatives, however, are actually the perfect link between the two. In fact, a closer reading will reveal a divine principle of openness and honesty that will bridge the discussions of suffering in verses 1-11 and reaching out for help in verses 13-20. To fully capture the meaning of James's reference to oaths and swearing, we are going to have to take the long way around. Trust me, it will be absolutely insightful and will help us understand James's meaning!

I. IMPERATIVE 46 AND 47 — VS. 12

> But above all, my brothers, **do not swear**, either by heaven or by earth or by any other oath, but **let your "yes" be yes and your "no" be no**, so that you may not fall under condemnation (Jas 5:12).

Our imperatives are found in the expressions, "Do not swear," and "Let your yes be yes and no be no." We can immediately recognize these expressions as quotes from Jesus's words in the Sermon on Mount (Matt 5:36–37), but how do these references fit with the context of the rest of the chapter? It's clear that this verse is not separate from the previous eleven verses because of the phrase James uses, "But above all." This puts verse 12 at the forefront of the existing conversation about suffering. This phrase is like James declaring, "I know that you are suffering unjustly. I know that many of you, like Job, have lost everything. Take hold of his example and the lessons he learned, *but above all*, understand this truth: do not fall into condemnation by being dishonest." I propose that the reason why James turned his attention to honesty is not because of the specific teaching regarding oaths, but because of the divine principle behind these teachings. Let me explain!

As we know from passages like Romans 10:4 that speak

of Jesus as being the *culmination* of the Law of Moses, there was more to Jesus's relationship to the Law of Moses than just fulfilling commandments and prophesies. Jesus fulfilled prophesy and carried out the commandments perfectly, but He also brought a better understanding of the divine principles behind the laws. The Law of Moses was a small translation and expression of God's divine character that was given to a specific people, at a specific moment in time, for a specific purpose. With the movement from the Law of Moses to the Law of Liberty came a necessary change in the divine translation since there was a change in recipients and a change in purpose for the Law of Liberty. Although the recipients and purpose of the new Law of Liberty changed from the Law of Moses, the divine principles behind the laws did not. Jesus alluded to this in Matthew 5:17, *"Do not think that I have come to abolish the Law or the Prophets; I have not come to abolish them but to fulfill them."*

Jesus's teachings were so insightful and authoritative that people could not help but marvel at His words (Matt 7:29). What was so special about the way that Jesus taught, when compared to the Scribes and Pharisees, was that He taught as one who had intimate knowledge of the thought processes behind the laws. To God, the laws were not just rules, they were expressions of His eternal character that were translated to finite and fragile human beings. Jesus's hearers, to include the religious leaders, were so focused on the specifics of the laws that any talk of the divine principles behind them seemed like a new teaching altogether. But as Jesus said in Matthew 5:17, His intent was not to destroy the divine expressions that they cherished, His intent was to fill their meaning full by giving the people the divine principles behind them. What a time to have been alive! Imagine hearing about the *why* behind the rules directly from the mouth of God.

In like manner, James is drawing from one such divine principle behind the oaths to strengthen those who were suffering. Now that we have established this foundation, let's seek to understand the divine principle itself behind the expression *"do not swear"* and *"let your yes be yes."*

II. BORROWED CREDIBILITY

There is a common misunderstanding when it comes to swearing and oath-taking in the Bible. The misconception is that God had forbidden the children of Israel from swearing in His name. But that's actually not true; He explicitly told them *to* swear in His name. Deuteronomy 6:12–13 and 10:20 says:

> *Take care lest you forget the LORD, who brought you out of the land of Egypt, out of the house of slavery. It is the LORD your God you shall fear. Him you shall serve and **by his name you shall swear** ... You are to fear the LORD your God and serve Him. Hold fast to Him and **take your oaths in His name**.*

The prohibition was not against swearing an oath, it was against swearing *falsely in His name*, as evidenced in the following examples:

> *You must not swear falsely by My name and so profane the name of your God. I am the LORD* (Lev 19:12).

You shall not take the name of the LORD your God in vain, for the LORD will not leave anyone unpunished who takes His name in vain (Exod 20:7).

Over time, this presented a problem for mankind because one of our trademarks as human beings is our struggle to be truthful because of fear, shame, or corruption. To keep His people honest, the Lord said swear by My name, but if you swear falsely, you will not go unpunished. This becomes an issue for someone who is not intending to keep their word because this means that there are consequences and risks to deception. Over time, God's people eventually came up with ways to get around explicitly swearing in the name of the Lord, while at the same time, borrowing credibility from the weight of God's name.

Rather than swear by the name of the Lord, loopholes were created that enabled oaths to be sworn on sacred objects that were connected to God to add fake divine weight to their promises. People began swearing oaths on their own heads, on the gold of the temple, by the altar of the Lord, on Jerusalem, by the earth, by heaven, etc. They were attempting to manipulate the holiness associated with God to inspire trust in their promises without having to go so far as to swear in His name and be punished for lying.

Jesus addressed this in Matthew 5, the very passage James quoted:

Again you have heard that it was said to those of old, "You shall not swear falsely, but shall perform to the Lord what you have sworn." But I say to you, Do not take an oath at all, either by heaven, for it is the throne of God, or by the earth, for it is his footstool, or by Jerusalem, for it is the city of the great

*King. And **do not take an oath** by your head, for you cannot*
*make one hair white or black. Let what you say be simply **'Yes'***
*or **'No'**; anything more than this comes from evil (vs. 33–37).*

Again, in Matthew 23:16–22, Jesus addressed this issue
once more. He said to the religious leaders,

Woe to you, blind guides, who say, "If anyone swears by the
temple, it is nothing, but if anyone swears by the gold of the
temple, he is bound by his oath ..." And you say, "If anyone
swears by the altar, it is nothing, but if anyone swears by the
gift that is on the altar, he is bound by his oath." ... Whoever
swears by the altar swears by it and by everything on it. And
whoever swears by the temple swears by it and by Him who
dwells in it. And whoever swears by heaven swears by the
throne of God and by Him who sits upon it."

Jesus is saying, "Bottom line: Operate with the understanding that God is everywhere and that He is connected to
everything in the creation because He created it! There's no
getting around that fact, and there are no loopholes to that
truth. If you swear on literally anything, it has the same
effect as swearing in the name of the Lord because He is
infused in all that He created!"

The surface-level teachings of Matthew chapters 5 and
23 and James 5:13 regarding oaths are pretty straightforward: be truthful with one another and keep your word. But
the divine principle behind these teachings is one that has
actually been brought up by James before. Namely, that
Christian speech isn't just our speech. It carries with it the
weight of God because we wear His name and we have been
called to mirror Him in all the creation as His first-fruits

people. Like the objects that were infused with God's divine name because of their ultimate Creator, we too are connected to Him in every aspect of our lives. This gives new meaning to Colossians 3:23–24, *"Whatever you do, work heartily, as for the Lord and not for men, knowing that from the Lord you will receive the inheritance as your reward. You are serving the Lord Christ."* Every aspect of our lives is connected to God because we wear His name and we are His first-fruit representatives in this physical world. This is the divine principle behind the expression: *let your yes be yes* and *do not swear an oath.*

III. "ALL THE PEOPLE OF EARTH SHALL SEE ..."

The children of Israel failed to see that the name of the Lord was meant to be more than just a name tossed about in conversation and the making of promises. It was to be a representation of the fact that they belonged to God! Allowing them to use His name was a way of saying, "In all things, reflect Me because we are bound to each other." This is why they were not just permitted, but commanded to use His name in their oaths to one another. God held them accountable and He invited them to invoke His will in their plans.

This truth should have produced visible works by the ancient nation of Israel that distinguished them from everyone else. This expectation was conveyed by God when He said: *"All the people of the earth shall see that you are called by my name"* (Deut 28:10). Instead, they defamed the name of the Lord in the sight of the nations and made it a profanity. In a shocking conversation with Ezekiel, the Lord said that instead of glorifying His name,

> when they came to the nations, wherever they came, they profaned my holy name, in that the people said of them, **"These are the people of the LORD, and yet they had to go out of his land."** But I had concern for my holy name, which the house of Israel had profaned among the nations to which they came. 'Therefore say to the house of Israel, Thus says the Lord GOD: It is not for your sake, O house of Israel, that I am about to act, but for the sake of my holy name ... (Ezek 36:20–22).

The oaths that they spoke were more than just verbal expressions. They were supposed to reflect a way of life and were to accurately tell a story about the God they served to the rest of the world. The Lord desired a people who would shine like bright lights in darkness, drawing attention to His name for the right reasons and not for mockery.

James's reference to the oaths should not simply be understood as a commentary on oaths or swearing, but instead should be interpreted as his call to live up to the divine principle behind the oaths. As Christians, we are called to be a "yes be yes" people, a people of honesty and truthfulness — not because we are forced to, but because the very name of God upon our hearts demands that level of integrity. In fact, the divine principle of representing God extends much further than just being honest. For those that were suffering, it meant walking away from taking vengeance because vengeance is another way of telling the world that the God cannot be fully trusted with our injustices. At the end of the day, God is enough for us and He is worthy to be trusted and humbly followed. This is why this principle appears here in the middle of these two major sections dealing with suffering and then vulnerability with others through prayer and confession.

III. GOD IS ENOUGH!

The nation of Israel missed the deep truth behind the original commandment regarding the Lord's name. Jesus did not teach a new twist on oath-making and rewrite the Law; He simply gave the substance behind the shadow, the reason for the rule! The ancient nation of Israel was supposed to have lived honorably, not just out of blind obedience to a rule, but because of the name they wore. In the Kingdom of God today, this divine principle is still very much still in effect: *"Whatever you do, in word or deed, do everything in the name of the Lord Jesus, giving thanks to God the Father through him"* (Col 3:17). This passage is not just about drawing authority from God for what we do, it also about honoring our responsibility to reflect Him in everything that we do. To see our hands and hearts as an extension of His.

If you go on to read the rest of Matthew 23, where Jesus addressed the oaths and all the loopholes that had been created, you will read the word "hypocrites" over and over and over again. Jesus called out hypocrisy among the religious leaders because that is what was really at the heart of the entire discussion. The oaths, the long robes that the Pharisees wore, the way they took certain commandments literally, all of these things were just symptoms of the disease of hypocrisy.

Hypocrisy causes us to be more concerned with pleasing

man than pleasing God, but confession is the cure for hypocrisy. James is going to bring up confession later in verse 16 of this chapter for that very reason. We cannot arrive at the point of openly confessing God's name and accurately reflecting His goodness to the world if we've spent a lifetime telling our Church family that we've got everything perfectly under control and we do not struggle with sin.

Hypocrisy, at its core, is about self-preservation either through deception or manipulation of the truth. Perhaps there were some among James's early readers who were plotting ways to take vengeance into their hands. James's imperatives in this section are reminders that if we are true to the divine principle behind oaths, the principle of accurately reflecting God's goodness and character, we will avoid hypocrisy at all costs. No wonder James invoked Job's example in the verses before. Job himself also learned that once every aspect of his identity or image was stripped away, God was still enough — the very thing that the name of God was supposed to symbolize and represent. There is no need for self-preservation and need for hypocrisy when we belong to God. Wearing the name of the Lord and living a *"yes be yes"* life of honesty means that we have arrived at the place of peace in our relationship with God where He is absolutely more than enough for us and we no longer feel the need to create something false to gain the approval of others or injure someone to wrongfully gain something from them. God is enough, He provides enough, and if we are suffering, we choose Him because we know that all things will ultimately work together for good! Watch how James masterfully weaves these truths into in the final section of this amazing book!

SPIRITUAL FORMATION SECTION

Are God and the identity that He offers enough for you? The way that you will know is if you feel compelled to act a certain way around one group of people and another way when in front of others. When our identity is not fully formed around God, we are forced to create alternative personas instead of enjoying the consistency that comes with yielding every aspect to Him.

Where are you with this idea? It is refreshing when we arrive at the point where God is enough because when we do, we don't need to keep track of who we are. We can be open and honest about our struggles, honest about our need for Him, and thankful for all that we have and are in Him!

CHAPTER 35

SPIRITUAL CONNECTION

JAMES 5:13–20

Imperatives 48–54
Let him pray. Let him sing. Let him call. Let them pray.
Confess. Pray for one another. Let him know.

INTRODUCTION

We all deal with pain and suffering in our own way. God wants us to infuse His identity and will for us into our suffering so that it has meaning and purpose. However, the frail part of our humanity may be tempted to turn toward hypocrisy. Projecting sinless perfection and invulnerability puts Christians into an unattainable and unsustainable box, especially when we're hurting. Suffering in silence is also another form of self-preservation. Perhaps it's shame that keeps us isolated and distant. Maybe it's fear of being rejected that keeps us inward. Either way, it is contrary to God's intent for His first-fruits people. When God is enough for us, we are able to do as He instructs and be open and honest about our deep need for grace and reach out for help. In our final section of Scripture, through the last seven imperatives from James, we will conclude our journey with that thought. There is strength found when the Christians who wear the name of God join together and strengthen one another. These seven final commands will each demonstrate what reaching out looks like in the Kingdom of God.

I. IMPERATIVES 48-54 — VS. 13-20

> *Is anyone among you suffering?* **Let him pray.** *Is anyone cheerful?* **Let him sing praise.** *Is anyone among you sick?* **Let him call** *for the elders of the Church, and* **let them pray** *over him, anointing him with oil in the name of the Lord. And the prayer of faith will save the one who is sick, and the Lord will raise him up. And if he has committed sins, he will be forgiven. Therefore,* **confess your sins to one another** *and* **pray for one another,** *that you may be healed. The prayer of a righteous person has great power as it is working. Elijah was a man with a nature like ours, and he prayed fervently that it might not rain, and for three years and six months it did not rain on the earth. Then he prayed again, and heaven gave rain, and the earth bore its fruit. My brothers, if anyone among you wanders from the truth and someone brings him back,* **let him know** *that whoever brings back a sinner from his wandering will save his soul from death and will cover a multitude of sins (Jas 5:13–20).*

Look at the commands that James gives in this passage and see if you notice a pattern.

- If you are suffering — pray to God.
- If you are happy — sing praises to God.
- If you are sick — call for the elders and let them pray over you.
- If you have sin — confess it to another and pray for one another.
- If Christians are doing the delicate work of rescuing an individual from the sea of chaos — encourage them so that they do not grow weary.

There is an important theme that weaves all of James's teachings together and it can be described in one word: Connection. Connection to God, connection to the elders, and connection to the church. Connection in happiness, connection in sickness, connection through confession, and connection in suffering.

Another way of looking at James's instructions here is through movement. If you are suffering bodily or with pain and sickness, have that pain and suffering move you to reach out to a fellow believer so that you can pray together. When we are connected in this manner, confident in reaching out to one another for help, we're fulfilling the heart of the Law of Christ which is, as Paul said in Galatians 6:2, to *"Bear one another's burdens ... ."*

Does the Lord have the power to lift every burden from us so that we don't have to rely on anyone else for help? Yes! But there's a deep spiritual lesson that He's teaching us by having us not only carry each other's burdens, but also confess our sins to one another. Reaching out to another allows our wounds to be uncovered and exposed for healing.

Our sins and our sufferings cannot heal without openness and authentic connection.

What often prevents us from doing that is fear and shame. We wonder, "If I did what James is talking about here and confessed my sin or invited my friends over to see me at my weakest state, what will they think of me?" Or, "If I spoke to someone about my past regrets that are still hurting me today, will they still love me? What will they think of me if they found out who I truly am?"

There is a real transfer of power that takes place when we let our guard down and open up to someone else. The world considers this transfer to be weakness, but this is the great paradox of Christianity: What the world considers weakness, God considers strength. The transfer of power is not within believers, it is to God. Again, this is another Christian paradox because when our perceived power is transferred to God, we are at our strongest spiritual state! Paul said,

> The Lord said to me, "My grace is sufficient for you, for **My power is perfected in weakness**." Therefore I will boast all the more gladly in my weaknesses, so that the power of Christ may rest on me. That is why, for the sake of Christ, I delight in weaknesses, in insults, in hardships, in persecutions, in difficulties. For when I am weak, then I am strong." (2 Cor 12:9–10).

Admitting that we need help is not a sign of weakness! It is part of God's design for His church family. There is strength in numbers, and in a family, we take turns being strong for each other! Meaningful connection, the kind of connection James is describing, cannot thrive where only superficial personalities exist. God has to be enough for each member and that must be expressed in a genuine way (Rom 12:9). When His opinion matters more than anyone else's and when we realize that even the loss of someone's approval or love does not eliminate our standing in His eyes, our confidence in Him can outweigh our insecurities regarding vulnerability. Then and only then will we be spiritually connected, under the shadow of His wing.

II. THE TWO ROADS AND RESPONSIBILITIES OF SPIRITUAL CONNECTION

Deep spiritual connection begins first within our hearts through humility. John writes,

> But if we walk in the light, as he is in the light, we have fellowship with one another, and the blood of Jesus his Son cleanses us from all sin. If we say we have no sin, we deceive ourselves, and the truth is not in us. If we confess our sins, He is faithful and just to forgive us our sins and to cleanse us from all unrighteousness. If we say we have not sinned, we make Him a liar, and his word is not in us (1 John 1:7–10).

Confession of sin and admission of guilt and regret is an invitation for God to heal us, but a heart that is unwilling personally insults Him and His grace. "We make Him a liar" when we deny that we need Him — when we ignore the fact that without Him, we have no hope of living eternally because we are sick with sin. Confession of sin — both to God and to each other — is not just about asking for forgiveness. It is a state of being before God where we openly admit our desperate need for His grace and mercy. Confession is not just an act; it is like a natural posture of humility that we take before the day even begins. The word "confession," in Greek, is *homologeo*, meaning "to agree with." Confession is not weakness, it's agreement with God that we need His grace!

As John just stated, confession unifies like-minded believers and builds the kind of spiritual connection that James implores us to have because it invites the precious *let there be light* work of Christ into our lives. If Paul were here, he would add,

> *Do not be unequally yoked with unbelievers. For what partnership can righteousness have with wickedness? Or what fellowship does light have with darkness? (2 Cor 6:14)*

Our partnership is with God and with fellow first-fruits believers and our mission is to bring new·spiritual growth into the world by displaying the righteousness of God and shining His light. Yokes attach to animals together so that their strength is harnessed and so that they travel in the same direction. Do not allow your precious time, effort, resources, and gifts to be unfocused. Align your life with the will of God and find strength in the Kingdom of God. This does not mean that unbelievers are to be ignored or shunned. This means that we understand that the nature of being God's first-fruits people means that we love and seek to rescue those drowning in the sea of chaos, not join them and certainly not create more chaos in the world through sin.

Deep spiritual connection with others is a sacred privilege that is earned. Each special first-fruits believer has value which comes from being created in the image of God.

We are co-equal and imperfect children of God, so our role in the Kingdom of God is not to speak down to or shame one another, but to strengthen each other. This is why humility and genuine love are vital. James is commanding us to have a special type of vulnerability that can only thrive in a place where individuals know that they are cared for and loved. The sacred privilege of speaking and receiving truth is purchased by traveling with others through the hills and valleys of life.

In this final section of the book, James invites his readers to pursue connection. Whether you are just starting out, are at the height of your career and accomplishments, or nearing the end of your life's journey, the Kingdom of God needs you! If you are in need of encouragement, the gifted first-fruits encouragers need you to be able to exercise their gifts! If you are strong, lend your strength to those who are struggling. If you are in need, allow your church family to bless you. No matter where you are at in your journey, allow your needs or strengths to move you to connection! That is what a church family does and that is what God expects from His first-fruits people!

The theme of connection in James chapter 5 is the perfect conclusion to the book because genuine connection empowers God's people to patiently endure and display God-honoring behavior in the midst of trials (Jas 1:1–18). Connections are formed with God's people when they live their faith by putting their belief and trust in action through obedience (Jas 1:19–27; 2:14–26). The connection grows when believers view themselves and others in perfectly balanced and humble state before God (Jas 2:1–13). Connections thrive when believers are aware of how delicate unity can be and how quickly words and selfish actions can erode these special bonds (Jas 3–4). James has given us a depth of rich teaching and guidance to build the connection that can and has changed the world!

YOU ARE LOVED, SO LOVE ONE ANOTHER

In this study, we have read through 54 imperatives, five chapters, and 108 verses. We have studied trials and the testing of our faith. We've looked at how to treat others who have more or have less possession than we do. We've discussed how to put our faith into action, how to avoid partiality, and the power of the tongue. We've seen judgment and boasting, how to understand our spiritual identity in pain and suffering, and the power of connection in the Kingdom of God. We have also learned what God's intention is for His creation and for His first-fruits people. We have learned that we are not spectators in God's plan for redemption and restoration, we are active participants. But if there is another word that could also perfectly capture every single teaching in this book, it would be *love*: love for self, love for our neighbor, and love for God.

I find it deeply insightful that James's final verse in this book says, *"Whoever brings back a sinner from his wandering will save his soul from death and will cover a multitude of sins."* This is a nod to Peter, a fellow servant of Christ and one who, like James, was a wanderer in need of restoration. It was Peter who said, *"Above all, keep loving one another earnestly, since love **covers a multitude of sins**"* (1 Pet 4:8). Without love, how can a wandering soul find their way back home? The violent waves in the sea of chaos are the voices that tell them that they are not good enough — they're terrible; they can't do anything right and they are unworthy!

But who is showing them the special love of the Lord? Love is the very essence of who God is and why He does what He does. What an absolutely fitting end to an amazing book!

In the quiet of your day, as you reflect on our brother James's incredible life and teaching, don't forget that love is why we were created and love is why we were given the free will to choose. Love is the reason why God sacrificed so much for us, and love is what binds us to God.

As you reflect on each of the 54 imperatives, I encourage you to take each spiritual formation section in this study and use them to help you develop a plan of change and action. Let us be the people that He desires us to be. If we are true to our purpose, we will show the world a love that is new and will draw people out of the sea of chaos by giving them a bright light to follow!

You are loved! Keep loving one another and may the Lord bless you and keep you, always!

SPIRITUAL FORMATION SECTION

In this study, what has surfaced for you? What rises to the top? What brought you moments of clarity, moments of tension, and maybe even moments of sorrow? Remember this above all: you are deeply loved by God and you are so special to Him. Never forget that! As you reflect on these questions, remember to also write down all the moments that the Lord provided for you and loved you so that you can share those with the generations to come. As Psalm 145:4 says, *"One generation shall commend your works to another, and shall declare your mighty acts."*

SCRIPTURE INDEX

CREDITS

ABOUT THE AUTHOR

Ismael Berlanga (DMin, Lincoln Christian University) currently serves as a Chaplain in the United States Army and is endorsed by the Chaplaincy Endorsement Commission. Ismael and Brigette Berlanga have been married for 14 years and have two children, Judah and Hadassah. Since 2006, Ismael has also served congregations across Texas in various capacities and has a passion for teaching and preaching.

ALSO BY CYPRESS PUBLICATIONS

Always Near: Listening for Lessons from God

by Bill Bagents

The Christian Life: Chapters for Bible Teachers

by Ed Gallagher

Cruciform Christ: 52 Reflections on the Gospel of Mark

by Travis Bookout

Easing Life's Hurts 2nd ed.

by Jack Wilhelm and Bill Bagents

Ecclesiastes: Designed to Disturb

by Coy Roper

Equipping the Saints: A Practical Study of Ephesians 4:11–16

by Bill Bagents and Cory Collins

The Holy Spirit: A Bible Study Guide

by Jack Wilhelm

Jesus the Christ: Chapters for Bible Teachers

by Ed Gallagher

King of Glory: 52 Reflections on the Gospel of John

by Travis Bookout

The Magnitude of God: Exploring the Divine

by Brian Poe

Rescue: God and Sin in the Old Testament

by John F. Wakefield

CYPRESS

To see full catalog of Heritage Christian University Press and
its imprint Cypress Publications, visit
www.hcu.edu/publications